PLAUTUS: THE COMEDIES

Complete Roman Drama in Translation

David R. Slavitt and Palmer Bovie, Series Editors

PLAUTUS:
THE COMEDIES
Volume III

EDITED BY
DAVID R. SLAVITT
AND PALMER BOVIE

THE JOHNS HOPKINS UNIVERSITY PRESS
Baltimore and London

© 1995 The Johns Hopkins University Press
All rights reserved. Published 1995
Printed in the United States of America on acid-free paper
04 03 02 01 00 99 98 97 96 95   5 4 3 2 1

The Johns Hopkins University Press   ·
2715 North Charles Street
Baltimore, Maryland 21218-4319
The Johns Hopkins Press Ltd., London

Library of Congress Cataloging-in-Publication Data

Plautus, Titus Maccius.
    [Works. English. 1995]
    Plautus : the comedies / edited by David R. Slavitt and Palmer Bovie.
        p.   cm — (Complete Roman drama in translation)
    Includes bibliographical references.
    Contents: v. 1. Amphitryon / translated by Constance Carrier — Miles gloriosus /
translated by Erich Segal — Captivi / translated by Richard Moore — Casina /
translated by Richard Beacham — Curculio / translated by Henry Taylor . . . [etc.]
    ISBN 0-8018-5070-3 (v. 1 : alk. paper). — ISBN 0-8018-5071-1 (v. 1 : pbk. :
alk. paper)
    1. Plautus, Titus Maccius—Translations into English. 2. Latin drama
(Comedy)—Translations into English. 3. Greece—Drama. I. Slavitt, David
R., 1935–   . II. Bovie, Smith Palmer. III. Title. IV. Series.
PA6569.S55   1995
872'.01—dc20   94-45317

ISBN 0-8018-5056-8 (v. 2 : alk. paper). — ISBN 0-8018-5057-6 (v. 2 : pbk. : alk. paper)
ISBN 0-8018-5067-3 (v. 3 : alk. paper). — ISBN 0-8018-5068-1 (v. 3 : pbk. : alk. paper)
ISBN 0-8018-5072-X (v. 4 : alk. paper). — ISBN 0-8018-5073-8 (v. 4 : pbk. : alk. paper)

A catalog record for this book is available from the British Library.

Acknowledgments of prior publication may be found at the end of this book.

CONTENTS

PREFACE

The five plays in this volume present broad variations on several of Plautus's favorite themes. A foreigner searching for his long lost daughters finally finds them. A father, abroad on business for some years, returns to discover that his son has dissipated the family wealth and is now overcome by shame and guilt, sorrowful at realizing what his self-indulgence has cost him in self-esteem. Another father, long away on business ventures, returns to find that his son has wasted all his money having fun and is now deeply in debt. Luckily for the son, his inventive slave guardian contrives to divert the father's wrath, until the truth gets out. In another comedy the resourceful intelligence of the slave Epidicus helps the son outmaneuver his father in the son's sincere and heartfelt pursuit of the girl he loves. But in another situation an entirely different pathway is found for a lecherous father to compromise his son and almost succeed in seducing the younger man's mistress. Parents and their grown-up children can be seen in wildly different lights. Smart slaves can come to the rescue. A comedy like *The Thirty-Dollar Day* can be deadly serious and heavily weighted—almost dragged down —with moral gravity. A comedy like *Asses Galore* can degenerate into farce like the degenerate father's abandoned antics on stage— until Plautus lets the players return to their senses and recover their good will.

Scipio defeated Hannibal at Zama in 202 B.C., ending the Second Punic War, so in the *Poenulus*, or *The Little Carthaginian*, produced in 191 B.C., Plautus can charitably accommodate a Carthaginian as his hero. The man even speaks Punic(!), the native language of Carthage's original colonizers, the Phoenicians. Hanno, the little Carthaginian, is not so little as he strides on stage at the opening of the last act, the image of intelligence and energy, deserving of sympathy for his untiring search for his long lost daughters. By finding them in this far corner of Greece the father rescues them from the clutches of the pimp who intended to sell them into prostitution as his slaves on this day being celebrated as the Feast of Love, the Aphrodisia, at the marketplace in Calydon. His mere presence confers a welcome identity on the two young women about to be victimized, and on his own nephew; the young women can become engaged to Agorastocles (Hanno's nephew) and Antomides, his boon companion. The father can only express (in Latin) his gratitude for the fate that has led him to the restoration of his family.

In contrast to the good feeling we get from the *Poenulus* is the bitter taste of the *Asinaria*. A foolish father is caught with his toga down (or up?—anyway, slipping). He is trying to share his son's new mistress for the night, and an informer tells his wife about the party. The wife bursts in on this ill-assorted trio and drags her whining husband home.

The Comedy of Asses comes from a plot by the Greek playwright Demophilus, and Plautus says in his prologue, "Maccus vortit barbare" ["Maccus translated it into a foreign tongue"]. Here Plautus twits the Greeks for their snobbish notion that any language other than their own is "barbarian," while he also makes an acute comment about the process of translation, which he calls "turning." The Prologue goes on to say that Maccus (Plautus's middle name) thinks this is a clever and charming comedy, and he asks for the audience's attention, expressing the wish that Mars will now, as at other times, be on their side—an allusion to the conflict with Carthage.

Fred Chappell's version, called *Asses Galore*, is a boisterous rendition that emphasizes the slapdash and even slapstick quality of Plautine stagecraft, bending the language from the decorousness of the original to something closer to our own traditions of burlesque. The situation, surely, is indecorous enough. The procuress, Cleareta, and her daughter, Philaenium, are completely cynical. The daughter's disinclination to submit to her mother's wishes and her preference for a poor suitor who is barred from the premises, Cleareta sees as rebellious and, therefore, a violation of Roman piety!

Freud is said to have liked line 495—"lupus est homo homini" ["man is a wolf to his fellow man"]—although Plautus was referring here to the arrival of a stranger onto the scene and actually wrote in full:

> lupus est homo homini, non homo
> quom qualis sit non novit
> [Man is no man, but a wolf, *to a stranger*]

It seems that Freud shortened the saying to form an epitome of aggression.

There is a similar inversion of Roman pieties in the *Epidicus*, where the masterful slave of that name takes over and arranges the lives around him, playing the father's interest off against the son's. Instead of chaos, the result is restoration of proper order. A long lost daughter is found, along with her mother, whom the father can welcome into his widower's home. Psychologically, the comedy presents still another view of the father's affectionate bond with a daughter, a connection as prominent in Plautus's work as it is in that of Verdi. Plautus compensates, in a sense, for the husband's conventional boredom or contempt toward his wife. Weighing against this is the fathers' love for their daughters. The dads may grouse about their own marriages (as in the *Trinummus*) but they are nonetheless concerned to see that their sons are properly matched with suitable wives.

Recent scholarship has failed to find any Greek original on which the *Epidicus* could be based, and it has been suggested that this may be Plautus's original composition. He was fond of the play, as he reminds us in the *Bacchides* of "The *Epidicus*—a comedy I love as well as my own self."

For fathers to be concerned about their sons is not surprising, given the Roman piety and reverence for the institution of the family. One of the worst things that can happen to a family is for a son to go astray. Suppose the father has been traveling for some years on business and the son has good-naturedly but thoughtlessly squandered his patrimony—and you have the situation at the beginning of the *Trinummus*. Lest we fail to appreciate the seriousness of this predicament, there is a sonorous Prologue in which two allegorical figures, *Luxuria* (Luxury) and her daughter *Inopia* (Want), make it clear to us. Luxury explains that since the young man no longer has the wherewithal to live with her, she will send her daughter to live in his house. But Luxury will not give away the plot, and only remarks that Plautus derived the drama—in Greek, called *The Treasure*—from Philemon, turning it into Latin and naming it *Trinummus*, "The Three-Penny Day."

For three pieces of money—*tres nummi* or *trinummus* (a three-penny bit)—an unnamed idler in the forum, who is simply called "Sycophanta," is hired to convey a letter of credit for a thousand gold philippics. Plautus has shifted the emphasis of the Greek model from the "treasure" to the "trifle," as if money were of no consequence. The plot, however, makes it clear that if you have money and property, you are well regarded by your fellow citizens; if you are lacking in these assets, you become suspect. Managing your subsistence profitably is a sign of good character.

There is the usual business of misunderstandings and talking and acting at cross-purposes, until the sycophant retires, having earned his pay by doing nothing. But along the way, there is a great deal of moralizing and solid, bourgeois advice. The son sees the error of his ways; the father learns to accept his son's newfound sense of responsibility. At some cost in money and emotion, there is a reconciliation. The *Trinummus* is a comedy of morals and it postures with great earnestness, although Plautus reminds us that this is posturing. Indeed, Stasimus, the slave, speaks as if he were a stage manager or producer, letting us know what Plautus is up to.

Tranio, in the *Mostellaria*, *is* the stage manager. He is the engineer who directs, plots, and virtually produces the whole show until he is finally forced to admit the truth: that he has only been putting on an act. Money is lent and houses are put up for security. But whose money? And which house? Tranio must improvise, pulling the wool over as many eyes as possible, because what he is really interested in is having a good time. His pleasure seeking is un-Roman, and, indeed, Plautus uses the verb *pergraecari*, "to act like a Greek," three times during the course of this play.

The ghost story of the title, about a murdered corpse buried in one of the houses that haunts the premises, is a spur-of-the-moment invention, but it can be said that the gremlin that is loose on the stage prompting such desperate stratagems is the *mostellum* (the diminutive form of *monstrum*) in this *fabula mostellaria*. The mischief itself is the hero, responsible for the slave's extravagant improvisational freedom.

Palmer Bovie

THE LITTLE CARTHAGINIAN

(POENULUS)

Translated by Janet Burroway

INTRODUCTION

Plautus's *Little Carthaginian* concerns a young man who rescues his lovely girl from a loathsome pimp who is about to sell her into prostitution. The girl turns out to be a respectable, free citizen whose rich Carthaginian father appears to recover his long lost daughter (and her sister) after years of searching. This is a comedy about sex, prostitution, love, money, and slavery. The main heroine whose fate is in question is named Adelphasium (Sister), her sister is named Anterastilis (The Other Lovely), and they are the property of a pimp named Lycus (Wolf, or Jackal) who, out of sheer, rather than professional nastiness has so far thwarted every bid made by the wealthy young hero Agorastocles (Big Man in the Market) to purchase Adelphasium and free her to become his wife. The scene of the action is Calydon in the Aetolian region of northwestern Greece (a far cry from Carthage and Rome), the mythical provenance of "difficult" women like Althaea, who destroyed her son Meleager; Atalanta, who outraced all her suitors but the last one; and Deianeira, who conspired in the death of her husband Hercules.

The time of the action is the precise day of the Aphrodisia, a festival to Venus (Aphrodite)—a kind of reverse taking of the vows for negotiable and attractive women lacking social status, who were sold off as prostitutes after duly observing their vows to Venus.

Agorastocles and his slave enter, the young lover sighing like a furnace over his mistress's charms, the slave busy with a pragmatic scheme to outwit the slave dealer Lycus. It is a ruse whereby Agorastocles' farm overseer, a man unknown to Lycus, named Collybiscus (Moneybags) will ask for hospitality in Lycus's lubricious establishment and offer a fee of three hundred gold pieces for services about to be rendered. The transaction completed, Agorastocles will then claim his slave back and by Lycus's denial of the charge of sequester-

3

ing a slave be empowered to hale Lycus before the praetor and claim extensive damages, including the whole household, which will give him possession of the girls Adelphasium and Anterastilis. The plot proceeds as planned. Lycus takes the bait in the presence of three additional witnesses Agorastocles has summoned (impecunious lawyers), and when he emerges again from his house he is confronted by Agorastocles and the witnesses; Collybiscus's identity is proved; Lycus is told to be in court the following day.

The action of the play continues as Syncerastus (Mixer), the slave of Lycus, returns from the Aphrodisia and informs Milphio that the two girls are in fact citizens of Carthage who were kidnapped as children, with their nurse and sold illegally into slavery. The slaves confer about how to use this information for further leverage in detaching Lycus from his ill-gotten girls. And then Hanno, the father of the girls, appears, speaking perfect B.B.P. (Before the Bellum Punicum) Carthaginian, makes himself known in Latin, and all work together in pulling down the rest of the house of the nasty wolf. As Plautus first reminded his spectators in the lengthy Prologue to the play, Hanno had been engaged for years on his search across the Mediterranean littoral for his daughters, going to each of the brothels in the big cities and paying for a girl whose identity he then inquired into, in the hope of discovering his daughters' whereabouts. Hanno is also the cousin of Agorastocles' deceased father; Hanno's slave attendant is the son of the girls' nurse Giddenis. Agorastocles himself had also been kidnapped from Carthage and subsequently sold by the child stealer to "a certain rich old man of Calydon who wanted children but hated women." When his adoptive father died, Agorastocles inherited his wealth.

Plautus's version of an unknown Greek original, the *Carchedonius* or *Carthaginian*, was probably presented first in 194 or 193 B.C. in the long interval between the defeat of Hannibal in 202 B.C. (at the close of the Second Punic War) and the destruction of Carthage in the Third Punic War (149–146 B.C.). The plot seems to show that the Carthaginians were clever people despite their misfortunes. Hanno is a rather dignified, if tough, descendant of the Phoenician merchants; "the typical shrewd Carthaginian" Plautus calls him "who knows all languages, but astutely dissembles his linguistic ability." His obsession with finding his daughters conveys a sense of resistance to the mercenary traffic in human bodies that distinguished this era in Mediterranean culture. Hanno is a powerful prop for the second part of the plot and lends a spirit of affection and authority to the drama, as well as yet another wave of affluence.

In this comedy, as elsewhere, Plautus likes the double effect. The *Poenulus* or *The Little Carthaginian* carries an alternative title, *Patruus Pultiphagonides,* or *The Oatmeal-Eating Uncle.* Hanno, being the cousin of Agorastocles' father, can rescue both his girls and his nephew on a kind of double mercy mission. There are two girls involved: Adelphasium is spoken for by Agorastocles; but Anterastilis is also spoken for, at least in passing, by the "alternate" bragging soldier that Plautus has introduced into the situation, perhaps for this very doubling purpose. There are two slaves, Lycus's menial and the hearty Milphio. There are almost two plots—the outwitting of Lycus and the rescue mission of Hanno—but they are of course combined into one fell triumph of wit, legality, and money over the flesh merchant.

In style, Plautus's Latin verse here presents its usual intricate variety of meters, based on the dominant ground of six- and seven-foot lines. His language demonstrates a wide-ranging diction and abounds in verbal sound effects, geared to alliteration and assonance, treating the ear to an astonishingly extensive vocabulary. The tone very often assumes the "lightning-quick, sneering, out-of-doors manner" that Virginia Woolf ascribed to Greek tragedy. The humor is harsh, unforgiving, irrepressible. The purpose of the joking invective, like the course of the plot, is to pin the villain Lycus to the mast of his own sleazy vessel, and to let the merchant prince of Carthage, with his longlost entourage, overwhelm this sloppy sailor who traffics in people. Plautus the poet rises buoyantly to the occasion, orchestrating a comedy of revenge in Latin that is as unsparing and salty as the powerful words of the Prologue promise.

Palmer Bovie

many characters
good into
poor, boring plot
5

THE LITTLE CARTHAGINIAN

CHARACTERS

Prologues
AGORASTOCLES, a young man
MILPHIO, his slave
ADELPHASIUM and ANTERASTILIS, girls, slaves of Jackal
A MAID
JACKAL (Lycus), a pimp
ANTAMONIDES, a soldier
SHYSTERS, acquaintances of Agorastocles
SPONDULIX (Collybiscus), Agorastocles' agent
SYNCERASTUS, Jackal's slave
HANNO, a Carthaginian
GIDDENIS, nurse to the two girls
A BEARER, Hanno's servant

PLOTUS

Pinched from his pa at seven, a Carthage kid,
One day sold to a wool-dyed woman hater,
Ended up his heir. Two girl cousins, later,
Nurse and all, were snatched as well. And bid
Up to a good price, got knocked down to the slaver
Lycus, who now taunts the Punic lover
Until he's framed with a flunky and some funds.
So Hanno gets his whole family back at once.

7

PROLOGUE

I've got half a mind to make like Aristarchus,
The way he wails over poor old Achilles' carcass.
I think I will. How's this: LET THERE BE QUIET!
Solemnly please to dispel and quell your riot!
Look at ME! . . . if you'll graciously pardon my being blunt.
I bring these high commands straight from the front . . .
Office, where they hope you'll relax on your butt
Whether your belly's had its fill or not.
Frankly, you showed more sense if you fed your face.
If not, you'll soon be fed up enough with us;   10
For although I grant you a play is a trick that's a treat,
Only a fool wants nothing else to eat.
(*To Announcer-bouncer*)
Hey you! Climb up and make this crowd calm down.
I've been wanting to see you do your stuff, you clown.
Open your mouth! It's all you've got to live by,
And silence is just about golden enough to starve by.
That's *dandy*! Go sit down and I'll double your pay.
(*To audience*)
Obsequious thanks for that obedient display.
Now, we want no whores up here in the actors' laps,
And you brass-buttons can just button up your lips.   20
Ushers are instructed not to ush, or float
Around while the actors are trying to emote.
If you lay too long in bed, now you'll stand on the floor;
You won't find a seat. And if you must sleep, don't snore.
Any slaves in here, just back right out the door
And leave us room, unless you've got cash in your purse
And can buy yourself off; otherwise things'll be worse
By a hundred percent at home, with our welts on your back
And Master cracking the whip, to see you've been slack.
Nurses! We want no brats in here, so tote 'em   30
Back, every bawling bundle, wherever you got 'em;
Or else when the plot gets thick you may run dry,
And even if the little dears don't die

They'll bleat for Nanny's breast like a bunch of goats.
Housewives, hold your tongues down to your throats.
Watch *silently.* Laugh *silently.* And chirping is for the birds.
Chatter as much as you like in your own backyards,
But your husbands came here to hear some sweeter words.
    As for the judges: debate and adjudicate
Straight. Don't nominate a second-rate,   40
Or favor friends, or cater to your kin,
Or generally manage to make the worst man win.
Oh yes!—and it had nearly slipped my mind—
Lackeys! Off to the sweetshop! All you find
Is yours while we sit rooted to the spot;
Might as well take 'em while the tarts are hot!
    That's just about the gist of the management's advice,
And I'll thank you not to make me say it twice.
    Now, I'd like to go back and bone you up on the spine
Of the play, so your erudition matches mine.   50
I'll set its limits, I'll bound it, I'll plumb its line,
Because yours truly is surveyor-elect.
I'll give you the title first if you don't object,
Although, of course, I'll do it in any case,
That being the big idea with my boss.
All right, then. The monicker is Carchedonius,
Which gets translated, thanks to Plautus's genius,
As a Roman Oatmeal Consumer *The Uncle.*
And now let's get along to something vital,
Like my synopsis, which I must here submit,   60
Surrender, and defend just as if it
Was a tax return on my whole haul of wit,
My own Internal Relevance; and as if these flats
Were meant for the Bureau, and you the bureaucrats.
    So pay attention—in cash, please. There were a couple
Of cousins, very rich and ritzy people,
As upper as a Carthaginian cuts the crust.
One's quick, one's kicked the bucket. You can trust
Me in the matter of the latter's sad reverses
Because I had the info straight from the hearse's   70
Mouthpiece, the very fellow who undertook

To take him under. Well, a little tyke,
The only son of the aforementioned stiff,
Was snitched from his dad and palatial pad, and if
He was seven then, he was thirteen when his father
Pitiably passed—I do hope it doesn't bother
You if I say this just once more—away.
See, seeing his son was a goner, the sad dad lay
And languished, bestowed all his lands and lucre on
The cousin, and hopped the boat for Acheron,   80
Without a sou, or a stitch or a knicker on.
   The kidnapper nipped off with the kid he'd nabbed
And hawked his hide in Calydon, to a crabbed
Old moneybags, who was fretting about posterity
But couldn't abide the asininity and asperity
Of women. This old guy paid a pile for the lad,
Never knowing a former crony was his dad;
And he made him his son and, what's more, made him his heir,
And kindly died. And the rich kid now lives *there*.
   Now I'm off again. I've got my itinerary   90
For Carthage and environs, and I'll be very
Happy to trans any suitable actions you'd like me to,
Com any missions and buzz any nesses you'll . . . stake me to;
For of course you must grease my grasp if you want any good
   of it.
And you'll see what good you've had of it when you're rid of it.
   Meanwhile, back at the mansion, in Magara Heights,
Old Uncle Hanno was tending the tender lights
Of his doddery years, two nymphets, four and five,
And damned if the daughters didn't get taken alive,
And their governess gratis, nicked by a nasty knave   100
Who bore 'em to Anactorium and sold 'em
To a second man (on second thought it's seldom
A pimp *is* a man) who is the sourest pickle
That ever shackled the anklebone of a fickle
Female. You know what he's like: his best friends call him
   Jackal.
Then later the pimp cut out for Calydon
To seek a shack to hang his shingle on,

And that place there is his, er, um, *salon*.
   Our hero—remember him?—is strictly besotted
With one of the misses, not guessing they're related,   110
Not knowing her background or ever having a hand on
Her foreground, the pander naturally having planned on
Pitching him up to a desperate tone of vice for her,
Whereupon he can demand a double price for her.
And the little sister too: we've got a role for her:
A certain soldier's just asking to play the fool for her.
   But poor old papa—the one still above ground—
Has been dogging the burgled girls the whole world round.
In every new city he hustles to the bawdy house,
He pays his simoleons and he takes his choice,   120
Then queries the deary about her preprostrate position,
Folks, fatherland, manner of capture and submission,
And generally how she descended to this condition.
So, in this shrewd and supersubtle way,
He looks for his girls with an utterly private eye.
He's rather a linguist, too, but—wouldn't you know it;
Those cagey Carthaginians!—he doesn't show it.
   Only last night he came riding a fancy barge in
This harbor, dad of the victimized virgin,
Boss to the nurse and unc to our lovesick mate.   130
Did you catch that? Are you sure you've got it straight?
If you've got it, swallow it, but please don't bite:
It's a trifle fragile, and we have a right
To finis our Plotus, take our tale to its tail. Oh, yes!
I nearly forgot the last little twist to the mess!
Old moneybags—the second of the dads that died?—
He used to be chummy with uncle. And now, inside
An hour or two, the latter will get back his stacked
Siblings and his nifty nephew. That's a fact.
   Excuse me, now. I must wrap me up in my trapping.   140
Try to receive us with rather more clapping than napping,
Eschewing the chewing, the griping, the gabbing, and so on.
Here's the gist of it just once more, for something to go on:
A Carthaginian Gent Will Now Arrive
To Bring His Girls and His Nephew Back Alive.

Bye-bye. Keep listening. I'm going, I'm practically scarce.
I've got to go alter my ego—and face—for the farce.
As for the rest, the rest are just restless to play for you.
If you think them divine, they'll be only too happy to pray
    for you.

ACT I

Scene 1

(*Enter* AGORASTOCLES, *agitated, and* MILPHIO, *malevolent*)

AGORASTOCLES: Milphio, pal! My partner! My pillar of
    strength!   150
    When I think how many a tight squeeze you've unstrangled
    Me out of, and untangled with acute acumen
    And percipient perspicacity and sagacity
    And also apperception and penetration!
    I should set you free! I go down on my knee
    And greet you with the greatest grateful gratitude!

MILPHIO: If the old saw seems dull, hand me an axiom.
    Buddy, this baloney is a batch of gooey hooey.
    It's crumbs you're offering, with long sweeping strokes.
    Today I get a four-course meal of buttered bunkum.   160
    Yesterday you wore out half a cowhide
    To tan my backside, and you didn't so much as sniffle.

AGORASTOCLES: But, Milphio, I'm in love! You must expect
    A certain fluctuation in my temper.

MILPHIO: Oh, great! Lord, yes. Look, I'm in love myself.
    I'm smitten silly. Do I get to smite you?

I'll whop you proper, and then, me being in love,
You let it be bygones.

AGORASTOCLES: But I will! I swear it!
  If it will amuse, feather me! Quarter me!
  String me up! I give you authority.   170

MILPHIO: Uh-huh. And when you come unstrung I'll have
  A few Authorities stringing along with me.

AGORASTOCLES: Why, could I do that? To my very own Milphio?
  When I see you struck, you simply can't imagine
  The pain it causes!

MILPHIO: Imagination I don't need.

AGORASTOCLES: No, no! I mean the pain it causes *me!*

MILPHIO: You're welcome to it, I'm sure. All right, let's have it.
  What dirty work do you want from your dearest pal?

AGORASTOCLES: O Milphio, to you I can confess it.
  I'm drunk on the potion of passion beyond control!   180

MILPHIO: Amen to that from my blistered shoulder blades.

AGORASTOCLES: But I mean I'm in love with adorable
    Adelphasium,
  The sweet little slut next door, the virgin strumpet,
  Elder of two slave sisters kept by Jackal.

MILPHIO: Let me know when you're done with the exposition.

AGORASTOCLES: I'm on the rack for lack of her! I'm distracted!
  But that imp that owns here is lousy as a louse.

MILPHIO: Want to present him with a present he'll resent?

AGORASTOCLES: I consent.

MILPHIO: Send him me.

AGORASTOCLES: Go to the devil.

MILPHIO: On the level: do you want him to get a gift
    he'll regret?   190

AGORASTOCLES: You bet!

MILPHIO: Remit the identical yours idiotical.
    He'll regret and resent having me, I guarantee.

AGORASTOCLES: You crack jokes while my heart cracks.

MILPHIO: No wisecracks, wise tactics.
    What would you say to having your honeybunch
    As a free woman, free of charge, this afternoon,
    Legal and tender without legal tender?

AGORASTOCLES: What would I *say?!*

MILPHIO: I'm the man for the fray,
    I'm the fellow to pull it the way you want.
    Have you got three hundred pieces?

AGORASTOCLES: Or three times that.

MILPHIO: One G will do it.

AGORASTOCLES: Do what?

MILPHIO: Tut tut tut!   200
    I say that by supper you'll have that pimp proper
    And all his pimp-ly property gratis from me.

AGORASTOCLES: Do you really think you can?

MILPHIO: Bend an ear to my plan.
You know your agent Spondulix has blown into town,
And this pimp hasn't had the pleasure. Follow me?

AGORASTOCLES: I, er, I follow you, but I haven't got you.

MILPHIO: I wish you hadn't.

AGORASTOCLES: No, really!

MILPHIO: Okay, I'll spell it.
We'll have Spondulix lug the money to the pimp's
And say he's a tourist ready for a raring tear;
A little love and a little privacy   210
In a corner without a keyhole. The pimp'll be keen
To con the coins, and'll hustle him into the house.
We'll have the Jackal for harboring the Jack and the jack!

AGORASTOCLES: Yes, yes, it's very clever.

MILPHIO: Then you come in.
You ask for your slave, and of course he'll think of me
And say *subito* that your slave is not inside.
Poor perjured pander. Can't you see it now?
His lie makes him liable for double the stolen dough
And twice the price of Spondulix. He hasn't got it.
So then the court convenes, and the court consigns   220
The concubinary kit and caboodle to you.
How's that? We snap the pimp with his yap in our trap.

AGORASTOCLES: Yes, yes, it's very clever.

MILPHIO: Is it ever!
But it's rough. I'll buff it enough to make it shine,
And then you'll find it even finer.

AGORASTOCLES: Fine.
  Well, if you can do without me, I'll just amble
  To the temple of Venus. It's Aphrodisia day.

MILPHIO: Is it, now!

AGORASTOCLES: I need to feast my poor sore eyes
  On the sight of glamorous gals rigged up in glad rags.

MILPHIO: Do you think you could spare a pair of
      minutes first,   230
  To get this maneuver moving? Now, for instance,
  We've got to prompt Spondulix in his part.

AGORASTOCLES: Ah, me. I see. I suppose we have to start.
  Cupid, be still! I must gird myself to duty
  And prorogate the clamorous claims of beauty.

(*He lounges off into the house*)

MILPHIO: You'll be glad you did, I promise, Master mine!
  That poor sucker has a love-stain on his thumper
  It'd take a high-price laundry to get out.
  Well, well; so now my powder keg is packed
  With trouble for that putrid little pimp,   240
  And in a lick or two I'll light the fuse.
  But wait a sec! There are the sexy sisters,
  Adelphasium and Anterastilis. See the one
  In front? It's her behind my master's after,
  And half daffy with the chase. I'll call him out
  And you'll see yourselves. Hey, Agorastocles!
  Shake a leg if you want to catch the leg show!

AGORASTOCLES: What a hullaballoo!

MILPHIO: That's true, but I figure you
  Probably need time to give her the once-over twice over.

AGORASTOCLES: O Marvelous Milphio! Hallowed be
    thy handle. 250
  I kindle like a candle at the sight my fond eyes fondle.
  How I pine to coddle and cuddle that bridal bundle!

(*He pulls* MILPHIO *out of sight*)

Scene 2

(*Enter* ADELPHASIUM *and* ANTERASTILIS, *adorned, and a maid*)

ADELPHASIUM: Any fellow that wants to triple his trouble
  Should load himself with a boat and a broad, that's all.
  The *fuss* of rigging and fitting out those two!
  Gear and tackle and trim, did the fellow say?
  And as for apparatus enough to sate us,
  It can't be done. I know whereof I prattle.
  Ever since sunup we've been sprinting and panting
  From primping and prinking and kinking our hair, 260
  Getting soaked, stroked, slicked, tricked out, and trinketed.
  Yes, and four maids tuckered out with greasing our elbows
  And two lackeys collapsed smack under their water buckets.
  I ask you! Surely one filly is folly enough
  And two is too much! I'll tell you my opinion.
  Any city of any size can be kept on the run
  By two lone dames and their eternal everlasting
  Fussing and prissing and pressing and dressing up!
  I mean, what does a woman mean by a mean?
  (. . . Besides. What is the *use* of all that washin'
  If your whole entire outfit is out of fashion?) 270

ANTERASTILIS: Sissy, honestly, you astonish me!
  Such fiddledeedee from somebody so brainy
  And so . . . *mature* and *sensible* as you
  When, really, as much as we look after ourselves
  The fellows aren't looking after us near enough.

ADELPHASIUM: I s'pose. But, Sister, listen: Moderation
  Is always in the mode. Too much of a good thing
  Spoils the broth.

ANTERASTILIS: Yes, Sister, but now *you* listen:
  Our critics pick us to pieces like pickled herring.   280
  Too salty, it's always called, and without a soaking
  In a small sea's worth of water, it tastes too sharp.
  Women are just as fishy: unless we're stuffed
  And trussed and properly saucy and well garnished
  A man can't stomach us.

MILPHIO: Well, I'll be damned.
  Hear that, Agorastocles? The girl's a cook.
  I'll have to remember that about soaking herring.

AGORASTOCLES: Pipe down!

ADELPHASIUM: Hush up! You've said just about
    enough.
  Really, the way you go on a person'd think
  A man was putting words in your mouth.

ANTERASTILIS: I'm dumb.   290

ADELPHASIUM: That's better, dear, but now try to be bright
    as well.
  Glance over this stuff and tell me what you think.
  Have we got libations enough to bribe the gods?

ANTERASTILIS: An excess, I expect, after all my effort.

AGORASTOCLES: O day! O glorious celebratorious day!
  O day as dazzling as the gorgeous goddess
  We honor on it!

MILPHIO: Honest Agorastocles.
  Don't you think I'm entitled to a bit of a bonus

For shouting you out here? How 'bout one wee barrel
Of very fine fifty-nine wine? Agorastocles?   300
Half a barrel? A bottle? Agorastocles? Boss?
Mister, I guess you must've lost your licker.
(*Yelling in his ear*)
What's the matter, Master, are you mesmerized?

AGORASTOCLES: Shut up! Don't shout; leave me to love.

MILPHIO: I'm shut.

AGORASTOCLES: If you were shut you'd never have opened up
   On that superfluous shut.

ANTERASTILIS: Come on, now, Sissy.
   Let's get going.

ADELPHASIUM: What for? What's all the flurry?

ANTERASTILIS: What do you mean? Why, Jackal's at the temple
   And probably champing at the bit.

ADELPHASIUM: Let him champ a bit.

ANTERASTILIS: Ad? You're mad. Delirious.

ADELPHASIUM: I'm perfectly serious.   310
   There'll be an awful crush at the altar now.
   Surely you have no wish to be squashed and smashed
   By a hash of common garden variety strumpets;
   Peons' pickups and pets of the petty bourgeois;
   Scummy, slummy sluts that smell like a stable
   When they don't smell like a dive. Anyway I don't.
   A flock of flat-broke baggage that a fine free man
   Never gave the high sign, let alone took home with him;
   Cheap chippies scrounging for scruffy slaves.

MILPHIO: Of all the . . . ! To hell with you! Just who
    the blinking   320
  Brink do you think you are to be scorning slaves?
  A raving knockout I dare say. I dare say a dozen
  Kings are slitting their throats for you. Tall tales
  From a short eyesore! Why, I wouldn't slip you
  A cupful of smog to snuggle seven nights with her!

AGORASTOCLES: Almighty immortals, was there ever such
    an eyeful?
  What makes you all mightier than me anyway,
  If my eyes can ogle such a gorgeous prize?
  Oh, Venus isn't Venus! Here's the goddess
  I must go down to, and whose praise I raise   330
  In the hope she grants one glance in my direction.
  Oh, perfection! Milphio? Hey! Where are you?

MILPHIO: Right at your heel, Boss.

AGORASTOCLES: Heal? I'd rather you'd sicken.

MILPHIO: Oh, you're a quick'un, you are.

AGORASTOCLES: All I know,
  Or hope to, I owe to my angel Milphio.

MILPHIO: Izzat so? I suppose it's me who taught you how
  To moon for a minx you've never had your mitts on?

AGORASTOCLES: So what? I'm piously gone on the gods as well,
  But I haven't tried to pet them.

ANTERASTILIS: For pity's sake!
  When I see these rags we're rigged up in I could gag.   340

ADELPHASIUM: Well, that becomes you far worse than your rig.
  We're dressed as well as our master's assets ask for.
  I grant you the pickings are slim if you don't kick in

A little outlay first, but the purse is sparse
If expense is twice the gross. I assure you, Sister,
Enough is plenty, and more than that is paltry.

AGORASTOCLES: Oh, for the love of God, for the love
    of that Goddess!
A stone would have to love her!

MILPHIO: That may well be.
   I've never seen a stone as dense as you've been
Since you lost your marbles over her.

AGORASTOCLES: And to think   350
   That, nuts as I am about her, I've never touched
So much as the nail of her toe.

MILPHIO: So. Nuts and nails.
   He's got a screw loose. Listen, Boss, I'm off!
I'm going to bring you back a box of bolts.

AGORASTOCLES: You dolt, what for?

MILPHIO: To screw the two of you.

AGORASTOCLES: Oh, go to hell.

MILPHIO: I'm in it.

AGORASTOCLES: Can it, clown.

MILPHIO: Who, sir, me? I'm mute. I'm muzzled for certain.

AGORASTOCLES: For centuries, I hope.

MILPHIO: Good grief, a comeback!
   He's waxing witty, I'll have to look out for my job.

ANTERASTILIS: I'm sure your outfit suits you for the
   moment,   360
  Sister dear, but the second you see a better
  On somebody other, you'll bother and fret, I bet.

ADELPHASIUM: And yet, you know, dear Sister, I've never
suffered
  The slightest symptom of malice or jealousy.
  I prefer a first-rate mind to a first-rate mink.
  The one is earned, the other's just expensive.
  Diffidence, I think, is a girl's best friend,
  And modesty is the most effective fabric
  For her outfit. Believe me, Sister, a stable jade
  Is more salable than one in jade and sable.   370

AGORASTOCLES: Milphio! Be a sport.

MILPHIO: I'm always game.

AGORASTOCLES: Go home and hang yourself.

MILPHIO: That's not my game.
  What for?

AGORASTOCLES: For joy, for bliss, for ecstasy!
  You'll never hear so many winning words
  At once again. Go home and hang yourself!

MILPHIO: Okay, if you'll swing beside me and be another
  Bunch of grapes.

AGORASTOCLES: How I love her!

MILPHIO: How I love
  To eat and drink!

ADELPHASIUM: Sister, give me a hand.

ANTERASTILIS: What is it?

ADELPHASIUM: I had something in my eye.
   Is it gone now?

ANTERASTILIS: No, there's a mite of a mote in the middle   380
   Of this one.

ADELPHASIUM: Maid, will you try to take it out?

AGORASTOCLES: Oh, gods! Is she going to put those filthy paws
   On my angel's eyeballs?

ANTERASTILIS: Addie, wouldn't you say
   We lay down on the job today?

ADELPHASIUM: No, in what way?

ANTERASTILIS: We ought to have got to the altar before the
       sun did
   And lit the first flame to Venus.

ADELPHASIUM: Not at all!
   Only the ugly sacrifice their sleep
   To be Venus's vanguard at an empty altar.
   It's always the freaks and frights you see at night,
   Scuttling and skittish, anxious to be early
   When Venus herself has barely got to bed.   390
   Yes, and supposing the goddess was awake
   Those frumps are so frowzy they'd scare her out of her wits
   And Venus would vanish; she'd vault right out of her altar.

AGORASTOCLES: Milphio, Milphio!

MILPHIO: St. Milphio the Martyr,
   What is it now?

AGORASTOCLES: Man, hear those honeyed words!

MILPHIO: Oh, absolute waffles, Boss, with maple syrup;
  Apple fritters and flapjacks, buckwheat and blackstrap.

AGORASTOCLES: How does my honey look to you now?

MILPHIO: Expensive.
  She looks to me like Mercury'd put no stock in her.   400

AGORASTOCLES: Well, a lover is not supposed to speculate.

ANTERASTILIS: Let's go, Sister!

ADELPHASIUM: If you insist.

ANTERASTILIS: Come on.

ADELPHASIUM: I'm coming.

MILPHIO: They're going.

AGORASTOCLES: Oh, no! Shall we go along?

MILPHIO: If you must.

AGORASTOCLES: Oh, miss!—uh, misses. That is: first,
  (*To* ADELPHASIUM)
  To you, miss, first-class, A-1 prime rib greetings,
  (*To* ANTERASTILIS)
  And to you, how d'you do, red ribbon, and to you
  (*To* MAID)
  A niggardly nod.

MAID: Then I've squandered all my bother.

AGORASTOCLES: Where are you going?

ADELPHASIUM: Me? To the temple.

AGORASTOCLES: Why?

ADELPHASIUM: To placate Venus.

AGORASTOCLES: She can't be provoked at you.
    She's placid, I promise, I guarantee it. Hey, wait!   410

ADELPHASIUM: Please don't molest me, mister.

AGORASTOCLES: What a grouch!

ADELPHASIUM: Ouch! Leggo me, there's a lammykins.

AGORASTOCLES: But what's the rush? There's a crush there now.

ADELPHASIUM: I know.
    But I want to gawk at the other girls a bit,
    And I shouldn't wonder they'll have a gander at me.

AGORASTOCLES: Why should you go out to take in those eyesores
    And give them a sight for sore eyes in exchange?

ADELPHASIUM: I have to. The panders are having a harlot auction
    At the altar this afternoon, and I'm on display.

AGORASTOCLES: Junk and rummage you have to advertise,   420
    But goods like this should go from under the counter.
    When are you coming over to let me love you?

ADELPHASIUM: That'll be the day the dead get passes
    Back from hades.

AGORASTOCLES: I have a peck of shekels
    Burning a hole in my pocket.

ADELPHASIUM: Is that so?
    Hand them over, I'll douse the flame in no time.

MILPHIO: Good Lord, what a sweetheart.

AGORASTOCLES: You mind your beeswax!

MILPHIO: The more I scan her, the more I'm inclined to find her
  An awful hatful of hateful offal.

ADELPHASIUM: I'm off.
  I think we've exhausted the subject.

AGORASTOCLES: Adelphasium!
  Just let's set aside this excess textile . . .   430

ADELPHASIUM: Keep your hands off me, you ruffian!
   I'm purified.

AGORASTOCLES: Lord, where do I go from here?

ADELPHASIUM: Oh, you're such a booby!
  You could kibosh all this bother in one bold bash.

AGORASTOCLES: Huh? Baby, it's no bother to bother 'bout you.
  Milphio, Milphio!

MILPHIO: Milphio, Milphio, Milphio!
  Must you bore us with that chorus? What's it now?

AGORASTOCLES: Why is she sore at me?

MILPHIO: Why is she sore at you?
  Why should that worry me? Which of us itched
  To fuss about lusting after her in the first place?

AGORASTOCLES: Now, by God, you cad, you're a cold
    cadaver   440
  Unless you calm her. Tame her, tranquilize her.
  I want her as placid as a hatching halcyon.

MILPHIO: How do I swing that?

AGORASTOCLES: Coax, cajole, extol.

MILPHIO: Okay, I'm your postmaster. Just don't mistake me
  For your punching bag.

AGORASTOCLES: I promise.

ADELPHASIUM: Promises!
  That's all a gal can ask from Agorastocles.
  He brags, he stacks big talk like building blocks
  Half up to heaven. And what does it amount to?
  A hill of beans and baloney. A hundred times
  You vowed and vouched and swore you'd buy me off   450
  And set me up in style, and so I stand here,
  Stuck like a stick in a stock, not another prospect,
  And for all your projects, as craven a slave as ever.
  Come on, Annie, let's get out of here.
  Clear the path, please, buster.

AGORASTOCLES: Bu-bu-but . . .
  Good God, I'm a goner. Man! Go at her, gain her!

MILPHIO: Well-uh . . . my joy! My jam! My jelly bean!
  My life, my lips, my eyes, ears, nose, and throat,
  My little lotus bosom, my angel pie,
  The apple of my cheek, my peachy passion,   460
  My onion dip . . .

AGORASTOCLES: Do I have to stand here and hear this?
  Damme, if I don't send him to death and hell
  On the next stage out of here.

MILPHIO: Now there's a dear,
  Don't *stew so*. Don't bristle and bluster at my boss.
  For my sake. If you'll settle down I'll set him
  On to setting you free and setting you up

As a citizen: he'll pay a million for you.
Make up and let him make for you; he won't make you.
Why ain't you friendly to your friends? Suppose he fibbed
Once, just a weensy bit, he's really reliable.   470
All right, suppose he lied, he's tried and true,
I'll take my oath; I'll take you by the earlobes
And seal it with a kiss.

ADELPHASIUM: You silly ass,
   Get off of me! A miniature of his master!

MILPHIO: Oh, God, I'm had. Ad, do a fellow a favor.
   I've got to get you tranquilized, or the bossman
   Will get provoquilized and spanquilize me.
   You don't know how ornery he is when he's unhappy.
   Come on, let me convince you, that's a princess,
   That's a honey, that's a love . . .

AGORASTOCLES: That's the last straw!   480
   I'm a lead slug's worth of a lad if I don't slug
   That slicker's lid in.
   (*Hitting* MILPHIO)
               There's your jelly bean!
   There's your peach pie! There's your lotus nose!
   There's your ear! Your onion dip! Your lip!

MILPHIO: It's illegal! I've got diplomatic immunity!

AGORASTOCLES: Then here's an extra one for your exemption!
   Was that any way to woo her?

MILPHIO: What's wrong? I wowed her.

AGORASTOCLES: What's *wrong!* You hood, you should have said
   it this way:
   Oh, I beseech you, Master's passion pie,
   His life, *his* lips, *his* eyes, ears, rose, and lotus,   490

His little onion bosom, *his* cheeky angel . . .
You get it? You got it all screwed up in the pronouns.

MILPHIO: Yeah, yeah, oh, sure. And I absolutely do, too,
I do beseech you, Boss's passion pie
(And my shrew stew), *his* bustiluscious buddy
(My bitter botheration), *his* light (my blight),
His molasses (my harassment); I do indeed
Beseech, besiege, and beslaver you besides:
Don't hate my master (or if you must hate him, hang him
And yourself and your grandmother all together). Because   500
I've a notion I'll get short rations for the duration,
Not to mention a few contusions in three dimensions
I carry around on my back.

ADELPHASIUM: You break my heart.
Maybe you'd like to explain to me how I stop him
Flailing you when I can't stop him fooling me.

ANTERASTILIS: Honestly, honey, hand him a little hope
And get him out of our hair. Let's get out of here.

ADELPHASIUM: All right, we might as well. Agorastocles,
I'm not irate. You rate yet one more gamble.

AGORASTOCLES: You're not? I do?

ADELPHASIUM: Um-hmmm.

AGORASTOCLES: Let's have a kiss on it.   510

ADELPHASIUM: Not so fast, you fresh thing. After the ritual.

AGORASTOCLES: Then rush!

ADELPHASIUM: Let's hustle, ladies.

AGORASTOCLES: Hey! D'you hear me?
    Give my regards to Goddess.

ADELPHASIUM: Yes, yes.

AGORASTOCLES: Listen!

ADELPHASIUM: Well?

AGORASTOCLES: Well . . . don't waste words with your
        libation,
    And . . . Adelphasium, gimme one smile, please do.
    She did it! Oh, Venus is bound to beam on you!

(*The girls and maid exit*)

Scene 3

AGORASTOCLES: Cue me, Milphio. What should I do now?

MILPHIO: Knock me about some more and hold an auction.
    You hardly need this ritzy place to sleep in.

AGORASTOCLES: Why not?

MILPHIO: You're always laying into me   520
    Anyway.

AGORASTOCLES: Stop that! Can't you see I'm suffering?

MILPHIO: I see it all right. What am I supposed to do?

AGORASTOCLES: It's all fixed with Spondulix. I gave him a grand
    Before you bellowed me out here. Now, pal, I beg you,
    By your right hand and your southpaw and your sloe eyes,
    And by your liberty . . .

MILPHIO: My whichywhatzis?
   That isn't much of a quantity to beg by.

AGORASTOCLES: O my Milphiologist, my trump, my savior,
   Keep your promise and help me stomp this pimp.

MILPHIO: Now you're talking. Look, go scare up a pair   530
   Of shysters. Anyone willing to bear witness
   For a buck an hour. Meanwhile, I'll be drilling
   Spondulix in a few gymnastics of my own.
   Go on, now.

AGORASTOCLES: Yes! I fly!

MILPHIO: Don't strain yourself,
   Just run along.

AGORASTOCLES: If you can pull this off . . . !

MILPHIO: Don't say anything you'll regret, just *get*.

AGORASTOCLES: I absolutely swear . . .

MILPHIO: Are you still there?

AGORASTOCLES: You'll see! I'll set you free . . .

MILPHIO: Sure thing. Now spring
   Off into the wings.

AGORASTOCLES: Yes, by heaven! I'm ever so . . .

MILPHIO: Oh?

AGORASTOCLES: So . . .

MILPHIO: So-so. Could I ask you to exit?   540

AGORASTOCLES: Ask any soul in hell . . .

MILPHIO: Well, will you *go?*

AGORASTOCLES: Not for all the H_2O in the ocean . . .

MILPHIO: In motion, Master, please.

AGORASTOCLES: No, not for love . . .

MILPHIO: Shove off.

AGORASTOCLES: . . . or a million . . .

MILPHIO: Will you . . .

AGORASTOCLES: . . . billion bullion,
    No, not one or the other . . . whether . . . well, there
    Are more things in heaven . . . but I haven't even . . .
    In sober earnest, honest . . . why continue?
    Why not? You see my meaning? To make it short . . .
    Good Lord, by Jove, Gadzooks: you get the message?   550
    Enough . . . it's off the cuff, but just between
    Us, gods and fishes, you see the lay of—you listening?

MILPHIO: If you won't take your leave I'll take it for you.
    Good grief, that speech needs a gloss from Oedipus,
    Ex-interpreter for the Sphinx.

(*He exits*)

AGORASTOCLES: A jinx.
    He left in a huff. He's miffed. I must be careful
    I don't throw a monkey wrench in the works. I'll rush
    And rustle up some witnesses. Look how Love
    Makes a free lover labor for a slave!

(*He exits*)

ACT II

(*Enter* JACKAL, *jaundiced*)

JACKAL: May Olympus slam a comeuppance on any pimp   560
    That ever slits the throat of one mutton to Venus
    Or kicks in one stick of incense from now on!
    The good gods came down on me today, okay,
    In a stinking mood. Six lambs I gave them. *Six*.
    And not the sign of a kind sign did I see
    From that sonofa so-and-so Venus. But don't weep yet.
    I'm not wet behind the ears; she didn't get
    Away with it. I got my lambs away
    Before they sliced the meat. Well, see, I thought
    If the guts weren't good enough for a single simple   570
    Amiable omen, it'd be sacrilege
    To insist on hacking and packing 'em up to her anyhow.
    Heh? How's that? Is that crafty or is that cagey?
    That greedy grubbing goddess, she wouldn't call it
    Enough, so I called it quits. That's the sort I am.
    Yes, sir, that's me all over. I guarantee
    It'll be a cold day in August when another
    August goddess gets the bright idea
    Of pulling the lambswool over my sweet eyeballs.
    Pah! And that worthless soothsayer, forsooth!   580
    Just about worth his job, the way he whined
    And droned out how the omens were all awful
    And looked like lousy luck for me. That jackass!
    Such a punk is not to be trusted at a till
    Or a temple either. Why, only a half-hour after
    I picked up an easy tenner. Now that I mention it,
    Where's that silly soldier that gave it to me?
    He said he'd slip in for supper. There he comes.
    Good God, will you just look at the way he struts!
    Like a cock in a corset.

(*Enter* ANTAMONIDES, *a braggart soldier*)

ANTAMONIDES: To continue, pimpling.   590
   Where was I? Yes. Reviewing the particulars
   Of the Penetronic Operation, wherein I slaughtered
   A squadron of sixty thousand airborne adversaries.

JACKAL: Winged warriors, huh?

ANTAMONIDES: Such was my assertion.

JACKAL: Just let me check. You're saying there are fellows
   That *fly?*

ANTAMONIDES: I said there were. But I dispatched
   The batch of them.

JACKAL: How did you manage that?

ANTAMONIDES: As follows: First, I accoutered my platoons
   With slingshots and with pots of putty pellets.
   Second, I supplied the squads with weed-leaves   600
   The which they laid within the slings.

JACKAL: What for?

ANTAMONIDES: To preclude the cohesion of gluten to the
   munition.

JACKAL: That's what I like in a liar: professionalism!
   Please do go on. My breath is always baited
   For a fish story.

ANTAMONIDES: To continue, pimpernel!
   My outfit fit its slingshots out with shot,
   And as I issued the order, let fly at the flyers.
   To make a long sortie into a short shortie,
   When the stickum struck 'em, they tumbled down as thick
   As plums in summer, whereupon I took the field,   610

Plucked a plume from each of the incapacitate,
And impaled his encephalon.

JACKAL: Extraordinary!
If you ever made such a scene may Jupiter make me
Sacrifice every day and twice on Sundays
With only ugly omens.

ANTAMONIDES: You don't credit me?

JACKAL: Oh, I credit you. Just as I'd issue credit
On my credulity. Come on inside.

ANTAMONIDES: As long as the meat isn't here, I have a mind
To regale you with another tale of another triumph.

JACKAL: Gale away. I'm going.

ANTAMONIDES: Pimpernickel!
By Mars, I'll spatter your gray matter in the gutter   620
Unless you listen; or you can go hang yourself.

JACKAL: Thanks, I'll opt for the latter operation.

ANTAMONIDES: *You say so?*

JACKAL: Yes, I say so.

ANTAMONIDES: *Well I say . . .*
It's such a lovely Aphrodisia day,
Wouldn't you like to make me over that mopsy?
The small one?

JACKAL: All transactions have been postponed.
Today I can't take chances, the surly glances
My sacrifices got from that sulky goddess.

ANTAMONIDES: I don't distinguish sacred days from sexular.   630

JACKAL: Come off it. But you might as well come in.

ANTAMONIDES: Lead on. I'm temporarily your mercenary.

(*They exit*)

ACT III

(*Enter* AGORASTOCLES, *aggrieved. Following him at a distance are three legal advisers, mumbling together and moving very slowly.*)

AGORASTOCLES: Nothing is as provoking as a slowpoke,
    so help me God!
  Especially for a lover that lives in a constant rush.
  Me, for instance, with these witless witnesses,
  These moseymasters, slow as a sloop in a calm.
  And yet, good God, I picked particularly
  Among the youngsters, and cut my older cronies
  Exactly because I didn't want them dragging
  Their years along behind me. But what's the use?   640
  Now I've got this bunch of lead-foot fops,
  The world's slowest. Hey, get a move on there
  If you count on getting here by dark! Or else
  Get lost! What kind of boost is that supposed
  To be to the prospects of an anxious lover?
  I think you're shaking those footsteps through a sieve;
  Or else that's a shuffle they shackled you with as slaves.

SHYSTERS: Look here, mister, just don't get too sassy.
  We look like plebs to such a swell as you,
  But we tend to be testy, and if you get too crusty   650
  We're ready and able to make blue blood feel blue.
  We couldn't care less whom you hate and whom you fall for.
  We bought ourselves off, and *we* coughed up the dough,
  Not you. We're scot-free and we ought to be and we'll not

Play bootblack to your passion. We don't give a damn.
It suits a citizen in the city streets
To go at a sober pace. You look like a lackey
If you're always dashing around. Especially in peacetime,
When everyone's already done in that needs doing,
It's unrefined to run. If you're in a rush   660
Why didn't you hire us yesterday afternoon?
But now please don't expect us to go scrambling
And scuttling down the street like a bunch of loonies
And having the populace pelting us for our pains.

AGORASTOCLES: Okay, but if I'd invited you out to the temple
For a bite to eat, you'd've outdone a bat out of hell.
You'd've split the wind on built-in stilts. Too bad
For me that I only wanted witnesses.
Now you've got the gout and the gait of a snail.

SHYSTERS: Well, that seems perfectly logical to us.   670
Haven't you reason enough to race to a place
Where the drink runs even faster, and the food is free,
And another man pays and you don't have to pay him back?
Nevertheless, we may be lower class,
But we've victuals enough of our own to keep us vital.
It may be little, but it'll suffice us nicely;
We ask no handouts and we don't hand out any,
So kindly please don't walk all over us
Or expect man jack of us to walk so fast
He bursts his belly or pops his lungs for you.   680

AGORASTOCLES: Come on, you make too much of it; you're
     touchy.
Why, I was only kidding, kids.

SHYSTERS: Ha, ha.
Take our remarks as likewise jocular.

AGORASTOCLES: Now look, you get the setup: I've suggested
How you can help me make this pander prickle

Who's been having a laugh at me and my girl's expense,
And how we'll trap him with my money and my man.

SHYSTERS: That's all old hat to us; just tell the audience.
It's for their sake we're stuck up here at all.
That's the gang to harangue so they'll get the hang   690
Of whatever it is you're doing when you do it.
Don't fuss about us; we know the whole business backwards.
For heaven's sake, if we hadn't learned our lines
Along with you, how'd we know what to answer?

AGORASTOCLES: That's very true. But please, just ease my mind
And run once through your role in the deal.

SHYSTERS: You heel,
We're going to get the third degree now, are we?
You figure we forget you gave your spy
Spondulix a purse to plump down at the pimp's,
Pretending he's a footloose libertine   700
And when the pander has the cash in hand,
You'll storm in and demand your man.

AGORASTOCLES: That's grand!
Most memorable memories! My saviors!

SHYSTERS: The slaver, thinking you mean Milphio,
Denies he hides your spy, and by his lie
Incurs a double debit for the swindle
And the court'll settle his chattels all on you.
And all you want of us is to witness it.

AGORASTOCLES: That's it, you catch it!

SHYSTERS: Scratch it, maybe; touch it,
But it's hardly big enough to make a handful.   710

AGORASTOCLES: Marvelous! Here's Milphio right on cue,
   And Spondulix decked in a glorious bib and tucker:
   Exactly what we need to bait our sucker.

(*Enter* MILPHIO *and* SPONDULIX, *disguised as a soldier*)

MILPHIO: You've got your orders now?

SPONDULIX: In perfect order.

MILPHIO: Did you study them? Did you cram?

SPONDULIX: What d'you think I am?
   I'm as crammed as a clam.

MILPHIO: But are you letter-perfect?
   Have you got your part by heart?

SPONDULIX: By rote! By the roots!
   Good Lord, give over, I can quote you chapter and verse,
   I can reel it off like a heavy ham or a comic.

MILPHIO: A supertrouper!

AGORASTOCLES: Let's step in.

MILPHIO: The extras?
   To witness for us?   720

AGORASTOCLES: Doubtless.

MILPHIO: What a caucus!
   What a congress! You couldn't have pressed a better.
   There isn't a legal holiday in sight.
   There isn't a bottom among 'em that hasn't sat
   Itself fat in the witness box. They sleep on the benches.
   They put more hours in there than the local justice.
   No prosecutor knows his legal spiel,

His procedures, and his precedents like these gents:
If they're out of a case they lay out cash to get one.

SHYSTERS: You can burn in hell.

MILPHIO: Why, thanks, I will. And you . . .   730
Are nevertheless excessively benevolent,
In this case, to help my master catch a mistress.
Boss, do they really grasp the situation?

AGORASTOCLES: By the handle.

MILPHIO: Okay, lend me your attention,
Gentlemen. You know this pander, Jackal?

SHYSTERS: Like the back of my hand.

SPONDULIX: But I've never seen his pan.
You fellows have got to point him out to me.

SHYSTERS: We will, don't worry. We've been thoroughly drilled.

AGORASTOCLES: This man has three hundred smackers in his
    pocket.

SHYSTERS: Let us have a look at it, Agorastocles,   740
So we'll know what it is we're swearing to later on.

SPONDULIX: Sure, take a peek, then.

SHYSTERS: Lord, that is a packet!
    (*To audience*)
He has the funny money, everybody—bogus, naturally.
Stage stuff, strictly vegetable. But we bank
On your indulgence and let it serve for sterling.

SPONDULIX: And I serve as a tourist.

SHYSTERS: Admirably.
    And on your arrival, you accosted us
    And asked if we could point you out a place
    Where you could let your hair down and have a hoedown
    On your own with a bottle and a bit of skirt.   750

SPONDULIX: Astonishing! Aren't they accurate! Astute!

AGORASTOCLES: I tutored them myself.

MILPHIO: And who cued you?

SPONDULIX: Come on, Boss, get yourselves inside the house.
    We don't want Jackal chancing on us here
    And botching up our plot.

SHYSTERS: That's logical.
    Do as he says.

AGORASTOCLES: I'm on my way. But, witnesses . . .

SHYSTERS: We've wasted words enough. Be on your way.

AGORASTOCLES: I'm on my way, then.

SHYSTERS: For the love of heaven,
    Leave!

AGORASTOCLES: I'm on my way. I'm way away.

(AGORASTOCLES *and* MILPHIO *exit*)

SHYSTERS: Clever of you.

SPONDULIX: Quiet!

SHYSTERS: What's the matter?

SPONDULIX: (At JACKAL's door)
  This door did something shocking!   760

SHYSTERS: Shocking? What?

SPONDULIX: It let a loud sound behind!

SHYSTERS: Be damned! Here, stand
  In the rear.

SPONDULIX: All right.

SHYSTERS: Are you ready? We'll lead on.

SPONDULIX: Very saucy—leading men with their behinds!

(Enter JACKAL, jovial)

SHYSTERS: That's him! That's the pimp!

SPONDULIX: A prime example
  Of panderhood, to judge by the evil eye.
  So that's him coming out, the lout whose loot
  I'm going to lift without so much as touching him.

JACKAL: (To ANTAMONIDES, inside)
  Be back in a second, soldier. I'll go dig up
  A couple of rakes to join us. While I'm gone   770
  The holy lamb chops should arrive, and the ladies
  Will show as soon as the service starts to bore them.
  But what's this bunch parading my direction?
  Something for me, I wonder? And who the blazes
  Is that gay blade behind in the army outfit?

SHYSTERS: The Aetolian freemen offer you good morning,
  Jackal, although in fact in back of the offer
  Is the opposite wish entirely.

JACKAL: Thank you kindly.
  And may you be as lucky as isn't likely,
  For I know how Lady Luck looks on the likes of you.   780

SHYSTERS: A numbskull who has no income but his tongue
  Plays risky stocks insulting his superiors.

JACKAL: A man who doesn't know the way to the ocean
  Has to follow a river. I hadn't a clue
  How to be fresh with you till you played the freshet.
  Now I'm on your course: if you're very nice
  I'll trace your flow, and if you're low and coarse
  I'm ready to race all the way from the source to the sea.

SHYSTERS: A good turn done to a bad man is out of tune
  As a bad turn done to a good man.

JACKAL: How d'you figure?   790

SHYSTERS: Good done to a bad man is soft-pedaled.
  A good man wronged will harp at you forever.

JACKAL: Very cute, but I don't get the connection.

SHYSTERS: We've come here for your benefit, but in fact
  We have a lukewarm liking for procurers.

JACKAL: Oh, I'll be grateful enough if it's something good.

SHYSTERS: It's nothing good of our own we've got for you,
  Or brought for you, or promise you, or wish you,
  When it comes to that.

JACKAL: When it comes to that, by God,
  I believe every word of it. That's just the brand   800
  Of benevolence I expect from you. What then?

SHYSTERS: You see the guy in the uniform? He's under
  The curse of Mars.

SPONDULIX: You can call it down on your heads!

SHYSTERS: Now that he's here, pimp, we suspect somebody
  Is going to make mincemeat out of someone.

SPONDULIX: Good!
  Today this hunter's going to bag his limit;
  The dogs are yapping at the Jackal's heels.

JACKAL: Who is he?

SHYSTERS: Haven't the faintest. All we know
  Is, down at the docks this morning he descended
  From a merchantman and made direct for us.   810
  He said hello and, naturally, we answered.

SPONDULIX: Rascals! The way they handle this shows practice.

JACKAL: Naturally. What next?

SHYSTERS: Next he explained
  How he was a total stranger in the town
  And was looking for a nook he could relax in.
  We walked him straight to you—and listen, Jackal,
  If you've got the gods on your side, here's your sucker.

JACKAL: Perhaps.

SHYSTERS: He's panting for it, and he's loaded.

JACKAL: Hmm. A plump pigeon.

SHYSTERS: He wants wine and women.

JACKAL: He couldn't have come to a better place.

SHYSTERS: But wait: 820
He wants to lie low. Undercover—get it?
Private. No spies and scrutinizers. Listen,
Here's the story: he's a mercenary
Out of Sparta—told us so himself—
Under King Attalus in that attack
When the town got taken, which was slightly scary,
He showed his heels and showed up here.

SPONDULIX: Ah! Very
Nicely turned, that: Mercenary. Sparta.
Cunning!

JACKAL: May heaven shower you with honey
For bringing me this come-on!

SHYSTERS: He's *not* common! 830
You better treat him handsome: we know first-hand
He's had the *un*common acumen to accumulate
Three hundred clinkers in his purse.

JACKAL: I'm a king!
Oh, if only I can lure the lad inside!

SHYSTERS: No problem. He's already sold.

JACKAL: Persuade him
To bed and board here: excellent entertainment!
Lavish lunches!

SHYSTERS: Advertise for yourself, then,
If you're so eloquent. The tourist traffic
Isn't up our alley; it's beneath us.

   We've brought the pigeon right to the cote. It's up   840
   To you to trap him, if that's what you're planning.

SPONDULIX: Off so soon, friends? What about my business?

SHYSTERS: Transact it with this man, sir. He's a paragon . . .
   In the line of goods you're after.

SPONDULIX: (*Aside*)   Lag behind
   A little. You should see him snatch the loot.

SHYSTERS: (*Aside*) We'll take it in from a little further on.

SPONDULIX: You've been most kind.

JACKAL: My booty's coming to me!

SPONDULIX: (*Aside*) Yes, like a quick kick from a jackass, Jackal.
   A real booting.

JACKAL: Now for an unctuous greeting.
   A hearty welcome, sir, from host to tourist!   850
   I'm gratified to find you in fine fettle!

SPONDULIX: May the gods smile on you, since you smile on me.

JACKAL: I understand you need a room.

SPONDULIX: No rumor.

JACKAL: And a room, I understand, from the information
   Those gents just here imparted, free from . . . flies.

SPONDULIX: Far from it.

JACKAL: What?

SPONDULIX: If I wanted fly-free lodgings
   I'd have gone direct to jail.

JACKAL: Sir! You're a howl!

SPONDULIX: How'll I find a place, on the other hand,
   Where I'll be handled tenderly and sweetly
   As King Antiochus's eyes?

JACKAL: I have it here!   860
   By Jove, you've just described the very cranny
   I can supply you with, if you can suffer
   A cushy nook with a nicely cushioned sofa—
   So far so good?—and a cutie on the couch.

SPONDULIX: You've touched me, pimp.

JACKAL: A place where you can sprinkle
   Your soul with wine: Leucadian,
   Lesbian, Thasian,
   Chian—so well aged they've lost their teeth.
   And perfumes! You can shower in them! Listen,
   We'll set a scent shop up in your steamy bathroom.
   But every word I use is in the army.   870

SPONDULIX: What do you mean?

JACKAL: They're yelling for the payroll.

SPONDULIX: Oh, that. You can't be readier to peddle
   Than I am to pay.

SHYSTERS: How'd it be if the boss
   Himself came out, to be his own star witness?
   Hey, Agorastocles! Flatfoot! On the double!
   Come see for yourself: The pimp is getting paid.

(*Enter* AGORASTOCLES, *anxious*)

AGORASTOCLES: What's up? What is it, shysters?

SHYSTERS: Cast your saucers
   Over on the scene to the right. The pimp is ripe
   To take the shekels straight from your lackey's hand.

SPONDULIX: Here, sir, have this: three hundred cash in
     coins   880
   They call Phillipos. Tend to my satisfaction
   Out of that. I want it swiftly squandered.

JACKAL: You've bought a philanthropical factotum,
   Friend! Come in, come in!

SPONDULIX: *I'm right behind you*
   As anyone can plainly see.

JACKAL: Come on,
   Sir, do. We'll settle the details inside.

SPONDULIX: I'll slip you all the latest Spartan gossip,
   Too.

JACKAL: Yes, splendid, right this way.

SPONDULIX: Lead on.
   You have in me a . . . loyal servant, sir.

(They exit)

AGORASTOCLES: What should my next move be?

SHYSTERS: Appropriate.   890

AGORASTOCLES: And if that's too much for me?

SHYSTERS: Do what you're able.

AGORASTOCLES: You saw the pander palm the purse?

SHYSTERS: We did.

AGORASTOCLES: The giver being my menial?

SHYSTERS: That's right.

AGORASTOCLES: The which infringes sundry laws?

SHYSTERS: That's right.

AGORASTOCLES: That's great! Now see you bear that all in mind
  And bring it out later for the judge.

SHYSTERS: We'll bear it.

AGORASTOCLES: How about if I batter his door right now?

SHYSTERS: Bright idea.

AGORASTOCLES: But what if he ignores me
  While I batter?

SHYSTERS: Then his cake is crummy.

AGORASTOCLES: And if he comes, what then? Should I go right
up
  And ask him: Pimp, is my slave inside?

SHYSTERS: What else?   900

AGORASTOCLES: And he'll say: Certainly not.

SHYSTERS: Uh-huh, he'll swear it.

AGORASTOCLES: Which makes him an accomplice, right?

SHYSTERS: Accomplished.

AGORASTOCLES: To the theft of those three hundred pieces.

SHYSTERS: Why not?

AGORASTOCLES: Oh, go to hell, the lot of you.

SHYSTERS: Why not you?

AGORASTOCLES: I'm going to knock his door down, now.

SHYSTERS: Why not?

AGORASTOCLES: But wait! The time has come to keep our traps
    shut;
  His door is squeaking open: here's the pimp!
  Now keep your promise, stick with me!

SHYSTERS: Why not?
  If you want to you can give us a bit of headgear
  So that ruffian doesn't recognize the meddlers   910
  That got him in this mess.

(*Enter* JACKAL, *joyful*)

JACKAL: Just look at this!
  For all I care those puny priests can swing;
  They can string themselves up this minute for all I ever
  Intend to swallow a syllable again!
  Can you picture it? They said my sacrifice
  Looked sinister—some kind of scrape and setback—
  And look at me now, just rolling in simoleons!

AGORASTOCLES: Hello, pimp.

JACKAL: Lord love *you*, Agorastocles.

AGORASTOCLES: The sweetest salutation I ever had from you.

JACKAL: We've hit a calm, like a boat on a breathless ocean;   920
  I'm swinging the sails to catch the leeward breeze.

AGORASTOCLES: I hope your household is in health—or half of it.

JACKAL: We're fine, thanks kindly, for any good you'll have of it.

AGORASTOCLES: Send Adelphasium over this afternoon,
  If you don't mind, pimp. It seems appropriate
  Since this is the sacred, celebrated day
  Of the Aphrodisia festival.

JACKAL: Huh? Hey,
  Did you burn your tongue at lunch by any chance?

AGORASTOCLES: What makes you ask?

JACKAL: The way you wag it now
  You seem to want to cool it.

AGORASTOCLES: Look out, pimp!   930
  It seems my slave's inside your place.

JACKAL: *My* place?
  Not a trace of him, not a chance of it.

AGORASTOCLES: That's a lie.
  He came here with a heavy purse. I have it
  From a most reliable source.

JACKAL: Of course, of course,
  You reprobate, you rush up with some shysters!
  There's not a body or a bean belongs to you
  Inside this house.

AGORASTOCLES: Jot *that* down, counselors.

SHYSTERS: Jotted.

JACKAL: Ah, I've got it! Oh, I've got it!
  Now it clicks! This is that bunch of bunglers
  That brought me the Spartan sucker a short while back,
  And now they're itching jealous to think I'm rich.   940
  Not knowing this scalawag is my opponent,
  They set him onto saying he's lost a slave
  And a bit of mintage. Really it's all a trick
  Concocted to make off quick with the jack themselves!
  They think you can rip a lamb from a jackal's teeth!
  Bunkum!

AGORASTOCLES: But come, let's get your story straight:
  You claim you've got no man of mine, no money?

JACKAL: Why, yes, I claim! I'll declaim and exclaim the same
  Till I'm frogified in the gullet, if you ask me.

SHYSTERS: Pimp, you're finished. That fellow we called a
    Spartan,   950
  That chap that slipped you the three hundred Phillipos,
  That gent is agent to his honor here,
  And you're holding the cash in question in your hand.

JACKAL: A frame-up! The hell with you!

SHYSTERS: Reserved and ready
  For *you*, friend.

AGORASTOCLES: Drop that purse this instant, pirate!
  A bandit, caught red-handed! Gentlemen,
  Please focus closely on this episode:
  I'm going in to get my errant servant.

(*He exits into* JACKAL'*s house*)

JACKAL: Oh, God, I've had it; I'm certain it's curtains for me.
   They cooked this whole thing up to cook my goose.   960
   I've got to race! I've got to escape and go . . .
   Jump in the lake to save my neck from the justice?
   Jupiter! When I had my pick of prophets!
   Omens and Oracles! Oh, if they augur you miracles,
   Those creep along like a worm. If they promise you harm
   It's no sooner said than you're done for. Well, I'll go see
   If someone I know has the knack of knotting a noose.

(He exits. Enter AGORASTOCLES, *egging on* SPONDULIX, *stuffing himself.)*

AGORASTOCLES: Get a move on, you. Execute this exit
   Where they can see it. Say, isn't this my slave?

SPONDULIX: Absolutely, Agorastocles.

AGORASTOCLES: So!   970
   What do you say to that, you crooked pander?

SHYSTERS: Your foe has quit the field, friend.

AGORASTOCLES: For the scaffold,
   I hope!

SHYSTERS: We share your animus entirely.

AGORASTOCLES: Tomorrow early I drag that cur to court.

SPONDULIX: Anything more for me?

AGORASTOCLES: Take off that costume.

SPONDULIX: Yes, Boss.
   (Aside)
               But the choice was choice. A soldier
   Naturally has to pillage a little plunder,

From under the noses of the pimp's staff. While they napped
I fortified my belly with a bulk
Of consecrated mutton. . . . But my master   980
Gave me marching orders.

(*He exits*)

AGORASTOCLES: Much obliged to you,
Gentlemen, for that friendly turn. I'm under
Obligation to you. Much obliged.
Well, yes. See you in court tomorrow morning.
Coming, Spondulix? Good-day to you.

SHYSTERS: And to *you*, sir!
There's a disgusting crust of justice for us!
We play his slaves and pay our own expenses!
But that's no better than par for our plutocrats:
Help 'em and their thanks lie light as a feather,
Fail to, and their anger lands lead.   990
Well, what's the use? At least we've the satisfaction
That profligate loses his profits in the action.

(*They exit*)

ACT IV

(*Enter* MILPHIO, *from* LYCUS's *house*)

MILPHIO: I've come to get the picture on my frame-up.
How my mouth waters to slaughter that slimy pimp
Who's torturing my miserable master! . . .
Who naturally reacts by whacking me.
By kicking, cracking, socking, whacking me.
I tell you, it's hell to work for someone stuck on
Some little trick he can't get his hands on. Wait!

There's Syncerastus—Jackal's lackey—dragging   1000
His apparatus back from the sacrifice.
I'll drop back under the eaves and have a listen.

(*Enter* SYNCERASTUS, *weighed down with implements for
    sacrificing*)

SYNCERASTUS: It's clear: nor gods nor men don't care a damn
    For a poor old cur with that kind of cad for a boss.
    You won't find a bigger liar or a lower louse
    On the face of the earth than my crass, nasty master.
    I'd rather quarry stone. I'd rather a millstone
    Was strung around my neck, and a ball and chain
    Around my ankle; it wouldn't rankle as much
    As tracking after a pimp. What a shocking lot!   1010
    And the way those places debase the populace!
    Mercy on us! Every sort of person
    Can be seen there, same as you'd find in hell:
    Rich men, poor men, beggarmen, serfs; and vassals
    Of all descriptions—vestal, festal, wastrel;
    Welcome, all of 'em! Just so they've got the price.
    Mice or men, never mind, cram 'em in a nook,
    A grimy cranny where they can gorge and booze
    Like a grogshop, like a pothouse. It's disgusting!
    And get this: fools' names, like fools' dirty verses,   1020
    Get carved a half-yard long in the terra-cotta.
    Lovers' names like a wine list of vintage labels.

MILPHIO: That's a funny sort of speech for Syncerastus,
    Unless he stands to inherit Jackal's packet,
    Because, by God, it sounds like a funeral dirge!
    I'd hail him if I didn't want to hear him.

SYNCERASTUS: It breaks my poor old heart to see it happen:
    The best of bondsmen going home deboodled
    By a fling with us, and not a thing to show.
    But they're to blame. Easy come is easy go.   1030

MILPHIO: And there's a preacher makes a fine example!
   The fellow that teaches sluggishness to slugs!

SYNCERASTUS: Now poor old me must drag this equipment back
   All the way home from the shrine, where that old sinner,
   No matter what he gave her, got no favor
   From Venus at the festival.

MILPHIO: Good Goddess!

SYNCERASTUS: Although she winked at the wenches the very first
   Split of a sheep's throat.

MILPHIO: I repeat, good Goddess!

SYNCERASTUS: Well, I'll be getting on.

MILPHIO: Hey, Syncerastus!

SYNCERASTUS: Eh? Did somebody call my name?

MILPHIO: A friend did.   1040

SYNCERASTUS: Holding a loaded man is not so friendly.

MILPHIO: Call it a deal, then: if I delay you now
   I'll lay myself at your service when you need it.

SYNCERASTUS: Well, I'd know how to name my part of the
      bargain.

MILPHIO: How's that?

SYNCERASTUS: Next time Jackal wants to thrash me
   You can supply the backside. Now get out!
   I don't know who you are or what you are.

MILPHIO: I'm a thorough rotter.

SYNCERASTUS: Rot yourself.

MILPHIO: Hey, stop!

SYNCERASTUS: My back is breaking!

MILPHIO: Take off your pack and look.

SYNCERASTUS: Oh, well, all right, but I'm really in a hurry.   1050

MILPHIO: Salutations, Syncerastus.

SYNCERASTUS: Milphio!
    Why the devil didn't you tell me so!
    Well, heaven bless . . .

MILPHIO: Bless who?

SYNCERASTUS: Not me, not you.
    No, not the Jackal either.

MILPHIO: Who's to bless, then?

SYNCERASTUS: Anyone who's earned it, which we haven't.

MILPHIO: I do declare, he's making repartee!

SYNCERASTUS: As well I might be.

MILPHIO: What might you be up to
    With all that stuff?

SYNCERASTUS: Let's say I'm up to something
    Adulterers aren't up to once they're caught.

MILPHIO: What's that?

SYNCERASTUS: I'm making off with my tool   1060
    Intact.

MILPHIO: The gods confound you and your whore-hound.

SYNCERASTUS: They won't hurt me. But I could make 'em
        curse *him*
    If I had a mind to. Yes, indeed,
    I'd blast that blessed miser all to blazes
    If I . . . if I . . . if I had the guts for it.

MILPHIO: Hmmm. Provocative. I hear you talking.

SYNCERASTUS: Listen, Milphio: are you a rotter?

MILPHIO: Absolutely.

SYNCERASTUS: I feel rotten.

MILPHIO: But isn't that just the way things ought to go
    For the slave of a pimp? You've got your gall to grouse: 1070
    Your food and drink are on the house, and the girls
    Are yours for free. That's slavery!

SYNCERASTUS: Lord love me!

MILPHIO: How could he resist?

SYNCERASTUS: So help me, Scylla,
    I wish for the crash and smashup of this whorehouse!

MILPHIO: Then put a little muscle into the wishing.

SYNCERASTUS: A fish can't fly; my wings have got no feathers.

MILPHIO: Phee-uw! Stop taking a razor to your armpits
    And in two months' time your wings will beat a buzzard's.

SYNCERASTUS: Go lynch yourself.

MILPHIO: I'm saving that for you
And the old wench-monger.

SYNCERASTUS: That's another song. 1080
I'd sing that little ditty; I could crush him
Into little bitty pieces!

MILPHIO: How'd you work it,
Hmmm?

SYNCERASTUS: Oh, no! I wouldn't trust your muzzle
With a peppermint!

MILPHIO: But can't you see I'd cache it?
I'd stash it safer away than a tongueless woman.

SYNCERASTUS: You might soft-soap me if I didn't know you.

MILPHIO: Go on, just trust me once. You won't regret it.

SYNCERASTUS: I do already. But I'm too credulous.
I'm gullible as a gull.

MILPHIO: I'll tell you something.
My boss calls your boss his best enemy. 1090

SYNCERASTUS: Of course.

MILPHIO: On account of Ad . . .

SYNCERASTUS: Don't waste your breath.
You're enlightening the enlightened.

MILPHIO: Well, all right!
Doesn't it stand to reason the livid lover

Itches to pitch the pimp in a patch of brambles?
And if you provide the patch, so much the richer.

SYNCERASTUS: That's what makes me shaky.

MILPHIO: Bunkum. Why?

SYNCERASTUS: What if he botched it? What if Jackal catches
His lackey blabbing? I promise you he'll turn
Syncerastus into a broken-legged man named Shrunkshanks.

MILPHIO: I swear on a stack of sacrificial sheepskins,   1100
No one'll know from me except my master,
And I won't tell him until he takes the oath.

SYNCERASTUS: I'm gullible as a gull, but I'm going to do it.
Just keep it mum.

MILPHIO: Consider me Mum herself.
Speak up; we're all alone; the time is ripe.

SYNCERASTUS: Well, if your boss is bright, he can bring the pimp
To heel.

MILPHIO: How can he do that?

SYNCERASTUS: In a jiffy.

MILPHIO: Yes, yes, but couldn't we have a few *details?*
Just what's this jiffy we can bring him down in?

SYNCERASTUS: Here it is: you know this Adelphasium   1110
Your master's daffy for? Well, she's freeborn.

MILPHIO: What's that?!

SYNCERASTUS: The God's own truth, the same as her sister.

MILPHIO: Prove it!

SYNCERASTUS: Well, Jackal bought 'em off a pirate
  In Anactorium when they were tiny.

MILPHIO: What price would you say he paid?

SYNCERASTUS: The pair of 'em
  Brought seventy-two simoleons, and Giddenis
  The nurse fetched half of that. And this Sicilian
  Admitted he was selling stolen children,
  And said they were freeborn citizens of Carthage.

MILPHIO: Glory to God, what perfectly gorgeous gossip!   1120
  Why, that's my boss's birthplace, too. He too
  Was kidnapped as a slip of a thing and shipped
  To Calydon and peddled to my old master;
  But that one wanted a son instead of a strumpet.

SYNCERASTUS: Why, then it's a cinch to clinch; have him claim the
      wenches
  As freeborn fellow townsmen!

MILPHIO: Shhh! I'm thinking.

SYNCERASTUS: He can play his pawn and put the pimp in check!

MILPHIO: We'll rook that rogue before he gets his game out.
  Just watch me. I've got the whole scheme in my head.

SYNCERASTUS: Mercy on us, get me another master,   1130
  Milphio!

MILPHIO: With a little mercy on us,
  We'll be getting out of the slave game altogether
  And setting up as mercers.

SYNCERASTUS: Mercy goodness!
    I'm nervous. Do you need me?

MILPHIO: Just to speed you
    With a run of luck.

SYNCERASTUS: My luck rides on your back.
    But look, the thing I said, do keep it dark!

MILPHIO: You didn't say a thing.

SYNCERASTUS: On the other hand,
    You must strike while the iron is hot.

MILPHIO: You're not
    Going to turn sage on me, are you? I can strike
    When I like.

SYNCERASTUS: You can make a first-class article   1140
    Out of this stuff I've given you if you work it
    With a little skill . . .

MILPHIO: I thought you had to hurry.

SYNCERASTUS: Don't harry me. I'm hurrying.

(*He exits*)

MILPHIO: You're a paragon
    Of precipitate propulsion. Is he gone?
    Almighty immortals! Make my master prosper
    And clip this pimp! We'll massacre the bastard!
    The gun is cocked to blast the second bullet
    Before the first shot cracks. I'll cut this act
    And go inside to tell my master. After
    All, there's no percentage in repeating   1150

The info you just heard. I'd rather bore
One man backstage than hear the whole house snore.

(*He exits*)

ACT V

Scene 1

(*Enter* HANNO, *handsomely attended*)

HANNO: *I thoo my minalom and semicolon*
   Calakkie mum a scythe and sticky barka
   Liffo kannutbe but be edan oy
   By marob sillygism absobuttle
   Both lummocks tullate antidamasson
   And siblong muggle filliskon when liffle
   In dibbur occuous agorastocles
   Emanting hitchers allicot my nassup   1160
   By now you dillock illy gops of bisium.
   But he allee asylum noo oo-thisium

   Dear gods who hold this city dear, do hear me:
   Grant my request, grant that the quest that wrest me
   Out of my home to this strange town prove fruitful.
   Grant that I meet my beautiful plundered daughters
   And get my nephew back again. Amen.

   Well then. This is the borough we used to furrow
   When we were sowing our wild oats, Antidamas
   And I, when he was the family familiar.   1170
   And now they say the scythe has cut him down
   And left as harvest one Agorastocles.
   I'll have to pass this keepsake to the youngster.

Let's see: it says his place is hereabouts.
I'll ask these strangers.

(*Enter* MILPHIO *and* AGORASTOCLES, *abstracted*)

AGORASTOCLES: You say Syncerastus
  Claims they came from Carthage, Milphio?
  And that they're freeborn?

MILPHIO: That's the very story.
  And now if you've got punch and pep you'll pinch 'em
  Pronto back from the pimp. Why, it's a scandal
  To let that vandal handle compatriots   1180
  As harlots, and swindle 'em out of their bourgeois birthright.

HANNO: Immortal gods, stay by me! Am I dreaming?
  My ears devour delicious words! Those words
  Are chalkous chalk upon the blackidation
  Of my despair.

AGORASTOCLES: I'm dubious. A witness
  Or two would screw my courage up.

MILPHIO: The deuce!
  You don't need witnesses if you've got passion.
  Ginger! Vigor! Vim! Velocity!
  Luck backs pluck!

AGORASTOCLES: But it's easier breaking ice
  Than backing out of the fish pond.

MILPHIO: Hey, hold on!   1190
  What's this bird in the loony tunic?

AGORASTOCLES: Punic!

MILPHIO: D'you think he lifted that shift in a Turkish bath?

AGORASTOCLES: I'd swear, he's a Carthaginian! He acts like
    a Gog.

MILPHIO: And just take a good long look at his fusty trusties.

AGORASTOCLES: What do you mean?

MILPHIO: Those bellhops under the baggage.
    Very hoary. And I perceive, poor chaps,
    They've lost their fingers.

AGORASTOCLES: How do you figure?

MILPHIO: Easy.
    What else would make a man wear rings in his ears?

HANNO: First I'll try Punic on them. If it works
    I'll keep it up; if not I'll try another.   1200

MILPHIO: Say, do you remember any Punic?

AGORASTOCLES: Me? Fat chance! Why, I was in short pants
    When they kidnapped me from Carthage.

HANNO: Mortal carnage!
    Many a lad is nipped like that from there.

MILPHIO: Hey, Boss!

AGORASTOCLES: Yes?

MILPHIO: Shall I speak to him in Punic?

AGORASTOCLES: Do you know how?

MILPHIO: Why, I'm the puniest Punic
    That ever ground out of a bun, the lowest form of wheat.

AGORASTOCLES: Then I knead your help; get along with it, you
    thoroughbred.
    Find out where he's from and what it is he's come for.
    Who is he? What is he doing? What's he want?   1210
    His family tree, his birthplace; ask the works.

MILPHIO: Sure thing. Uh . . . *How!* Uh . . . Where are you folks
    from?

HANNO: *Anobun myth am bull, yoo dratit aunnuch.*

AGORASTOCLES: What did he say?

MILPHIO: He says his name is Hanno.
    Er . . . comes from Carthage, son of Mythembull.

HANNO: *How!*

MILPHIO: He says hello.

HANNO: *Hondutti.*

MILPHIO: Yes sir!
    Listen to that; he is offering you a handout.

AGORASTOCLES: Tell him hello from me.

MILPHIO: Right. *How hondutti,*
    Boss says, from him to you.

HANNO: *Moy harta vocka.*

MILPHIO: Yeah? Well, sooner you than me. He says   1220
    He aches in the vocal cords. I think he takes us
    For nose and throat men.

AGORASTOCLES: Let him know we're not.
    We mustn't mislead tourists.

MILPHIO: Are you listening?

HANNO: *Refain my cockissam.*

AGORASTOCLES: You set him straight.
   Make sure he gets it. Ask him what he needs.

MILPHIO: Hey, beltless! What's your business? What's your
   beeswax?

HANNO: *Mufrucka.*

AGORASTOCLES: What's he say?

HANNO: *Misoo lay manna.*

AGORASTOCLES: What's he here for?

MILPHIO: Can't you hear him talking?
   He's . . . er . . . importing mice from Africa.
   Wants to present 'em to the city circus.   1230

HANNO: *Shaston noot a deeking shaw.*

AGORASTOCLES: What now?

MILPHIO: Shoestrings, nuts, and drinking straws, he says.
   Wants you to help him sell them.

AGORASTOCLES: He's a peddler,
   I guess.

HANNO: *Agrossam.*

MILPHIO: Yes, sir; very gross.
   Fat and sassy.

HANNO: *Pale shoovarg a dertha.*

AGORASTOCLES: Well? What's that?

MILPHIO: Uh-huh! Some pails and shovels
   For digging in the earth somebody gave him.
   Clearly in the farm equipment line.

AGORASTOCLES: What's that to me?

MILPHIO: He's taking inventory
   So later you can't say he filched the goods.   1240

HANNO: *Stomifid cretam!*

MILPHIO: Oh, oh. Watch out, Boss.
   I wouldn't do it.

AGORASTOCLES: What? What does he want?

MILPHIO: Fellow says he wants to be stoned and crated.

HANNO: *Gunnible sam in lerier!*

AGORASTOCLES: Translate that!

MILPHIO: I can't! Oh, Lord, I'm lost, I shut up shop.

HANNO: Perhaps I'll help you out and speak your language,
   Reprobate of a scrapegrace that you are
   To twit a tourist and a gentleman,
   By God.

MILPHIO: By God, a conniving con man *you* are   1250
   Too, for a gentleman to come and trap us
   With your double talk, you two-tongued snake in the grass,
   You miggledix!

AGORASTOCLES: You, shut your mouth! I warn you,
   Milphio, put the brickbats down. This man

Is kin of mine and I won't have him batted.
May I say, I'm a Carthage boy myself,
Your honor.

HANNO: Is that so! Well met, my townsman!

AGORASTOCLES: By Jove, hello, your honor, whoever you are.
Whatever you need, you let me know. I'm breathless
To do your bidding, on account of our common country.

HANNO: I thank you. And you could perhaps acquaint me   1260
With a young man here called Agorastocles.

AGORASTOCLES: Without a step from here, if the chap you mean
Would be the adopted son of Antidamas.

HANNO: What is that you say?

AGORASTOCLES: I'm Antidamas's boy.

HANNO: Good heavens! Look, compare this keepsake, then,
A token of the family fellowship.

AGORASTOCLES: Of course! Imagine! It's the spitting image
Of one I have at home.

HANNO: Let's have a hand on it!
Hearty hail! Why, lad, your dad and I
Were sidekicks in the old days.

AGORASTOCLES: Any friend   1270
Of Father's . . . come on in, you'll hang your hat here.
Hospitality and my hometown are two things
I don't disclaim.

HANNO: God bless you! But, boy, listen!
How can it be you came to light in Carthage.
If you have an Aetolian dad?

AGORASTOCLES: I don't have.
   I got abducted. Then I got adopted.
   When Antidamas bought me and brought me here.

HANNO: Ah, yes, of course, he was himself adopted
   By old Demarchus. But enough of him.
   Tell me about yourself. Do you remember   1280
   Your folks? Or what their names were?

AGORASTOCLES: I remember.

HANNO: Reveal them then; you never know. You know
   The world is small. They may be kin or cronies.

AGORASTOCLES: My mother's Ampsigura, and my father
   Was Iahon.

HANNO: Aha! A pair of parents
   I'd give my ear to have alive and here!

AGORASTOCLES: They're dead then?

HANNO: In the grave, and it was grievous
   Hard on me, your mother being my cousin
   And Iahon the son of my old uncle.
   Oh, I can tell you it was rough on me
   The way he died and left me all his money.   1290
   However, if you're who you say, hold out
   Your hand: there ought to be a mark a monkey
   Left in the left one when you got too chummy.
   Hold it out, don't hide it.

AGORASTOCLES: Here you have it.

HANNO: Open wide! Good God! Dear lad!

AGORASTOCLES: Dear uncle!
   Bless your heart.

HANNO: Bless Agorastocles!
   How this reunion does rejuvenate me!

MILPHIO: Lovely to see such a stroke of luck on stage,
   Ain't it? But, sir, I have a small suggestion.   1300
   You wouldn't mind if I made it?

HANNO: With my blessing.

MILPHIO: Well, sir, it seems to me, sir, a fellow's son, sir,
   Ought to get back the paternal property,
   If you see what I mean. I mean, the family funds, sir.
   It's only fair.

HANNO: Exactly my opinion.
   He'll have the whole inheritance at once,
   Entire, intact, when he's back in Africa.

MILPHIO: Oh well, but couldn't he have it and stay here?
   Pretty please?

HANNO: And a pretty penny of Hanno's
   To add to it, in the case of my demise.   1310

MILPHIO: Hmm. You know, I just had a bright idea.

HANNO: What is it?

MILPHIO: How'd you like to lend a hand?

HANNO: Nothing could suit me better. What's your plan?

MILPHIO: Can you be cagey and canny? Can you be cunning?

HANNO: I can with an antagonist. With a crony
   I scorn to scheme.

MILPHIO: I'm thinking of a stinker.

HANNO: Let's have at him.

MILPHIO: My master is in love
   With a strumpet.

HANNO: Clever. Never a better choice.

MILPHIO: The pimp lives over here.

HANNO: Well, let's have at him!

MILPHIO: He has two sister slaves he's making over   1320
   Into minxes, but the clever devil
   Never lets my master near the sister
   He hones to hover over as a lover.

HANNO: Severing's acidulous to a suitor.

MILPHIO: The pimp is playing him.

HANNO: It's his profession.

MILPIIIO: But Master wants to ruin him.

HANNO: His duty.

MILPHIO: Now here's my brainstorm, here's my proposition.
   Supposing you pretend the drabs are daughters
   Of yours that someone plundered out of Carthage
   When they were kids. That's it! Go in and claim them   1330
   As freeborn offspring. Get it?

HANNO: Ah, too readily!
   I had two whippersnappers that were snatched
   In just that way, and whisked away one day
   With their nanny.

MILPHIO: Damme! Doesn't he do it proper?!
   It's a pleasure to witness your performance, sir.

HANNO: Oh, I could wish to do it worse!

MILPHIO: That's first-rate!
   My word, ain't he wily! Look at the way he
   Weeps! Now, that's what I call method acting!
   The pundit of the perfect perfidy!
   Better at brisk bamboozling than the master   1340
   Craftsman—myself, of course.

HANNO: But wait, the nurse!
   Describe the girls' attendant!

MILPHIO: She's resplendent!
   Tawny, and not too tall.

HANNO: That's her exactly!

MILPHIO: A looker. A dark-eyed blackbird.

HANNO: By my word,
   A perfect portrait.

MILPHIO: Want to have a look?

HANNO: I'd like to see my girls, of course—but yes!
   Let's have her out here; if she's who I'm hoping
   She'll play a recognition scene directly.

MILPHIO: Hey! Halloo! Anyone at home? Giddenis!
   Get on out here! You've got visitors!   1350

(*Enter* GIDDENIS, *grumpy*)

GIDDENIS: What's the racket?

MILPHIO: Look at what I've brought you.

GIDDENIS: What?

MILPHIO: Don't you know this goat in the pendent
    poncho?

GIDDENIS: I can't believe it! Do my eyes deceive me?
    Hanno the Carthaginian, my patron
    And pater to the waifs!

MILPHIO: Why, that old slyboots.
    I never would've thought she had it in her.

GIDDENIS: Oh, Master Hanno, heaven bless you heavily!
    We never hoped to see you more. God bless you
    And . . . Master, don't be all aghast and agog.
    Don't you know your governess Giddenis?   1360

HANNO: Yes . . . my head's awhirl . . . where are the girls?
    I must see my daughters!

GIDDENIS: They're at the temple of Venus.

HANNO: Which one? What for? What are they doing there?

GIDDENIS: This is a special feast of Venus, sir,
    It's Aphrodisia day. They gone to pray
    To ask the goddess to assist their fortunes.

MILPHIO: I guess she must have heard them if this bird's
    In earnest after all.

AGORASTOCLES: Giddenis! Is he
    Really their dad?

GIDDENIS: Indeed he is! Oh, Master,
    Your search was worth whatever you had to suffer!   1370

You came in the nick of the eleventh hour,
I swear! This very day those two sweet virgins
Were going to be forced to forsake their names and natures
Turn prostitute and taint their patronymic.

BEARER: (*Bearing down on* GIDDENIS)
  Ooh, amma dilly!

GIDDENIS: *Hoo! been silly musting.*
  Mepstatim, das dummit lan a coshen!

AGORASTOCLES: What are they saying? What's going on?

HANNO: A meeting.
  Mother and son are greeting. Now, Giddenis,
  Stow that snivel; spare the female furniture.

AGORASTOCLES: What's furniture for girls?

HANNO: Their lusty lungs.   1380

AGORASTOCLES: Oh, let her howl.

HANNO: (*To* MILPHIO)   Escort my employees
  Inside, sir, and assume the nurse among 'em.

AGORASTOCLES: Get a move on.

MILPHIO: What about the women?
  Who's going to introduce him?

AGORASTOCLES: I can manage.
  I'm qualified.

MILPHIO: I'm going to miss the climax!
  Okay, though, if you say so. I'll just exit.

AGORASTOCLES: Execute it, don't articulate it.
I want a banquet cooked up for my uncle.

MILPHIO: *Yeah cheena,* everybody! But I'll prod you
From here to the mill and from there to the jail and from
there   1390
To the big black auction block. I'll bet a nickel
You'll gripe and grouse at the housewarming I can fix you.

(*They exit*)

AGORASTOCLES: Uncle! Don't suppose I unprotest
My protestation! Proffer me your daughter!

HANNO: Agreed.

AGORASTOCLES: You give your word?

HANNO: I do indeed.

AGORASTOCLES: Oh, what a duck of an uncle! I detect
An undeniable family likeness now!
Now I can chatter and prattle at my pleasure
With the precious pet! But we'd better be getting on
If you want to see your daughters.

HANNO: If I *want* to!?   1400
I'm greedy for it.

AGORASTOCLES: Gracious! They're just coming.

HANNO: Ah! How's that? My heart! Are those my daughters?
My little toddling tots? Those great adults?

AGORASTOCLES: Uncle, they're actresses, so naturally
They're up on buskins.

(*Enter* ADELPHASIUM *and* ANTERASTILIS, *airy*)

ADELPHASIUM: Now if you ask me,
  That was a festival to feast aesthetic
  Eyes on! The way the altar was embellished!
  There's nothing as courtly as a cute cortege
  Of courtesans when they're courting Venus's favor;
  And a stack of sacrifices decked in gimcrack   1410
  And bric-a-brac, fit for the Queen of Passion,
  Mashes, and fashionable infatuation.
  Today her ascendancy was in evidence:
  Such quantities of such quiddities of such quality!
  And the altar ambrosial in attar and ambergris!
  Well, Venus, good Goddess, you know how to put on a show,
  And to gather a crowd of the Calydon courtesans, too.

ANTERASTILIS: Excuse me, Sister. *If* I might add a footnote,
  I'd say not one of the slave girls gained her favor
  And got such a wink from Venus as we two did.   1420
  And on the subject of winking, I just might add,
  Ad, the men weren't mocking us by a long shot,
  The way they were some others.

ADELPHASIUM: Well, but rather
  Than hear you say so and boast of yourself so, Sister,
  I'd like to think others were thinking it.

ANTERASTILIS: I hope so!

ADELPHASIUM: Oh, dear. And so do I. When I think of our birth
  And the worth of our stock and the lack of it in those others,
  Well, I could cry. We owe it to our ancestry
  Never to give one tongue a cause to wag.

HANNO: O Jupiter, who supports and succors mortals,   1430
  Who gives us breath and broth and who our hope is,
  Let me prosper and repossess my losses,
  Restore my two sweet stolen daughters: show
  A father's fondness reaps its fruits below.

AGORASTOCLES: Don't fret, I'll see to it; Jupiter's my pet,
  Uncle. I've got him wrapped around my finger,
  By Jove!

HANNO: Don't joke! How can you?!

AGORASTOCLES: Don't cry, Uncle.

ANTERASTILIS: Isn't it glorious to be victorious,
  Sister dear, the way we were today?
  And have the whole world wanting to adores us   1440
  'Cause we're so nifty?

ADELPHASIUM: And one of us is a ninny!
  Sister, sister! You fancy you're fascinating
  The minute you notice nobody's mocking you
  But marking you up with bootblack.

AGORASTOCLES: Uncle, Uncle!

HANNO: Don't bother me, boy. What is it?

AGORASTOCLES: Let's just face it.

HANNO: I'm facing that.

AGORASTOCLES: Oh, unclemost Unc of uncles!

HANNO: Well? Out with it.

AGORASTOCLES: She's such a pretty petkins!
  And such sagacity.

HANNO: Hereditary,
  That. She had it from her dad.

AGORASTOCLES: I doubt it!
  Why, man, she wore out all the wits you gave her   1450

An age ago! Whatever apprehension
And IQ she lays claim to now, she owes it,
Every iota, to me and my devotion.

ADELPHASIUM: Shackled we may be, Sister, but our extraction
Exacts that we act so as never to raise a snicker
Or shock a soul. We women are always weak,
But the worst of faults is called complacency,
And taking too little trouble to attract.

ANTERASTILIS: Oh, I agree. But, Sister, wasn't it super
The way our signs were kinder than anyone else's?   1460
And Venus was certainly pleased with our sacrifice
If the soothsayer said the truth!

AGORASTOCLES: I'd give my youth
To know what he said about me.

ANTERASTILIS: That we'd be free
A few days from now, at most, no matter for Master.
But I hardly see how that can be, unless
A god or our dad is going to assist us.

AGORASTOCLES: Listen!
I'm certain that soothsayer had myself in mind
When he made that promise; yes sir, that's the fact.
He knows my passion.

ADELPHASIUM: Let's pass in.

ANTERASTILIS: I'm coming.

HANNO: If you please, just hold your ground a moment.   1470
I'd like to have a word with you.

ADELPHASIUM: Who are you?

AGORASTOCLES: This fellow is philanthropic.

ADELPHASIUM: Opportune,
   If true. Who is he?

AGORASTOCLES: He's your boon companion.

ADELPHASIUM: Who supplies the boon?

AGORASTOCLES: I promise, baby,
   He's straight as a die.

ADELPHASIUM: My! Better that than crooked.

AGORASTOCLES: If you have one chum in the country, let it
     be him.

ADELPHASIUM: Suppose you compose your own prayers.

AGORASTOCLES: Adelphasium!
   He wants to treat you females very sweetly.

ADELPHASIUM: Sweets to the sweet from the sweet, sir!

AGORASTOCLES: See her, Uncle?
   If I were Jupiter I'd appropriate her   1480
   And kick Juno out of my house on the spot. Such sunny speech!
   Such decent, dulcet, dainty turns of phrase!

HANNO: My daughter, Adelphasium, not a doubt.
   Did you catch my shrewd approach?

AGORASTOCLES: Felicitous
   And apposite, by jeeze.

HANNO: Well? Shall I tease them?

AGORASTOCLES: Be brief; the audience has got the fidgets.

HANNO: Right, let's get on with it! I wish to issue
    A summons to you strumpets!

AGORASTOCLES: That's the spirit,
    Uncle! Shall I pinch this one?

ADELPHASIUM: Don't touch me!
    Agorastocles? He's your relation?   1490

AGORASTOCLES: I'll let you know as soon as you need to, lady.
    Meantime say your prayers; here's where I settle
    My score with you for life. You'll be . . . my wife!

HANNO: Done! To the court! No appeal and no reprieve!
    I'm your witness: have her!

AGORASTOCLES: You're my witness . . .
    And then she's mine to kiss . . . that is to say . . .
    No, that's exactly what I meant to say.

HANNO: You! Don't delay, you're due in court; unless
    Abduction suits you better.

ADELPHASIUM: What's the summons?
    Why must we go to court? What have we done   1500

AGORASTOCLES: You'll find out when you get there.

ADELPHASIUM: Thank you, traitor!
    I see my own dogs snap at me.

AGORASTOCLES: I'm a lap dog,
    I need a lot of petting. Try a kiss
    To pacify me, with a taste of tongue
    For a special treat. Why, I'll eat out of your hand,
    I'll be at your feet, I'll melt like a bite of butter.

HANNO: Get along there!

ADELPHASIUM: What have you got against us?

HANNO: You stole from me.

ADELPHASIUM: What, us?

HANNO: Yes, you!

AGORASTOCLES: It's so!

ADELPHASIUM: What stealing does he mean?

AGORASTOCLES: Why not ask him?

HANNO: For lo these many years you've hid my kids   1510
   Hugger-mugger; highborn, freeborn females.

ADELPHASIUM: Good heavens! Don't believe such evil of us,
   Sir! I swear you'll never prove it, never!

AGORASTOCLES: Let's have a little bet on your veracity,
   Loser to pay in extended osculation.

ADELPHASIUM: Let go of me! This isn't your affair!

AGORASTOCLES: You're my affair, if you think it fair or not.
   This man's my uncle and I must back his business.
   I'm going to tell him all about your intrigues
   And how you keep his girls as poor as churls   1520
   Although you know they're stolen and nearly noble.

ADELPHASIUM: Where are they? Who do you mean, for pity's
   sake!

AGORASTOCLES: Are they nettled enough?

HANNO: Shall I tell them?

AGORASTOCLES: Go on, spill it.

ADELPHASIUM: Oh, Sister, this is tragic! I'm distracted!
I'm flabbergasted!

HANNO: ⸗   Pay attention, ladies!
My first prayer, if I thought the gods would hear it,
Would be that nothing undeserved should fall . . .
To the undeserving.

AGORASTOCLES: Hey!

HANNO: However, now,
The gods are good, and deserve the gratitude
Of me and you and your mother, since their mighty   1530
Bounty blesses our affection for you.
Girls, get ready for the revelation:
You sisters are my daughters; I'm your father
And this fine boy is a cousin, once removed.

ADELPHASIUM: They wouldn't think a trick like that was funny,
Would they, if it wasn't true?

AGORASTOCLES: No fooling,
Honest, I tell you, Ad, the man's your dad.
Why don't you take his hand?

ADELPHASIUM: Oh! It's my father?
My really unbelieved-in, out-of-the-blue
Papa? May I hug you?

ANTERASTILIS: Daddy *darling!*   1540
How I've prayed and pined!

ADELPHASIUM: He's got two daughters.

ANTERASTILIS: Well, come on, there's hugging room for two.

AGORASTOCLES: Now I'm left out. When do I get my loving?

HANNO: Oh, I'm a mountain of joy! I found a fountain
    Of youth to wash my old ex-woes away.

ADELPHASIUM: It all defies belief!

HANNO: But I have proof!
    Giddenis recognized me in a minute.

ADELPHASIUM: Our nurse! Where is she?

HANNO: Safe inside his house.

AGORASTOCLES: Now that's enough of that nonsense on his neck!
    What's the point prolonging the hanging posture?   1550
    You there, on the left, let go!

ADELPHASIUM: Oh! Cheeky
    Pest! What makes you think he'll give his blessing?

AGORASTOCLES: Okay, I quit.

ADELPHASIUM: In which case I'll kiss *you*,
    That's for the man that I wanted all along.

HANNO: I sentence us all to a jailhouse of embraces.
    Now where under heaven have you ever seen such bliss?

AGORASTOCLES: Just deserts for the deserving, Uncle?

HANNO: My fondest fantasy's become a fact!

AGORASTOCLES: O Apelles and Zeuxis, peerless painters!
    Why did you die two centuries too soon   1560
    To do this family portrait? I won't trust it
    To any recent artist.

HANNO: Mount Olympus
  And all inhabitants thereof, I love you
  Just as I ought, my gratitude is utter
  That Fate has requited the faith of a doting pater,
  That heaven was waiting to play the benevolent plotter,
  That I am permitted my daughter . . . and my daughter.

Scene 2

(*Enter* ANTAMONIDES, *adamant*)

ANTAMONIDES: I'll have my mammon's worth of those finances
  I slipped the pimp or I herewith give permission
  To the local jokers to take me for their monkey!   1570
  The idea! The in*dig*nity of that dawdler
  Issuing extortionate invitations
  To luncheon, and then sashaying out of the back
  And leaving me like a butler; not a bottle
  Or a broad or a bawd or a pander or a pickle!
  I lifted a little collateral on my losses
  And left. That's how I operate. I'll have
  Some heavy military taxes levied
  On that sweet sourface! Oh, he picked his victim
  This time! All I need to bring my choler   1580
  To consummate quintessence, is the presence
  Of that bold bitch. By God, I'd fetch a punch
  Would make her the color of a crow. I'd dye her dark
  As an Ethiopian waterboy at the circus!

ANTERASTILIS: You dear, you darling, squeeze me, please. I'm a
    skittish
  Little thing, always afraid of buzzards!
  And afraid one might come looking for your chick!

ADELPHASIUM: Oh, Papa, hold me tight!

ANTAMONIDES: I'm wasting time.
  I can do a decent meal with the booty here.
  But what? What's that? What's this? What's up?
     What on?   1590
  What's this congress? What's this concentration?
  Who's the barboy in the shapeless apron?
  Hey? Am I going blind? Is that my baby?
  My Anterastilis? It is! It is!
  I always knew she was stringing me along
  But I never thought I'd see her stand in the street
  Cuddling a common barkeep, on my honor!
  I'll pass that ass to the executioner
  This instant for triple torture, I will, by God!
  These tunic-toters think they're plenty sexy,   1600
  But I can cool an African amoroso's
  Ardor, when I'm started. Watch me. You!
  I'm speaking to you, slut! What? Why aren't you blushing?!
  And you, dad! What's your business with my baggage?
  Answer me sharp!

HANNO: Good afternoon, young man.

ANTAMONIDES: Don't try to sidetrack me, you side of bacon.
  What do you think gives you the right to touch her
  With the tip of your little finger?

HANNO: I enjoy it.

ANTAMONIDES: *Enjoy it*, do you?!

HANNO: I enjoy it, boy.

ANTAMONIDES: Go and hang yourself with your sandal
    thongs,   1610
  Mister! Do you presume to impersonate
  A gay deceiver, toenails? Do you suppose
  To seduce the whore of a hairy-chested he-man?
  You peeled sardine, you sementiated sarpis!

You hide, you brine, you masticated mango!
You reek of leeks like a row of Roman rowers!

AGORASTOCLES: Excuse me, sir. The way you cast aspersions
On this personage, it occurs to me you might
Have an itching chin. Are you looking for a licking?

ANTAMONIDES: Won't somebody give this lad a tambourine   1620
So he can set that poetry to music?
You look to me more like a ballerina
Than a man.

AGORASTOCLES: Oh? Would you like to see me dance?
(*Calling inside*)
Guards! Come out here armed!

ANTAMONIDES: No harm, no harm
Intended, sir! Say, can't you take a joke?

ANTERASTILIS: Just what sort of fun does it afford you,
Antamonides, to affront my father?
For in fact, this gentleman's our progenitor,
If you want to know. He's just now found it out,
And found the "ballerina" is his nephew.   1630

ANTAMONIDES: Well, I'll be blowed. Isn't that a lovely show?!
I'm satisfied and gratified to find
The pander isn't prospering.

AGORASTOCLES: Propitious!
I see our hero just now hobbling home.
Let's drag him off to court to get his due.

HANNO: Oh, no!

AGORASTOCLES: Why not?

HANNO: Rather, to get his drubbing.

(*Enter* JACKAL, *jaded*)

JACKAL: There's comfort in confiding in your comrades,
  There is indeed. they never disappoint you.
  Mine were unanimous in their opinion.
  I'd have to hang myself to save my shekels.
  That's consolation.

AGORASTOCLES: Jackal! Quick! To court.   1640

JACKAL: Be altruistic, Agorastocles,
  Let me noose myself to the nearest post.

HANNO: You! To court!

JACKAL: You too? What's your complaint?

HANNO: Quite plain. I proclaim these damsels are my daughters,
  Born free in Carthage and spirited away
  As minors with their nurse.

JACKAL: Oh, worse and worse!
  That's nothing wonderful. I only wondered
  Why nobody came to claim them long ago.

AGORASTOCLES: I want a restitution presto, pimp!
  Double the stuff you took.

JACKAL: You'll have to take it   1650
  Off my neck.

HANNO: And I'll have vicious vengeance
  Before I've had enough.

JACKAL: Take what you like
  From here. I'll pay my debts with my neck and back
  From now on, like a porter.

ANTAMONIDES: Hey, procurer!

JACKAL: The pimp is occupied. Is it important?

ANTAMONIDES: I mean to procure the repair of my petty cash
    Before they stash you away in jail.*

JACKAL: The devil!

ANTAMONIDES: My mind's made up; you sup on bread and water.
    You're slated to settle three simultaneous scores:
    Money for me, and money for him, and your neck   1660
    In a noose for justice.

HANNO: What's the best procedure?
    If I really insist on an absolute reprisal
    I must risk my neck on an unknown equity
    After all I've heard of scandalous Calydon.

ADELPHASIUM: Father, a favor to me: don't fool with him.

ANTERASTILIS: Listen to Sister, Dad, and let's depart.
    Let the reptile be.

HANNO: Attention, pimp!
    You ought to get your comeuppance in so much hemp.
    But I'll not pursue the matter.

AGORASTOCLES: No, me neither.
    As long as I get my jack back, Jackal, why
    As soon as you're out of stir you can go to . . . hoosegow.   1670

JACKAL: I'm glad to see you're running true to type.

---

*Two versions of the last scene are given in the manuscripts, and the numbering and ordering of the lines are in dispute. The translator has followed Paul Nixon's (Loeb Library edition) reconstruction of the scene.

ANTAMONIDES: My Carthaginian friend, I beg forgiveness
  If in my ferocity I was offensive.
  I guarantee I'm gratified to see
  You've got your girlies back.

HANNO: Sir, I believe you
  And I forgive you

ANTAMONIDES: You're another issue,
  Pimp. I'll have a mopsy or my money.

JACKAL: How would you like my flute-girl?

ANTAMONIDES: Not a chance!
  You can't tell her cheeks from her chest.

JACKAL: You'll have the best.   1680

ANTAMONIDES: I'd better!

JACKAL: And you'll have your dough tomorrow.

AGORASTOCLES: Don't let it slip your mind!

JACKAL: Come inside, soldier.

ANTAMONIDES: I'm right behind you.

(*They exit*)

AGORASTOCLES: Now then, Uncle Hanno!
  When do you set your sights and your sail for Carthage?
  I'm going too.

HANNO: Immediately, or sooner!

AGORASTOCLES: But give me a couple of days to hold an auction.

HANNO: As you wish.

AGORASTOCLES: Let's go and have refreshments.
  Please follow me inside. I'm tired and dry,
  And I think we've earned ourselves a nip and nap:
  Now you folks—clap!   1690

ASSES GALORE

(ASINARIA)

Translated by Fred Chappell

INTRODUCTION

Scholars assure us that despite their apparent similarities, the Plautine plays are nothing like our modern musical comedies. I have appreciated this intelligence, but I am not so overcome with gratitude that I have allowed it to define the nature of my translation—which, in any case, is more properly denominated an "adaptation."

I turned this play into musical comedy for two reasons: I wanted to produce lively and interesting scenes, and I needed a way to overleap some of the deficiencies of the original work. Songs—whether or not they bear much formal or practical resemblance to the Roman canticae—provide a pleasant method of skirting around some of the faulty maneuvers and illogic of the *Asinaria*.

Plautus's lack of verisimilitude here is easy to remark. Demaenetus (our "Manny") is at first described as a good father willing to make personal sacrifices for his son. Yet before long he insists on a sexual and financial arrangement that might raise a blush even in our confused century. Argyrippus ("Rip") is shown in the beginning as dying for the love of Philaenium ("Lena"), but soon enough accepts his father's gross proposal—and so does Lena, his courtesan-lover, who is supposed to be smitten with Rip. Lena's mother, Cleareta, is at least consistent in her behavior: she will lease her daughter only to the highest bidder—and seems to think that this principle makes her a paragon among parents. Manny, who would be notorious in the largest metropolis for his lowlife habits, has managed for decades to deceive his wife and friends as to his true character. Rip, although still a young man, is described as being both a sailor and a lawmaker.

These egregious inconsistencies may help explain why the *Asinaria* has never achieved popularity in later ages, has been performed only rarely, and has not been imitated by later playwrights. Molière knew the play, yet lifted but a single line from it; the French

95

taste for inexorable dramatic logic is cruelly frustrated here. And though this play, like the others of Plautus, is a storehouse of Roman proverbs, only one has achieved later currency: "homo lupus homini" ["man is a wolf to man"]. Our latter ages have given this adage a much more mordant tone than Plautus's casual context provides.

There stands another and nearly insuperable obstacle to its finding popularity: the relentless scurrility of the story. My wife, Susan, remarked that this play is like one of Shakespeare's dark comedies except that it lacks the "noble" parts of the action. Even that description may be too mild, for there is not one admirable character here, and hardly any likeable ones—though the slaves, Libanus and Leon, possess energy and some charm. The piece displays an unsettling lack of an ethical center until the final scenes, when Manny's wife, Artemona ("Big Mona"), shows up to put affairs in order with an iron hand. She is hardly drawn as a figure; the playwright feels that he can depend on her role being so easily recognized as a stock character that he has not bothered to fill in her outlines. This detail may imply a satirical point—that Roman morality had fallen completely to the care of the powerful Roman matron ("Artemona" is an anagram of "matrona")—but even she is drawn in none too friendly a fashion, portrayed as a sanctimonious bully.

There are other problems, too: slave-beating is no longer regarded as automatically funny, as it was in Plautus's time—and in Shakespeare's. The final scene in the brothel must be rather difficult to stage convincingly. And we lose the humor of the Latin puns, though this loss sometimes may be accounted merciful.

These dramatic shortcomings gave me the temerity to take a few liberties, to make consistent some of the poetic conceits, to clear up some of the alliterative nonsense verse, to add a couple of songs unjustified by the Latin text.

But for all my quibbles in this introduction—and quibbles are what they amount to—I found the play entertaining to read and fun to try to put into American English. I kept very strictly to the sequence of action; I kept as much of the Roman idiom as I could make comprehensible and colloquial; I used the songs to underline the text and not to transfigure it; and I preserved as much of the knockabout atmosphere as I could get onto a printed page. I learned that if I gave the play its head and left off judging it by standards utterly alien to its author, the scenes achieved real interest. The play has outlasted all its purse-mouthed detractors and will of course outlast whatever damage my version may have wreaked upon it.

The *Asinaria* is after all a self-confessed minor play with goals that are modest. These qualities are part of its charm, just as Prologus tells us in his diffident *vade mecum:*

> My friends, I hope you'll be attentive
> To this new play by the inventive
> Plautus—and that experience of it
> Will be to your and our own profit.
> The brassy herald now will sound
> His horn to halt your milling around.
>
> (Thank you, Herald. Now keep still.
> I'll pay you when you send your bill.)
>
> My purpose here is nothing vital:
> Merely to inform you of the title,
> That in the original was *Onagos,*
> By the Greek Demophilus,
>
> Of whom remains now but his name—
> Such a fragile thing is fame.
> Our Latin Plautus never shirks
> The chance of cribbing Hellenic works
> And, finding the Greekish tongue no barrier,
> Calls this piece his *Asinaria.*
>
> Our Senex droll, our ingenue kissable,
> We think you'll find the play is risible
> And think you'll be diverted by it—
> If you will sit down and be quiet!

Fred Chappell

ASSES GALORE

CHARACTERS

LIBANUS slave of Manny
MANNY (DEMAENETUS), an old gentleman of Rome
RIP (ARGYRIPPUS), son of Manny
CLEARETA, a madam
LEON (LEONIDA), another slave of Manny
MR. MARCHAND (MERCATOR), a trader
LENA (PHILAENIUM), a courtesan and daughter of Cleareta
MR. DEVLIN JR. (DIABOLUS), a young gentleman and Rip's rival for
    the favors of Lena
MR. LEECH (PARASITUS), Mr. Devlin Jr.'s attorney
BIG MONA (ARTEMONA), Manny's wife

ARGUMENT

Athens formerly, but now Rome
Serves as setting for this play:
Senex, wanting to have his way,
Excited by an itch to roam,
Steals some money from his spouse;

Gives it to his son to bless
A yearlong sexual excess
Laid in a famous madame's house.

99

Oh what silly lives we lead,
Riotous with lurid mess,
Engorged in folly toe to head.

SCENE: *A street in Rome. Enter* MANNY *from his house. With him is his slave,* LIBANUS.

ACT I

Scene 1

LIBANUS: We call him "Rip," this only son you love so much. I know you'd like for him to be prosperous and live a long and happy life. But now you're getting along in years, Manny—and you're frightened of your wife, Big Mona. So tell me no lies. If you lie to me, I hope she lives to tango on your tombstone.

MANNY: Wish me no calamities, then I'll tell you no lies. What is it that your little brain wants to know?

LIBANUS: You've got to be serious. Don't jerk me around.

MANNY: Ask your question, my highly familiar slave.

LIBANUS: You won't send me to the place where stone grinds stone?

MANNY: Come again? Where are you talking about?   11

LIBANUS: To the Moaning-Groaning Den, where dead oxen torture men.

MANNY: Ah, yes . . . Those bullhide whips down at the grain mill. That's the grist of what you mean, that's what you're aiming at.

LIBANUS: That's exactly where I'm *not* aiming at. Spit that word *slave-mill* out of your system. Spit it out and stomp on it.

MANNY: (*Amused*) Yes, Master.

(*Spits*)

LIBANUS: You're not even trying. You've gotta hawk it deep and spit it far. All the way down and all the way yonder.   20

MANNY: How far yonder?

LIBANUS: To the grave.

MANNY: Hey now. Better watch your mouth, Crowbait.

LIBANUS: Not your grave. I never said yours. Your wife's. Big Mona's.

MANNY: That's better. Always speak your mind.

LIBANUS: Thanks. I hope that soon you'll acquire one to speak.

MANNY: Let's get to it: I need your advice. We've got a situation. I know that most fathers would be angry, but I don't want to be mad at Rip.

LIBANUS: (*Sarcastic aside*) That's it, bring your problems to Libanus. He's a slave, so he must have a lot of free time.   31

MANNY: You know Lena, that call girl who lives with her mother in Cleareta's House of Ill Repute? Well, Rip's in love with her. Have you heard anything?

LIBANUS: Only that he's hit hard times.

MANNY: Why's that?

LIBANUS: She wants more than he can supply. . . . More money, I
mean.

MANNY: Why don't you help him out now and then?

LIBANUS: Well now, I do help him. And my buddy Leon helps me
help him.   41

MANNY: Good. I don't usually give bonuses to slaves, but you fellows
deserve one. Even so, we've got to keep an eye out for my wife.
You know how Mona is.

LIBANUS: I feel I know Big Mona pretty well. (*Flinches and rubs his
buttocks*) I know I feel her very well. You're a lucky man to get her
blows firsthand. All I get are hand-me-downs.

MANNY: Yes, she's rather temperamental.

LIBANUS: That's half right. She's got temper. Mental, I don't know.

MANNY: She just needs to lighten up. The trouble these days is that
parents are too hard on their kids. That's no fun. I want my son to
like me as his buddy. I want to be the best friend Rip ever had.

(*Song: "I Want to Be My Son's Best Friend"; "Volo amari"*)

My father used to try to win my love   53
By giving me anything I ever wanted;
And though his plan is sometimes thought ill of,
I think of him enrolled among the sainted.

   For I agree with how my dad
   Brought me up as his darling lad.
   No matter what the present trend,
   I plan to be my son's best friend.   60

He gave me all my little heart desired;
He gave me candy and expensive toys;

He found a girl who all my senses fired;
If I had asked, he would have paid for boys.

He gave me gifts no other kid could have;
He bought the best, he never purchased junk;
The day he bought my personal household slave
Together we came home kneewalking drunk.

    And I agree with how my dad
    Brought me up as his darling lad.   70
    No matter what the present trend,
    I plan to be my son's best friend.

And when at last my dear old daddy died
I mourned him just the way he would have said:
I partied till the liquor cured my hide
And every chance I got, I got laid.

    So I resolve to follow his plan
    Until my son becomes a man;
    To follow Daddy I intend:
    I want to be my son's best friend.   80

So now just this morning Rip comes and tells me that he's in love
with this neat little piece by the name of Lena. And he asks for a
lot of money. Okay by me. His mother can do the moralizing; she
likes that. But it's not my style. I'm proud that he leveled with me,
so I'll make it easy for him. I want to give him the money so that he
can have a good time with his little honeypot.

LIBANUS: The trouble is, you don't control the money. Your wife put
her dowry-slave, that guy they call Saurea, in charge of the whole
business. You're left out in the cold.

MANNY: True, I sold my masculine authority for money. . . . But
let's get down to it. Here's the deal: my son needs a thousand
dollars. You see that he gets it.   92

LIBANUS: How?

MANNY: By cheating me out of it.

LIBANUS: That cart won't roll. I can't steal the pants off a man who's stark raving naked. You don't have a dime, unless you've defrauded your wife. If you've swindled Big Mona for a bundle, then I can swindle you.

MANNY: It's okay to swindle me. It's better to swindle her. Best of all would be to swindle that sorry-ass Saurea. Fleece whoever looks fleeceable. Do it soon and we'll be buddies, you and I.   101

LIBANUS: You're asking me to fight a killer whale with a toothpick.

MANNY: Get Leon to help you out. Think, man, think. Improvise! But get the cash for Rip to give to Lena.

LIBANUS: Well, okay, but—

MANNY: But what?

LIBANUS: Suppose they call the cops and I wind up in the pokey. Will you bail me out?

MANNY: Naturally.

LIBANUS: Then your worries are over. Are there any other little impossibilities you'd like to see performed? If not, I'll go on to the forum.   112

MANNY: Have a nice day. (*Calls him back*) Just a minute, though—

LIBANUS: (*Returning*) Always at your beck and call.

MANNY: Where will you be if I need you?

LIBANUS: (*Aside*) I'll be taking my big fat ease in any place I damn
well please. Because from this time forward, I'm a man with no
master. You've shown me what you're made of and it's shoddy
stuff. If I get away with what I've got in mind, you'll be nobody's
sweetheart anymore. (*To Manny*) Don't worry. I'm going off to
hatch a plot.   121

MANNY: Good deal. You can find me at the moneychanger, Bullion
Bill.

LIBANUS: In the forum?

MANNY: Yes. Just in case you need me.

LIBANUS: All right.

(*He exits*)

MANNY: (*Sings "My Man Libanus"; "Non esse servus peior"*)

> Now when you need a scurvy trick,
> Don't call for Slug or Dirty Dick.
> The chap who'll do it good and slick—
> My man Libanus.   130
>
> He's our Johnny on the spot,
> Especially if the spot is not
> Legitimate but you-know-what!
>   Johnny Libanus!
>
> *Ban ban Libanus—ban*
> *Crooked master, crooked man*
>
> He's the one you want to see
> For a jot of forgery
> Performed for quite a modest fee—
> "Novelist" Libanus.   140

To perpetrate a crafty fraud
Just tip the guy a knowing nod:
He'll get it done today, by God!
          "Softsoap" Libanus.

> *Ban ban Libanus—ban*
> *Crooked master, crooked man*

Hear the stroke of midnight break!
He is lying wide awake,
Planning, plotting—for your sake.
(So says Libanus.)   150

His the character so black,
His the creepy sneak attack—
Never ever turn your back
          On my man Libanus!

> *Ban ban Libanus—ban*
> *Crooked master, crooked man*

Scene 2

(Center stage a housefront all gaudy and froufrou with a prominent sign above the door: CLEARETA'S HOUSE OF ILL REPUTE. *Suddenly the door flies open, and* RIP *is catapulted out to land flat on his butt in the street. The door slams shut.)*

RIP: *(Furiously addressing the door)* So you think that's it, eh? Throw me out into the street. After I've given you the best weeks of my life. I know the gist of your philosophy: Be nice to me and I'll be nice to—me. Well, that's all over now. I'm going to the cops. I'll tell them how Cleareta has made her daughter Lena into a whore. You're a menace to society. You're as deadly as a typhoon at sea . . . Worse. I made money at sea. But in your house I lost every dollar. You ungrateful bitch! You've got my money and I've got nothing. But I'm going to have one thing. One thing I'll make damn sure of.

(Song: "Revenge!"; "Male quod potero")

Revenge! Revenge! I'll have revenge!
Before this sordid story's told,
Your daughter and yourself I'll send
Back to the gutter from which you crawled!   170

For in your House of Ill Repute
I squandered all my worldly goods;
But now I'm broke I get the boot—
Do you call that gratitude?

When first we met you lived in squalor
Without two dimes to rub together.
I've spent with you my final dollar;
I'll see your ass shine in the weather.

You treat me like a dog, a pig;
And if I perish, you don't care;   180
Cleareta, you've grown too big,
Too big for the britches you don't wear.

You've robbed me blind, your soul is black;
You've taken all my silver and gold.
Now I'll work to send you back,
Back to the gutter from which you crawled!

(Enter CLEARETA *from the house)*

CLEARETA: Rip, I want to thank you for your warm regards. Your
    compliments are worth as much as silver. I wouldn't sell them for
    any price. Cupid has taken your brains and locked them up in my
    House of Ill Repute. And only Cupid has the key. You're a sailor
    boy, but as fast as you sail away, the tide will float you right back to
    port. Our port.   192

RIP: Damn you and your Cupid and ports. No matter how it stings and hurts, you're going to get your just deserts.

CLEARETA: You speak loudly, but you carry an extremely little stick.

RIP: You owe me. If I was Lena's one-and-only, you'd still owe me. Who saved you from bankruptcy? Me, myself, and I, that's who.

CLEARETA: Slip me the money and the three of you can have her. Lena will be your one and only when your bankroll gets some size on it.　　　　　　　　　　　200

RIP: How much do I have to pay? You never get enough. As soon as I pay you once, here you come again.

CLEARETA: Give to the amount that you love. You're the one who never gets enough. As soon as you go out the door, we hear you knocking again.

RIP: I paid the fee.

CLEARETA: And you got the girl. All fair and square.

RIP: You've done me wrong.

CLEARETA: I do the way I have to do. Read the plays and novels and tell me if you come across a madame with a heart of gold. Believe me, we're all alike. We're not here to develop your amatory skills. We have to look out for ourselves.

RIP: But if you're nice to me now, I'll keep on coming back in the future.　　　　　　　　　　　212

CLEARETA: Try to understand. The girl who gives it away hasn't got a future.

(She sings and accompanies herself with castanets "The Day the Bill Is Due"; "Quasi piscis")

I offer but a single crumb;
Like flocks of birds the suckers come;
And though they like to bill and coo,
There comes the day the bill is due.   220

They don't know why but still they do;
The guilt is sharp, the pleasures too;
Our lives are short and time's a thief—
And screwing seems a true relief.

And to my House of Ill Repute
They flock to taste exotic fruit,
But when the reckoning is due
I don't accept their billets-doux.

I know to Trot they're always Hot To,
But *I take cash* is 'Reta's motto: 230
And though they swoon and bill and coo
How soon the noon the bill is due!

(*Whispers*)
On easy love your heart is set;
I take you in my silken net:
You'll find your will's deserted you—
Then comes the day the bill is due!

And that's our watchword: Every man for himself.

RIP: I paid a lot of money to learn that tune.

CLEARETA: And if you had any money left, you'd sing a different
   tune. But if you can't get up the cash, I won't stay here talking
   trash.   241

RIP: I won't let you get away with—

CLEARETA: And I won't give my girl away for free. . . . But look
   now: young as you are, you're an old customer. We understand

how you feel. So just slip me a thousand dollars, put it right here in
my hand, and I'll see you get a freebie with Lena this very night.
No charge. Gratis. On the house.

RIP: And if I say I don't have the money?

CLEARETA: I'll accept your word: I'll believe you don't have any. But
Lena will be with somebody who does.   250

RIP: What happened to the money I already gave you?

CLEARETA: All gone. If I still had the money, you'd still have the
girl. Water is free, the sun and moon and stars are free. Nobody
charges for the time of day. But for a loaf of bread and a bottle
of wine they want cash on the line. That's what the baker says
and the vintner says, and that's our policy too. Cash on the line.
Seeing is believing. A buck in the hand is worth a hand in the
bush . . . I don't need to go on, I'm sure. I wouldn't want to
bore you.

RIP: You used to take a different tone with me. When I had money, it
was honey honey honey. Sugar and spice and everything nice. You
were all happy to see me come in.   262

(*Song: "I Was Your One and Only"; "Me unicum unum"*)

Do you remember how, back in the golden days,
I was your one and only? You said so all the time.
Now you come to tell me we must go our separate ways.
Oh, the way Time treats us is a mortal crime.

    As lovely as the moon,
    As warming as the sun,
    Love shines on us today
    And is tomorrow gone.   270

You'd flutter all about me like a cooing dove;
Whatever I desired, my wish was your command;

You had a Horn of Plenty I took plenty of;
Your lovely daughter Lena came easy to my hand.

The Age of Paradise has fled this world of sorrow,
With Autumn in the fields and Winter on its way.
I weep and cannot bear to think about Tomorrow:
I was your one and only—only yesterday!

> As burning as the sun,
> As distant as the moon,   280
> Time takes our one and only
> All away soon.

But now you don't care any longer. You dreadful bitches!

CLEARETA: Temper, temper . . . Our profession is just like bird
catching. The bird catcher has an area that he sweeps and scatters
with expensive bird seed. After a while the birds get used to
feasting there. If you want to make money, you have to spend
money. Day after day the birds eat for free. But then! . . . And
once they're caught they're money in the pocket . . . That's how it
is with us: the seeded area is my House of Ill Repute, the expensive bait is Lena, and the bed is the bird catcher's net. And you,
my able seaman, are the pigeon.   292

(*Resumes tango and castanets. Song, reprise: "The Day the Bill is
Due"; "Amatores aves." Whispers.*)

Like flocks of birds the lovers come;
I try to make them feel at home;
The bait is laid, the snare is set—
And then I quickly cast a net!

(*Louder*)
No matter how they fret and rage,
They go into my gilded cage.
Long may they sing, the little dears:
Their notes are banknotes to my ears.   300

Now you come weeping, as sure as rain,
But on what grounds can you complain?
You always loved to bill and coo,
And now, my dear, the bill is due.

How can you forget what took you so long to learn?

RIP: That's not my fault. You tossed me out before I graduated.

CLEARETA: Come back and matriculate when you've got your tu-
ition fee. But now—run along.

RIP: Wait a minute. If I wanted Lena to myself for a whole year,
mine alone, how much would that cost?   310

CLEARETA: Exclusive rights? One thousand dollars. But don't forget
that we have other bidders. There's a young Mr. Devlin Jr., who is
quite interested. If someone else brings the thousand first, you're
out of luck.

(*Turns to leave*)

RIP: Just one more thing.

CLEARETA: Let her rip, Rip.

RIP: I'm not completely broke. I saved a little back. I can get you
your thousand. But I set my own rules, right? Let's get it straight:
for one whole perpetual year Lena's mine, all mine, and mine
alone. No other man of any description to be admitted.   320

CLEARETA: Whatever you say. If you insist, I'll have my baritone
slaves turned into sopranos. Think up your rules and write them
down. Your wish is our command. Just give me solid cash to feel,
and you and I can make a deal. My house is just like a gambling
club. If you've got the dough, you're in the game; if not, no dice.

(*She exits into the house*)

RIP: I'll just curl up and die if I don't get that money. Lena's all I want; it's my money or my life. I'll go to the forum and see if I can't borrow from my pals.

(*Song:* "*My Friends Won't Let Me Down*"; "*Supplicabo, exobsecrabo*")

So I'm going out
          Upon the town   330
I know my friends
          Won't let me down
  They're generous souls
  To a guy on the dole
They're kinda free
          To a guy on a spree
  Who's in a hole.

I think I'll visit
          My old pal Jimmy
With a mouthful of "Please"   340
          And a handful of "Gimme"
  I'm sure he'll be
  A bankroll for me
If he refuses
          Why then he loses
  My sweet company.

If that's what it takes
          To get my girl
I'll beg my way
          Around the world   350
  If that's the game
  I'll take the blame
To be in love
          Is reason enough
  To have no shame.

Now I know Marcus
         Doesn't like me much
So I'd better develop
         That magic touch
  Got to tell him lies   360
  Till there's tears in his eyes
Got to make him weep
         Till we're ankle-deep
  In sobs and sighs.

To get my Lena
         I'll have to borrow
From all my buddies
         Like there's no tomorrow
  Got to let them know
  That I love her so   370
They'll think it's queer
         That I hold her so dear
  But they won't say No.

My mama would stagger
         If she but knew
That I'd turned beggar
         Just to be with you
  So, Lena, do right
  By me tonight
I'm passion-gripped   380
         I'm pussywhipped
  I'm all uptight.

So I'm going out
         To ask around
I know my friends
         Won't let me down
  I'll be here, honey,
  With a barrel of money
Oh, what a trip

                              For Lena and Rip
        To snugglebunny!

ACT II

(*Several hours later. Enter* LIBANUS, *talking to himself.*)

LIBANUS: Libanus, you'd better get on the stick. I've got to dream
    up a scheme to get that thousand bucks that Manny wants. I've
    been hard at it. I went down to the forum and loafed hard and
    napped hard. But now I've got to get my brains a-cooking. Other-
    wise, I'm slaving just for the privilege of being a slave. I need to do
    my master some good. What I need is some luck, some chance to
    work a dodge. The old long arm of coincidence. Luck is what I
    need.

(*Song: "A Bit of Luck"; "Unde sumam"*)

My luck was always dreadful bad   400
And every hour it just gets badder;
I think the day that I was born
My mother walked beneath a ladder.

    I'm looking for a bit of luck
    A horseshoe or a four-leaf clover;
    I'm flying like a busted duck—
    On one lame wing and half seas over!

I take a list of VIPs
And scan it over A to Z.
I do not find virtue rewarded—   410
Successful saps are what I see.

If you have opportunity
To choose among the gifts of the gods,

Turn down Talent, pass up Wisdom,
Plump for Luck, and play the odds.

A bit of luck is what I need;
My fate's a chain of doleful states;
In the same old muck I'm always stuck—
And Luck goes by on roller skates!

But here comes my old buddy Leon. Huh-oh, he's running. I'll
bet this isn't the kind of luck I was hoping for.   421

(Enter LEON. *For a long while he's unaware of* LIBANUS's *presence.)*

LEON: *(To himself)* I wonder where Libanus is? Or young Master
Rip? I'm bringing home the bacon for them. Seeing as how we
drink together and whore around together, maybe we ought to
share our loot.

LIBANUS: What's he going on about?

LEON: He couldn't find another chance like this with a bloodhound.
If this doesn't work, our master will be at the mercy of his wife.
But if it does, we'll pull off the dingdong daddy of all dandy
diddles. Then Manny and Rip will owe us one and we'll all get
along together fine.   431

LIBANUS: He's going to get us both in trouble. Look at him, talking
to himself. By the itching of my bum, heavy trouble's going to
come.

LEON: But I'd better trust'to my feet and not to my mouth. I'm
talking 'way too much.

LIBANUS: Don't run down your mouth, old son. It's your mouth that
saves your ass.

LEON: I'd better go back and lock up before the money's stolen.

LIBANUS: Money? What money? Let's just find out what's going on.
 (*Loudly to* LEON) Hello! Hello there! Helllllooooo!   441

LEON: (*Sees* LIBANUS) Oh. Howdy there, Stickyfingers.

LIBANUS: Howdy to you, Sleazeball.

LEON: Tell me, Libanus, old man, how much do you weigh?

LIBANUS: I couldn't say. How much do you think?

LEON: Well, I'll have to take your measure. Let's see now. If I strip
 you down, and hang you from a crossbeam, and tie an anvil to
 your feet, and hitch a boulder to the anvil, you'll weigh—let's see:
 put down three and carry seven . . . Aha. You'll weigh exactly as
 much as a genuine Grade-A Blue Ribbon Asshole.   450

LIBANUS: You're asking for trouble.

LEON: That's simply the description they put out every time you run
 away.

LIBANUS: Let's have less bull and more meat. What kind of dodge
 are you up to?

LEON: Can I trust you?

LIBANUS: I'm as trustworthy as a savings and loan company.

LEON: Okay, if you want to help Rip get his Lena, there are some
 chances we'll have to take. We must boldly go where no con man
 has gone before. We've got a golden opportunity to be the coolest
 cats that ever got whipped.   461

LIBANUS: How can I turn down a chance like that? Tell me all.

LEON: It's a case of big gain or big pain.

LIBANUS: I live for pain. That's why I decided on a career as a slave. Tell me all.

LEON: That's it. Keep your pecker up. It takes nerve.

LIBANUS: I've got nerve. When they catch me I'll pine and whine and decline. I'll lie and lie and lie and lie and lie.

LEON: Good deal. That's my brand of manly courage.

LIBANUS: So, tell me all.   470

LEON: All right. Just let me get a breath.

LIBANUS: If I know you, you'll steal mine. And I don't care if it's your last.

LEON: Where's the master?

LIBANUS: Master Major's in the forum. Master Minor's in the House of Ill Repute.

LEON: Okay. . . . Do you remember the flock of Arcadian asses our steward Saurea sold to that merchant from Pella?

LIBANUS: Indeed I do. So?

LEON: So, he's sent along the money to pay for the animals. A young fellow has just brought the cash and is looking for Saurea.   481

LIBANUS: Where is this dear young treasure?

LEON: Think you can grab his gold with a single snatch?

LIBANUS: Without blinking an eye. You *are* talking about all those broken-down, busted-up asses with their legs worn off to the knee joints?

LEON: The very same. The ones that ruined their health carrying the canes it took to teach you some manners.

LIBANUS: No, they loaded them with a week's worth of the lies you tell. That brought 'em down.   490

LEON: Always some smart remark, eh? Look, I was in the barber-shop and in comes this bozo and asks if anybody knows our master Manny. Only he calls him Demaenetus, the son of Strato. And I says, Sure I do, and he says his thing and I says mine and finally he got me to give him our address.

LIBANUS: And so?

LEON: And then he sez and I sez and he sez and I sez and it comes out he's carrying our thousand smackeroos. He'll turn them over to Saurea. He doesn't know Saurea, but he knows Manny.

LIBANUS: And so?   499

LEON: How do you ever learn anything if all you do is talk? Here's what I did. Very cleverly I improvise myself into a snooty kind of high-horse dude and I tell this sucker: "Look no farther. I'm it. I'm the steward Saurea, servant to Manny, and descended from generations of stewards." But he says, "I don't know you. You bring Manny here and I'll hand the money over." I told him I'd do that very thing and meet him at our house. He's going to the bath-house, then he's coming here. . . . So what's your plan, genius? Tell me all.   508

LIBANUS: Umm . . . Well . . . Hmm . . . We'll figure out how to duck Saurea and get the moolah. But we have to plan it now because if the trader gets there first, we're sunk. This morning Manny took me aside and said, "Libanus, you and Leon have got to come up with one thousand skins to give to my son Rip. Otherwise it's your skin that'll be ripped. Cheat Saurea, cheat Big Mona. It's all right, I'll stand by you." So now, you go down to the forum and when the trader shows up, you pretend to be Saurea.

LEON: Yes, Master. I hear and obey.

LIBANUS: If the trader comes by here first, I'll delay him.

LEON: All right, but—

LIBANUS: Now what?   520

LEON: Well, if I'm going to play the part of the steward, and if I'm
going to be convincing, I'd better kick the menials around pretty
good. Give 'em a bruise or two to show authority. I'm sure you
won't mind a contusion here and there.

LIBANUS: Contoot me no contusions. If you lay a hand on me, even
your mother will call you Lumpy.

LEON: We have to make this trader believe us.

LIBANUS: I'll make a believer out of you. I'll make you believe my
foot is all the way up your esophagus. And you'll be believing the
truth.   530

LEON: Promise me you'll do it right.

LIBANUS: I'll give my promise and keep it too: Lay a hand on me and
you're black and blue.

LEON: I have to go now, but I'm not worried. If there's cash in it,
you'll play your part. As long as money comes to you, you won't
mind a lick or two . . . Hey, look! Here comes our man, the
trader. Mr. Marchand is his name. You keep him here while I go
find Manny.

(*Enter* MR. MARCHAND *with his slave*)

MARCHAND: Well, this is the address. This is where Manny is supposed to live. (*To slave*) Knock on the door, boy, and find out if
Saurea the steward is in. If he is, call him out.   541

LIBANUS: (*Answers door before the knock*) Who is breaking down our nice door? Lighten up. Lighten up, I say. Can you hear me?

MARCHAND: What's your problem, buddy? My man hasn't touched your door.

LIBANUS: But I could tell he was going to, with that threatening way he came at it. This door is my friend. I don't like to see my friends knocked about.

MARCHAND: Your friend is in no danger, as long as you answer beforehand.   550

LIBANUS: This is an educated door. I trained it to give me a whistle whenever it sees some heavy knockers coming. (*Whistles lewdly*) Now, what are you here for?

MARCHAND: I have business with Manny.

LIBANUS: If he was here, I'd be the first man to give you the news.

MARCHAND: How about Saurea the steward?

LIBANUS: He said he was going out for a haircut.

MARCHAND: I ran into him at the barbershop. Isn't he back yet?

LIBANUS: Afraid not. What do you want with him?

MARCHAND: If he was here to take the money I'd give him a thousand dollars.   561

LIBANUS: For what?

MARCHAND: He sold a flock of asses to a trader from Pella.

LIBANUS: Oh yeah, I heard about that. And you've brought payment? He ought to be here soon.

MARCHAND: What does this Saurea look like?

LIBANUS: Skinny-legged and egg-headed, paunchy and raunchy, greasy and sleazy. Middling size with squinty eyes.

MARCHAND: That's him, all right. Down to the last nose hair.

LIBANUS: (*Pretending surprise*) Well, I'll be a centipede's mother! Here he comes now! He's just waiting for some poor slob to give him an excuse. Look at him huffing and puffing.   572

MARCHAND: I don't care if he huffs and puffs like a dragon. If he fools with me, I'll shut his damper.

(*Enter* LEON, *posing as* SAUREA)

LEON: (*Irascibly*) All right, where is he? Where's that Libanus? I ordered him to meet me at the barbershop. No show. If he can't follow orders, I'll stomp that sucker's candy ass.

MARCHAND: (*Aside*) What a blowhard!

LIBANUS: (*Exaggeratedly*) Oh Lord! I'm in big trouble!

LEON: (*To* LIBANUS) I see you're not taking orders these days. Got your manumission papers all in order, have you?   581

LIBANUS: Have mercy! Please, have mercy!

LEON: You're going to wish you were on a desert island. Why didn't you meet me?

LIBANUS: I was going to, but this gentleman detained me.

LEON: (*Pretends not to see* MARCHAND) I don't care who or what detained you. I don't care if you've got eyewitnesses. You're going to pay for it with your hide.

LIBANUS: Help me, stranger! I'm in trouble!

MARCHAND: Now listen to me, Saurea. This slave had good reasons—

LEON: (*Ignores him*) I wish I had a hickory stick; I'd lay it on you hot
     and thick.   591

MARCHAND: Come on now, simmer down.

LEON: Since your hide's been tanned to leather already, I guess I'll
     have to break your bones. (*To* MARCHAND) Pardon me, sir. Just
     stand back and give me room to stomp this pissant. I have to tell
     him what to do a hundred times. I get totally exhausted—while
     he's so lazy he stays fresh as a daisy.

(*Song: "The Laziest Slave"; "Iussin sceleste"*)

The laziest slave that ever there was
Is our Libanus because because   600
    The way that a slave
    Ought to behave
Has always given him pause.

He's slow as molasses, as lazy as cheese,
Too trifling to scratch in his armpits for fleas;
    He's a total disaster
    And never moves faster
Than boiling water can freeze.

Tardier always than language can utter,
Too lazy to loaf, too languid to putter,   610
    One day he lost,
    To his master's stiff cost,
A race with melting butter.

So I have to beat some natural rhythm into him.—Like this.

(*Whips up on* LIBANUS)

LIBANUS: Help me, stranger.

LEON: (*To* LIBANUS) Now did anyone ever show up to pay for that
olive shipment?

LIBANUS: Yes, sir.

LEON: Where's the money?

LIBANUS: Stichos has it. They placed it with your aide, Stichos.

LEON: All right, you'd better be straight. Stichos is the best there is,
the best man Manny has. What about the wine that went to Vinnie's Vine Street Vino? Has Vinnie settled with Stichos?   622

LIBANUS: All square, I think. Vinnie was here with his accountant.

LEON: Good. The last time I gave him credit he took a year to pay.
When I cut him off, he shows up with his accountant and writes a
check on the spot. Has Philo come by with those goblets we lent
him?

LIBANUS: Hasn't shown up.

LEON: No? Well, that's what they say: "Lend to a friend and you will
see you've done your bit for charity."   630

MARCHAND: What the hell is this, the noonday stock report?

LIBANUS: (*To* LEON) That's enough. I think he's taken the bait.

LEON: (*To* LIBANUS) All right. Now I'll set the hook. (*To* MARCHAND)
Oh, pardon me, sir. When did you show up? I hope you won't be
angry that I kept you waiting. Sometimes I get so mad at this slave
I can't see straight.

MARCHAND: Yeah, I can see you can't see. What I'm here for is to see Manny.

LEON: Libanus tells me he's out. But go ahead and count me out the money and I'll close the deal for you. 640

MARCHAND: I think I'd better wait for Manny.

LIBANUS: Saurea here is our master's right-hand man.

MARCHAND: I'll wait.

LIBANUS: Don't worry, I'll take the responsibility. The old man would get huffy if you didn't trust his steward. Saurea here looks after everything.

LEON: Hey—who cares? It's not important. Let the man wait if he wants to.

LIBANUS: (*To* MARCHAND) Please, Mr. Marchand. If he thinks I've told you not to trust him, my ass will be beaten more than all those you bought. Go ahead, give him the money. Everything will be fine. 652

MARCHAND: I'm sure it will be—as long as I've got the money. I just arrived; I don't know any Saurea.

LIBANUS: (*Anxiously*) Please: I'll be glad to introduce you.

MARCHAND: That would be nice of you. But I still won't know and still won't give the money.

LEON: (*To* MARCHAND) So who gives a velvet-lined camel fart? (*To* LIBANUS) Don't you dare beg this jerk. He's just too damn pleased with himself and his thousand dollars. (*To* MARCHAND) Go away. We don't want your piddling little money. Get outta here.—Scat!

MARCHAND: My, what a big mouth! I just love it when alley cats try
   to roar like lions.   661

LEON: (*To* LIBANUS) Give this guy a piece of my mind. Otherwise,
   I'll have a piece of you.

LIBANUS: (*Loudly to* MARCHAND) You greasy streak of slime! (*Softly*)
   Can't you see how mad he is?

LEON: Come on, talk to him!

LIBANUS: You miserable syphilitic microbe. (*Whispers*) Please, sir,
   give him the money. I hate to cuss you like this.

MARCHAND: You boys are in deep doodoo.

LEON: (*Calmly, to* LIBANUS) All right, for a start I'll shatter your
   shinbones and nutcracker your kneecaps. For starters. So give
   this guy some lip.   672

LIBANUS: (*Gloomily, hesitantly*) You pustulant, piss-dripping, maggot-
   oozing mass of mouse turds!

LEON: What are you, his boyfriend? I said, Lay it on him.

MARCHAND: I don't believe this, a slave insulting a free man.

LEON: (*To* MARCHAND) Get stuffed.

MARCHAND: That's the kind of stuff that'll get *you* stuffed till your
   stuffing runs out. Wait till I see Manny.

LEON: Do you think we're afraid of our master, Donkey-Breath? Go
   ahead and find this master you threaten us with.   681

MARCHAND: All right. And not one thin dime goes to you till Manny says so in person.

LEON: Okay, let's go. You think you can insult me and not get insulted back? I'm a man the same as you.

MARCHAND: I hear you talking.

LEON: So we'll let it go . . . Except I'll just say that no one's got anything against me. I'm the most trusted man in town.

MARCHAND: I hear you talking . . . But you won't catch me handing money to somebody I don't know. A stranger takes what care he can, For man is ever a wolf to man. 691

LEON: Okay, so we're off to find Manny. I knew you'd learn to trust me. I don't mind an insult or two. Maybe I don't look like a merchant prince, but I've got money that hasn't seen the light of day.

MARCHAND: I hear you talking.

LEON: Do you know Mr. Perry, that rich trader from Rhodes? We were all alone in an alley and he gave me five hundred for Manny. He understood I'm an honest man.

MARCHAND: I hear you talking. 700

LEON: And after you've been around here for a while, you'll trust me with your money.

MARCHAND: I . . . fear your talking.

(*They exit*)

ACT III

Scene 1

(*Enter* CLEARETA *and her daughter* LENA *from* CLEARETA'S *House of Ill Repute, stage center*)

CLEARETA: And so you won't do as I tell you. Your heart's set on disobeying your mother.

LENA: I can't be a good girl if you're in charge. I'd better not practice what you preach.

CLEARETA: But when you disobey me—then you're a good girl?

LENA: It's right to do right and wrong to do wrong.

CLEARETA: Oh my, oh my. So now you're a philosopher, my little jellyroll.   711

LENA: I do what I have to do. And when I fancy I can, I can get quite fancy.

CLEARETA: You need all the scolding you get.

LENA: I don't want to disobey. But you're keeping me from the man I love.

CLEARETA: May I get in a word or two—before my sunset years?

LENA: Say your say. Say mine too, for all I care. But if it wasn't for me you'd have nothing to say anything about.

(*Song: "I Carry This Business"; "Sola ego in casteria"*)

You taught me how to whisper guff   720
That makes them want to see my stuff;
You taught me how to say the words
That shuck the trousers off these nerds;
But surely we must face the fact:
I carry this business on my back!

You taught me how to slink and strut,
To bat my eyes and wiggle my butt,
To stroke the suckers till they come
Across with our complete income;
I hope you will admit the fact: 730
I carry this business on my back!

I hate to complain, but don't you see
That we'd be paupers if not for me;
I've mastered such an amorous skill
They fling their silver in our till,
And tell me, "Honey, it's a fact:
You carry this business on your back!"

So I really ought to have some say about the men I see.

CLEARETA: You are without doubt the silliest girl ever born. How
many times do I have to tell you? Don't waste time chatting up
that Rip. Stop making eyes at him. He's out of money. He talks
sweet, but you can't spend words. Quit hanging on him; find a
fatter sheep.   743

(*Song, to same tune as preceding:* "No Sucker Gets an Even
Break"; "Illos qui dant")

Before you dream of True Romance
Consult the state of our finance.
Do you think a handsome face
Will pay the mortgage on this place?
The world's a slough of gray heartache:
No sucker gets an even break!

On your back you're one of a kind;   750
Our trouble starts when you use your mind.
Control your feelings, let good sense
Banish all Romances hence.
Remember, Lena, for your own sake:
No sucker gets an even break!

Go through our list and search out one
Who's recently fleeced a savings and loan.
He's the man to pay the fiddler,
And we're the girls to diddle the diddler.
As for the homeboys, let 'em eat cake!   760
No sucker gets an even break.

And as for Rip—unless he brings that thousand bucks, he's out in
the cold. He's a wealthy man—if lies and sighs and hoping and
moping make money. But today he's yesterday. Let him go.

LENA: Oh, Mother!

CLEARETA: Find a man who loves to give you—anything but love.

LENA: But what if my heart belongs to another?

CLEARETA: Do what I do. Worry about your heart after you've covered your ass.

LENA: Even the shepherd who feeds the sheep someone else possesses has a little pet lamb of his own. Please let me have my Rip,
my one and only. For true love's sake.   772

CLEARETA: Don't talk back. Get in the house.

LENA: (*Bitterly resigned*) Look at me, Mother. I'm the daughter you
created.

(*They exit*)

Scene 2

(*Enter* LIBANUS *and* LEON *from the forum, with a large money pouch*)

LIBANUS: Victory to Perfidy! Thanks be to Fraud! They tan our hides but we skin 'em alive; I take the lash but also the cash. Leon, my hero, you have triumphed. I did more than my share, but you deserve some credit. Now what nice things were you going to say about me?   780

LEON: Oh, I've got plenty of things to say about you. I've made a little list.

(*Song: "Forty Strokes"; "Ubi fidentem fraudaveris"*)

> Always you're willing
> To make a quick killing;
> They'd better be feeling
> The goods that you're selling;
> They'd better be telling
> Over your billing;
> Your weird wheeler-dealing
> Is nothing but stealing—   790
> And yet your tricks and little jokes
> Always earn you forty strokes.

Now haven't I got you down about right?

LIBANUS: Pretty near, I have to admit. You've got it straight, for the first time in your crooked life. But I've been taking notes on you. Let's see what we see.

(*Produces long scroll. Sings "Forty Strokes," as above.*)

> You've libeled and slandered
> And perjured and pandered;

The money you've squandered
Would feed nigh a hundred;   800
How much you have plundered
Everyone's wondered;
When policy's pondered
Fraud is your standard—
And yet your tricks and little jokes
Always earn you forty strokes.

Now, is that a just description or not?

LEON: It bears a resemblance, I gotta admit. We're two of a kind,
you and me, and that's the truth.

LIBANUS and LEON: (*Song: "The School of Hard Licks," with a final
chorus from "Forty Strokes"*)

There are colleges of marble,   810
    Colleges of bricks,
But we matriculated from
    The School of Hard Licks.

We learned philosophy,
    We sorely learned ethics—
But there ain't no Aristotles in
    The School of Hard Licks!

We're magna cum laude
    With complicated tricks,
And we owe all we are to   820
    The School of Hard Licks.

So look out all you honest blokes
Here come the Boys of Forty Strokes!

LIBANUS: All right, let's get to work. Tell me true now—

LEON: What?

LIBANUS: Where is that sweet beautiful virgin one thousand bucks?

LEON: (*Shows pouch*) Here it is, every penny. Old Manny fixed that Marchand fellow. Made him believe I was Saurea, Big Mona's steward. I almost ruined the whole thing by laughing when he chewed that trader out for not trusting me. He never slipped, called me "Saurea" every time.   831

LIBANUS: Shhh.

LEON: Why?

LIBANUS: Isn't this Lena and Rip coming out of the house?

LEON: Yeah. Let's eavesdrop. Keep real quiet.

LIBANUS: Look at them mugging and hugging. I wonder what they're up to.

LEON: Lend me your handkerchief.

LIBANUS: What for?

LEON: Because money talks. I'd better have a gag for this thousand bucks.   841

(*Enter* LENA *and* RIP *from the House of Ill Repute*)

RIP: Don't be a drag. Let go.

LENA: I love you. I can't stand for you to leave.

RIP: Goodbye.

LENA: Nothing good about it.

RIP: Take care.

LENA: Why don't you stay and take care of me?

RIP: Your mother has cast me off.

LENA: She may as well have cut my throat.

LIBANUS: (*To* LEON) I see. They've barred him from the whore-
   house.   851

LEON: (*To* LIBANUS) Looks like it.

RIP: (*Tries to disengage*) Stop now. That's enough.

LENA: Don't go away. Please. Stay here.

RIP: Well, if you'll let me stay all night—

LIBANUS: (*To* LEON) His night is a year long. Can you believe this
   joker is a politician who writes the laws for us poor buggers to
   follow? Sometimes he's so drunk his days are nights.

LEON: He keeps saying he's leaving. But he don't go.

LIBANUS: Shhh.   860

RIP: Farewell!

LENA: But where will you go?

RIP: Farewell forever and ever. We'll meet again in heaven. This
   world I must bid adieu.

LIBANUS: (*To* LEON) What kind of books has Master Rip been reading?

LEON: (*To* LIBANUS) The kind of stuff that sailors' wives pack in the
   duffels.

LENA: But don't kill me by saying goodbye. I'm innocent.

RIP: Never would I kill you. I'd give my life, my very soul, for yours.

LENA: But you mustn't say you'll do away with yourself. I'd do the
same. You know I would.   871

RIP: O Lena, you're the sweetest little sweetmeat that ever strutted
a street!

LENA: For sure, you're my very own life. Gimme kissy.

RIP: Without delay.

(*Kisses her*)

LENA: Oh, if only we could expire in one another's dear embrace!

LEON: (*To* LIBANUS) Libanus, I gotta say. The most miserable man in
the world is a man in love.

LIBANUS: No, no. A slave taking a whipping is worse off.

LEON: (*Recollects*) Of course! You're right, I almost forgot . . . Tell
you what: you stand over there and I'll stand right here. When
I count three (makes a gesture), we'll waken them from their
trance . . .   883

LEON and LIBANUS: (*Together*) *Hello, there!*

(RIP *and* LENA *startle apart*)

LEON: (*To* RIP) Are you kissing a girl or an onion?

RIP: Onion?

LEON: Well, she seems to make your eyes water.

LIBANUS: Howdy, Lena.

(*Makes eyes at her*)

LENA: I hope you boys are having a nice day.

LIBANUS: I'd rather have a nice night. With you.   890

RIP: All right, slave. Watch your mouth.

LIBANUS: No, no. I meant you. You should have a nice night with her.

RIP: Okay. You can say that if you like.

LIBANUS: (*Indicates* LEON) What I'd *really* like is to beat this guy's butt.

LEON: You and who else, Cockroach-Muncher? You mess with my butt, I'll bust your beater.

RIP: I'd trade places with you, Libanus, even though you are a lowly, miserable slave. At least you're alive. But this very day, today, I must expire.   900

LIBANUS: Say what?

RIP: Because I love Lena and Lena loves me. But now I'm penniless. Her mother won't let me see her again because another fellow offered a thousand dollars for exclusive rights to her. So that's what I need—a thousand bucks.

(*Song:* "*A Thousand Bucks*"; "*Argenti viginti*")

I'm no miser racked with greed,
A thousand bucks is all I need.
With that money in my hands
I can satisfy my glands.

I don't care to call on Venus,   910
That old bawd is just pure meanness;
I don't want to call on Cupid,
The little runt looks mighty pooped:

So I pray to powerful Lucre
Who knows the way to hook a hooker.
To this omnipotent god I plead:
One thousand bucks is all I need.

Now you see, now you understand.

LIBANUS: Well, has this other guy already paid up?

RIP: Not yet.

LIBANUS: So don't worry about it.   920

LEON: Libanus, come here. I need you.

LIBANUS: (*Sarcastically*) Coming, Master. Night and day, from here
to eternity, now and forever, I'm at your beck and call.

RIP: Why do you guys always squabble? You do better by acting
friendly.

LIBANUS: Different stripes for different types, sir. Billing and cooing is all right for you and Lena. But he doesn't like my coo and I
won't take his bill. So you two please do what you two like to do.

RIP: Good suggestion. Why don't you boys watch how it's done?

(*To* LIBANUS) Let's shake 'em up, whatcha say?   930

LIBANUS: What have you got in mind?

LEON: How'd you like for me to get you—right here on this spot
with no delay—a kiss from Lena?

LIBANUS: I swoon at the thought.

LEON: Let's go.

(*They approach the lovers*)

RIP: (*Leaves off kissing*) There. Did you get the idea?

LEON: Did I ever get ideas! Now, listen up. We're slaves, me and
Libanus, right? That's our station in life. But for a thousand bucks
how would you classify us?

RIP: Free men.   940

LEON: Is that the best you can do? How about—boss men?

RIP: Sure, fine. Boss men.

LEON: It just so happens that a thousand bucks is what I've got.
Right here in this pouch. How'd you like it if I gave this money to
you?

RIP: Oh, may the gods adore you, hero of the age! Comfort of your
master! Example to the citizenry! Cornucopia of generosity! Em-
peror of love! Idol of my soul!—Put it right here. Hang that money
pouch upon my manly chest.

LEON: Oh no. The slave totes the burden, not the master.   950

RIP: Give yourself a holiday. I shall bear your every burden.

LEON: I'm the ass, so I must carry. You walk before me, empty-
headed as befits your station. Excuse me, I meant empty-handed.

RIP: Come on now. Hang that money pouch upon my manly breast.

LEON: You'll just give it to Lena. Make her ask me for it; get her to *beg* me for it. I'll take pleasure in hanging it upon her . . . manly chest.

LENA: (*Not yet serious*) Please let me beg you for it, Leon. You're the apple of my eye. My beautiful rose of forever, my own true soul, my supernal joy in life. Don't keep two lovers apart. Hand over that cash to me. 961

LEON: You're doing it wrong. Here's what you say: "Oh, Leon, I'm your little bitsy-birdy oopsy-poopsy lamby-pamby silly-willy woo-woo gal. Grab me by my ears, you gorgeous side of beef, and put your little mushy-wushy to my little mouthy-wouthy."

RIP: You want her to kiss a slave!

LEON: Ain't I a stinker? But not a drachma in your drawers from me. Not until you get down down down on the ground and lick my ——foot.

RIP: What! (*Reluctantly*) Well . . . A man's gotta do what a man's gotta do. I'll kiss your foot. (*Does so without enjoyment, then leaps up*) Now where's the treasure? 972

LENA: Leon, you must save us. Rip loves me. Be nice and you'll go free. Give him the thousand.

LEON: You're one goodlooking piece, you know that? If the money was mine you wouldn't have to beg me for it. But actually I'm just keeping it for my friend Libanus, and I'd better give it back. (*Tosses the pouch*) Now he's the one you've got to schmoozy-woozy.

RIP: All right, you fellows. Quit horsing around. 980

LEON: Oh Master Rip, if only you'd licked my foot a little cleaner. And with a little more feeling. Appassionato—that's how I like it. (*To* LIBANUS) Your turn to wheel and deal and feel.

LIBANUS: (*To* LEON) Stand back. genius at work.

RIP: (*To* LENA) Oh well, why not jiggle his jollies for just a jiffy? He can't be as gross as Leon.

(*Spits*)

LIBANUS: (*To* LEON) Get ready. Here I go.

RIP: Libanus, old man, I say. Don't hang me out to dry. Slip me that grand. I'm in love!

LIBANUS: Well, let's think about it. Why don't you tell Lena to be real nice to me? I'm a magic lamp. If she rubs me in the right spot, she'll find the treasure.   992

LENA: Does my iddle slave want a iddle hug? A iddle kissy-wissy?

LIBANUS: Just a teeny weeny iddle tiny.

LENA: (*Feels him up*) Here you go, get it while it's hot. So now—the thousand.

RIP: Libanus, old chum, give me the dough. I don't like to see you bent under its weight.

LENA: O Libanus, Ban-ban Libanus. Little moneyballs, little honeyballs, little honeymoney. I'll love you a way you never had. Just fork, fork, fork me—that money.   1001

LIBANUS: Well . . . maybe. But first you have to call me sweet names. Your iddle widdle tiddle piddle diddlekins. And kiss me, kiss me with double-forked asp-tongue. And hold me tight, imprisoned in your arms.

RIP: (*Aside*) That's not the kind of prison he'll be getting used to.

LIBANUS: (*Overhearing him*) Just listen to you. Treat me like a pig.
Well, if you want this money, you'll be giving this little piggy a
piggyback ride.

RIP: What, me? Let you mount me?   1010

LIBANUS: That's the only strategy that'll let you get the currency.

RIP: Damn damn and double damn. Well, that's the way it goes
these days. The master supports his servants.

LIBANUS: Lo, how the mighty are fallen! Just bend over now. Like
that. Remember when we were kids together, playing leapfrog? . . .
There. You're doing fine. I always knew you had some real horse
sense.

RIP: Come in, let's get it over with.

(*Bends over*)

LIBANUS: Here goes. (*Mounts*) Giddy-up go. Hey, can't you set a
smoother gait? Don't forget I've got the money.   1020

RIP: All right, enough. (*Ominously*) O Libanus, how I love you!

LIBANUS: No time for that now. We've got to gallop uphill and down,
riding through the dale. (*Digs in his heels*) Spurring on to victory.
All the way to Naples. Okay, whoa up, bonebag. I'll dismount
here.

RIP: Now you've had your little joke. Where's the mazoolah?

LIBANUS: Not yet. First you must worship me. I am the great god
Save-Your-Hide. Set me up an altar and a statue and sacrifice me
one of your oxen. Then we'll see.

(*Tosses* LEON *the pouch*)

LEON: (*Brandishes it*) Libanus is not the god he claims to be. I'm the
  god you gotta please. With a monument or two.   1031

RIP: And what, pray tell, is your divine cognomen?

LEON: Good-Luck-or-Kiss-My-Ass.

RIP: Oh, you are the superior god, then.

LIBANUS: What's better than saving your hide?

RIP: I'll need Good Luck to save my hide.

LENA: (*Sarcastically*) These are fine gods, Rip.

RIP: The only good gods are the ones that are good to me. That's my
  philosophy.

LEON: Now wish for something you'd like.

RIP: Why?   1040

LEON: I'll make it happen.

RIP: I want Lena's services to be mine alone this whole year in
  and out.

LEON: (*Oracularly*) Hocus Pocus. Abracadabra. Bite My Rutabaga
  . . . It is done.

RIP: Really?

LEON: Truly.

LIBANUS: Now come over here to me. Wish for something you want
  most of all.

RIP: I wish I had that thousand bucks for Lena's mother.   1050

LIBANUS: Voodoo Hoodoo. Buzzard Doodoo. It is done. Your wishes have come true.

RIP: You guys are too much.

LIBANUS: (*To* LEON) Okay, we've had our fun. Let's own up. (*To* RIP) Listen to me, dear Argyrippus, with all your flaming little heart. Here's the money your funny old daddy sent us to deliver to you.

RIP: Well, not a moment too soon.

LIBANUS: Ill gotten gains, every penny. All yours upon the terms agreed.

RIP: Come again? What terms are you talking about?   1060

LIBANUS: You've got to let him have the first night with Lena. And besides that, you must buy him an oyster dinner.

RIP: (*Cheerfully*) No problem. Tell him to be here. We'll show our appreciation.

LEON: You don't mind your daddy dorking your darling?

RIP: (*Kisses the money pouch*) Not with this in my hands. Leon, run home and invite him over.

LEON: No need. He's in the Ill Repute already.

RIP: He didn't come this way.

LEON: No, he sneaked around back, trying to hide. He doesn't want Big Mona to find out. You know how your mother is.   1071

RIP: I do. . . . But times have changed since she was young.

LENA, RIP, LEON, and LIBANUS: (*To the tune of "Anything Goes"*)

In olden times, the days of Cato,
Folks sat around discussing Plato;
    Now, heaven knows,
    Everything goes.

In those proud days a son would rather
Box a bear than vex his father;
    Now everything shows   1080
    The way it goes.

A man would bring to Zeus an offering
That he might have virtúous offspring;
    Now well he knows
    There's none of those.

In our hard times the sons are dastards
Because their dads are horny bastards;
    You may well suppose
    Everything goes!

    It used to be   1090
    That honesty
    Was our policy,
The one for which we fought.
    But now, we guess,
    Success will bless
    Our crookedness—
If only we don't get caught.

In those good days the man was master,
The other arrangement sheer disaster—
    But, as Jupiter knows,
    Feminism grows!

Mules give milk and lions are browsers   1100
When the females wear the trousers,

And everyone knows
Everything goes.

I'd rather room with ticks and fleas
Than love again through times like these—
    When everyone knows
    How deep it flows—
    Up to the nose!—
    Buddy, it's gross!—
    That's how it goes . . .   1110

LIBANUS: (*To* RIP *and* LENA) You two had better go in now.

RIP: Okay. Bye bye.

LEON: And get it up, Lover Boy, get it up.

(RIP *and* LENA *exit into the house*)

ACT IV

(*A short time later. Before Cleareta's house. Enter* MR. DEVLIN JR., *with his attorney,* MR. LEECH)

DEVLIN: All right, Mr. Leech, suppose you read me that contract you drew up for me and Lena and her mother. Let's hear the terms. You're the one lawyer in the world I'll ever trust.

LEECH: Mr. Devlin, Cleareta will have a fit when she sees these rules you've laid down.

DEVLIN: I don't care. That would serve her justly.   1119

LEECH: Very well then, here we go. (*In a pompous, officious voice*) "Mr. Devlin Jr., only son and sole heir to Mr. Devlin Sr., his father, has to Cleareta, licensed proprietress and sole owner of the knocking shop—" No, wait (*Erases and scribbles*) " . . . sole owner of the business establishment known as Cleareta's House of Ill Repute, has to her, we say, this day conveyed currency in the amount of one thousand dollars, in consideration of which sum she stipulates that her daughter Lena shall spend with Mr. Devlin Jr., all her days and nights during the coming fiscal year to begin forthwith today, at nine P.M. in the evening."

DEVLIN: And not with any other person whatsoever.   1130

LEECH: Shall I put that in?

DEVLIN: Inscribe it and underscore it twice in red ink.

LEECH: (*Writes and mumbles*) " . . . whatsoever." (*Louder, proceeding*) "She will admit no other masculine presence into the house, whether this presence be denominated priest, guardian, friend, brother, cousin, or Bull Dyke. Her door is barred to all but Mr. Devlin Jr., and on this door she must hang a sign reading in letters no less than four inches tall OCCUPADO. She shall have no letters delivered, nor shall there be any letters within the house, nor anything found to write with, nor anything to write on, nor anything that looks, sounds, feels, tastes, or smells like a letter. If she possesses any male nude art studies she must sell them. If, within four days of receiving the aforesaid money, she keeps anything not to the liking of Mr. Devlin Jr., then he may jump up and down on it with both feet and then proceed to destroy it utterly. She may invite no guests; Mr. Devlin Jr. will invite them all. If she happens by accident to look upon the person of another man, she must wash her eyes out with soap and water and retire immediately to a dark closet."

DEVLIN: The terms are satisfactory to this point.   1150

LEECH: "Always above suspicion, she must not play footsie during card games. She must accept no aid in going up or down stairs. She must never under any circumstances present her hand to

be kissed." Let there be no mistake about what she can and cannot do.

(*Song: "Terms of Contract"; "Alienum hominem"*)

She shall not wink or even blink
   Until you say she may;
She shall not ever try to think
   Until you've had your say;
And if she plies those goo-goo eyes   1160
The girl will get a sad surprise.

When dancing she shall not be glancing
   In that certain little way;
She'd better not let her eyelids flutter
   To signal a gent "okay";
And to forestall *if, and,* or *but*
She might just keep those brown eyes shut.

She shall desert her miniskirt
   And dress up like a nun;
And if the light burns down at night   1170
   She shan't move muscle one;
She must sit as still as the Palatine Hill—

DEVLIN: Stop! Hold on! In the dark with another man I'd insist that
she keep still, of course. But when I'm her company in the dark,
it's a different matter. Strike that clause, Mr. Leech. Here's the
way those terms ought to read:

(*Sings*)

If the light is spent by accident
   When she's with someone else,
She has no leave to even breathe
   Or emit attractive smells;   1180
But when it's me, lasciviously
She can be as free as she likes to be.

LEECH: I see. You want to close all the loopholes.

DEVLIN: All of them. Except the one in her panties.

LEECH: Very good. (*Scribbles*) Now that part is taken care of. Do you
　　want to hear the rest?

DEVLIN: By all means.

LEECH: As follows herewith:

> She shan't be leaning to suggestive meaning
> 　　Or employ a double entendre;　　　　　　　　　　　　　1190
> Ambiguities are superfluities
> 　　That bring a shame upon her;
> She must commence with plain good sense
> And end without ambivalence.
>
> In short, she oughta do nothing naughty
> 　　Or ever give the appearance;
> She must strongly assure that she'll act demure
> 　　And forget her cousin Clarence—
> And she agrees to be your dear
> Until the end of the fiscal year.　　　　　　　　　　　　1200

DEVLIN: Exactly! Beautifully written. My dear Mr. Leech, you are
　　a legal genius, a true Solon.

LEECH: I believe you'll find this document watertight.

DEVLIN: In we go, then. We'll tender this contract to Cleareta.

LEECH: Once we procure her signature, the terms are in force.

(*They knock and are admitted to the house. The door closes. For
some time the stage is empty and silent. Suddenly the door flies open
and* DEVLIN *and* LEECH *are flung out, landing together on their
butts.*)

DEVLIN: (*Rises and adjusts himself. Shakes his fist at the door.*)
Don't think this is the end of this affair!

(*Song: reprise of* RIP's *song in Act I, "Revenge"*)

Revenge! Revenge! I'll have revenge!
Before this sordid story's told,
Your daughter and yourself I'll send
Back to the gutter from which you crawled.   1210

We drew a contract, made a deal;
The terms were set and almost signed.
Have you no pity for how I feel?
Do you belong to humankind?

Your words are vain, your deeds are false;
Upon my rights you meanly infringe.
You think you've got me by the balls—
But I'll have my toute sweet revenge!

All right, Manny, you've had me thrown out. You were there first
with the thousand dollars. But I'm not lightly to be reckoned with.
I'm going off right now to talk to your wife. Big Mona will be very
interested to hear about this. In the House of Ill Repute you're a
hot rod stud, but when you get home to Mona you're a limpwrist
dud. You've paid a madame to give your son a yearlong free ride
with her daughter—and now you want the first night with both of
them yourself.   1226

That is immoral.

And so I'm going to tell Big Mona you're robbing her to pay for
your orgies.

LEECH: (*Has meticulously readjusted himself*) Now, Mr. Devlin, I
believe you might wish to reconsider this plan. It will, I think, be
better for me to go to Manny's wife to represent you in this matter.

If you approach Big Mona, she'll ascribe your motive to jealousy. She won't believe your version.

DEVLIN: Hmmm. You're correct, Mr. Leech. You think of every-thing. But when you tell her, be sure to paint Manny in the worst colors. You must make sure that she's extremely upset. Describe her husband's three-way orgy that includes their son. And make absolutely certain she knows she's footing the bill.

LEECH: You may trust me completely.   1240

DEVLIN: Very good. I'll wait at home. Please report to me at first opportunity. I'm anxious to know the conclusion.

ACT V

(*A short time later, in the House of Ill Repute. A drinking party is in progress with* LENA, RIP, *and* MANNY *sitting close together on a couch. There is a lot of byplay, with* LENA *trying to avoid* MANNY'*s advances while getting close to* RIP.)

MANNY: Now, Rip, surely you won't mind my snuggling up to Lena just a little? Just a teensy-weensy little bit?

RIP: I consider, Father, that it is my filial duty to look upon the spectacle with a sad permissive eye. I'm sure I'll be able to accus-tom myself, no matter how much I love her.

MANNY: Young folks must respect their elders, Rip.

RIP: I'll never forget your example, Father.

MANNY: So come on. Let's live it up a little. Songs. Booze. Don't hang back. I want to be my son's best friend.   1251

RIP: And I feel that I should behave as a good son must.

MANNY: So lighten up, why don't you?

RIP: Do I seem sad to you?

MANNY: No sadder than a convict who spots his hangman.

RIP: So sad as that?

MANNY: You look like a bloodhound with a hangover.

RIP: Well, okay. Here goes—a cheery smile for you.   1258

MANNY: The embalmer puts better ones than that on corpses.

RIP: Well, I made a bargain. I receive a year with Lena all my
own, but first we share her for a single night. And tonight's the
night. . . . This arrangement does rather get me down. I want you
to be happy, and with another girl I wouldn't care. But not with
Lena!

(Song: "Three's a Crowd"; "Verum istum amo")

I don't want a gruesome threesome,
I just want a toothsome twosome;
Let my Lena play with me some,
Let some other play with you some.

Now I'm not prudish, but surely it's bad
To join in a threesome with your dear old dad.   1270

I know what the old song says:
"I want a girl like Daddy has."
But I can tell you it's no fun
When you want to share my only one.

Your years are many and your hair is gray;
Lots of girls must have come your way.
You know my feelings, you see my plight—
Why not rest on your laurels tonight?

The senate avers, the people complain
That the morals of Rome go down the drain;   1280
The examples that our elders set
Are the only ones we youth shall get.

I'm no moralist, I can be had,
But I want no threesome with you, dear Dad!

MANNY: One of these days you'll look back on tonight and laugh.
    Don't forget you've got a whole year ahead, thanks to the money I
    filched from Big Mona.

RIP: We made a bargain. I remember.

MANNY: All right then. Let the good times roll!

(*Enter* BIG MONA *and* LAWYER LEECH. *Unseen by the orgiasts, they
comment upon the party.*)

MONA: You say my husband Manny is here? And my son Rip? And
    that Manny stole the money we got for selling that herd of asses?
    And he spent it all on this girl Lena?

LEECH: I cannot tell a lie. One hundred asses went for a single piece
    of ass.   1292

MONA: I simply don't understand. I thought he was the best man I
    ever knew, a real leader of youth. Sober, industrious, upright,
    worthy. Honest all the way. I thought he loved me most of all
    forever.

LEECH: Well, the truth is, he's a drunk, a letch, a crook, and the
    lowest lowdown loser I ever met. As for the youth, I wouldn't trust

him with them either. His passion for you is true—but it's a
passionate dislike.   1302

MONA: I suppose you're right. I find him in this place—

LEECH: He's clever. He had me fooled. But drinking it up and getting on a threesome with his son! What a sad old sod!

MONA: It's beginning to come clear. Every night a business dinner.
With Arthur or Barter or Carter or Darter or Farter. Someone, he
says, every night. And all the time he's teaching Rip how to make
it with Cleareta's whores . . . Well, his life is going to be a living
hell.

LEECH: Isn't that the definition of marriage?

MONA: Think of all the lies he's been telling. Says he's busy in the
senate or busy with a client. Busy, he says, busy busy busy.

(Song: "A Busy Little Bee"; "Ibi labore")

So Manny's been a busy bee,   1312
    Slaving by the hour?
Well, I believe it now I see
    His chosen type of flower.

For when at home he comes to bed,
    He just lies there and snores;
I'm sure he's worn out, as he said—
    Worn out by his whores.

Busy busy busy busy   1320
    Busy busy busy busy,
A busy little bee:
But he's as crazy as a punchdrunk daisy
    To think he can honey me.

I know that he's been wandering far
    In the flowery fields about;

I'll stop his flings and clip his wings
  And pull his stinger out.

From here on out he can dream about
  The things that he has seen;   1330
No more he'll roam, he'll stay at home
  Paying tribute to his queen.

Busy busy busy busy, etc.

LEECH: Let's search around here. Maybe we'll catch him in *flagrante delicto.*

MONA: In whom?

LEECH: In *flagrante delicto*—in the very act. Redhanded. It's a term from the Latin.

MONA: Well, can it. I never studied Latin. Let's find my husband.

LEECH: Wait here.   1340

(*Goes about looking.* Spies RIP *and* LENA *and* MANNY *and scurries back to* MONA.)

MONA: What news?

LEECH: If you saw your man sozzled to the eyebrows, stretched out on a sofa with a girl pawing him all over—would you believe your eyes?

MONA: Try me.

LEECH: *Ecce homo!*

(*Points*)

MONA: (*Annoyed*) More Latin? (*Looks*) Oh, Lord. I'm dying. Dying, I tell you.

LEECH: Let's see what's going on.

RIP: (*To* MANNY) Father! Really! Don't you think you two have had enough?   1351

MANNY: Well, Son, I've got to tell you—

RIP: Yes?

MANNY: I never get enough.

LEECH: You hear?

MONA: I hear.

MANNY: (*To* LENA) You've stolen my heart, so I'm going to steal over to my house and steal Big Mona's best stole. Then I'll steal back here with the stolen stole and the stole will be yours solely. I'll do it, I swear on my wife's grave: Which I hope to see before long.

LEECH: (*To* MONA) It's not the first time things have been missing, is it?   1362

MONA: So that's where all my furs have gone. My jewels, my linens. To think how I've beaten the servants for thieving!

RIP: Pass us the wine, Father. I sorely need a drink.

MANNY: (*Passes the jug*) There's a nip for little Rip. (*Annoys* LENA) And here's a nip on a bit of a tit.

MONA: Uh-huh. And at home he's as hotblooded as a tombstone.

MANNY: (*Kisses* LENA) Wowsah wowsah wowsah. Now that's what I call a kiss. Not like the ones I get at home.

LENA: Doesn't Big Mona kiss you nice?

MANNY: About as nice as a fish on ice.   1370

MONA: I'll remember that. It's not real smart to insult the wife who has the money.

LENA: (*To* MANNY) Oh, you poor dear.

MONA: (*Aside*) Poor—that's his future. Penniless.

RIP: But, Father, don't you love my mother?

MANNY: I love to worship her from afar.

RIP: And when she's near?

MANNY: I adore to think of her surrounded by flowers. Big wreaths of lilies.

LEECH: (*To* MONA) You hear how much he loves you.   1380

MONA: (*To* LEECH) I hear. Wait till we get home. I'll give him a nice fishy kiss that'll pickle his herring and dry his cod.

RIP: (*Passes a dice cup to* MANNY) Here you go. Let's toss to see who pays for the next jug.

MANNY: You bet your ass. I would too, but I've already bet one hundred of mine. (*Laugh*) Come on, bones, to Mr. Jones! Ha! Seven. (*Offers a toast*) Here's to me. Here's to you. Here's to Lena. And let us drink to a glorious hope: Here's to the spirit of my dear departed wife.

MONA: I've had enough.   1390

LEECH: It takes a bit of getting used to—like making your living emptying privies. Why not remove his eyeballs for him?

MONA: (*Reveals herself to the trio. To* MANNY *she speaks in icy, deliberate tones.*) Well, Husband, my dear Demaenetus, I thank you very warmly for my funeral oration. I feel unworthy of it—since I'm still alive. Still, your words were wonderfully chosen, and I'll be glad to help you remember them from here on out.

LEECH: (*Aside*) Call an ambulance!

RIP: (*Meekly*) Hello, Mother.

MONA: Not "Hello Mother." You can call me Mother Hell.   1399

LEECH: (*Aside*) Good enough. I'll leave them to squabble while I run to Mr. Devlin Jr. to tell him how well I've carried out his orders, to the last iota. He'll treat me to dinner. Tomorrow we'll go to Cleareta with the thousand dollars and propose that Rip go halves with Junior on Lena. I'll need to work some sort of deal or he'll hire another attorney. Because Mr. Devlin Jr. fancies himself the last of the red-hot lovers.

MONA: (*To* LENA) Where do you get off, letting my husband entertain you in this joint?

LENA: You think this old fool is entertaining? Oh, you poor poor poor poor dear thing!   1410

MONA: (*Threatens* MANNY) Hey, get it up, Lover Boy. Get it up and take it home.

MANNY: (*Abashed*) Call me Mr. Zero.

MONA: Not zero. Number One. On my shit list, you're Number One. Don't sit there till you lay an egg, Cuckoo-Bird. Get it up, Lover Boy, get it up and take it home.

MANNY: Woe is me.

MONA: Your gift of prophecy makes a piker of Cassandra. So get it up, Lover Boy, get it up and take it home.

MANNY: Please, Big Mona. Please please please. Honey-darling, lambie-pie. Lighten up a little. Please.   1421

MONA: Get it up, Lover Boy, get it up and take it home.

MANNY: Yes, all right, I'm coming, wifey dear.

MONA: So now you remember I'm your wife. But just a minute ago I was a pimple on your nose, a thorn in your flesh, a hemorrhoid.

MANNY: Oh Lord.

MONA: How is it I kiss? As nice as a fish on ice?

MANNY: No no no. I said . . . it's awfully nice to kiss you twice.

MONA: And have you steeled yourself to steal that stole you told you'd steal?   1430

LENA: He stated that he'd steal the stole—and stole a smooch to seal the deal.

MANNY: (*To* LENA) Will you shut up?

RIP: (*Primly*) I tried to reason with him, Mother. I talked till I was blue in the face.

MONA: (*Sarcastically*) Of course you did, Mr. Morality. (*To* MANNY) So this is the sort of thing you want to teach your children, eh? Have you no shame at all?

MANNY: Only you, my darling wife.

MONA: Come along, Mr. Cock-a-Doodle. Drag your gray hairs out of here.   1441

MANNY: Can't I just stay till supper? They're serving coq au vin.

MONA: There'll be plenty of poultry at home. I'll cook your goose and watch you eat crow.

MANNY: And I'm the turkey.

RIP: Now, Father, don't you wish you'd followed my advice and done as Mother says to do?

LENA: Oh, Manny dear, don't forget to steal the stole.

MANNY: Don't you forget to go to hell.

LENA: Be nice now. Let's have one last little itsy-bitsy teensy-weensy oochy-goochy-poochy-woochy-smoochy.   1451

MANNY: (*Dispirited*) To hell, Lena.

LENA: Well, not quite so far. In fact, just into the bedroom with Rip. (*To* RIP) Come along, darling.

RIP: Yes. You first—and I'll bring up your rear.

(*Everyone exits*)

EPILOGUE

(*Song: "Get It Up"*)

MANNY: I'm no creature made of wood,
             Just a man of flesh and blood;
             I take my pleasures as they come—
             Sometimes I must look abroad
             For what I never get at home.   1460

BIG MONA: You think that you've found someone good
            Who'll do what your wife never would—
            But, dear, before you start to roam
            Remember that your name is mud
            By the time that you get home.

CLEARETA: If you pay to bill and coo
            And screw until the clock strikes two,
            You know your wife has prepared your doom:
            A fierce and bloody hullabaloo
            Will start the minute you get home.   1470

LENA: The suckers come in, rain or shine,
            And when they come their money's mine;
            They complain the beer's all foam
            And that they cannot drink the wine;
            Still—they're reluctant to go home!

RIP: From our elders we receive
            Examples that we must believe
            Since they're set by those in whom
            We've trusted always to behave
            Out in public as at home.   1480

TUTTI: When you think you'd like to do
            As the pagans used to do,
            As the Romans did in Rome—
            Lover Boy, get it up,
            Get it up and take it home.

THE THIRTY-DOLLAR DAY

DAY

(TRINUMMUS)

Translated by Daniel Mark Epstein

INTRODUCTION

For three pieces of money—*tres nummi, trinummus*, a three-penny bit—an idler in the forum is hired to convey a letter from an Athenian merchant abroad on business to a citizen of Athens named Callicles. The letter authorizes the payment of a thousand gold Philippics to the absent merchant's "well-thought-of" friend ("Callicles") at home, as a dowry for the absent merchant's daughter. The merchant's son has run through his father's money and sold the family house to Callicles. All that the son has left of his father's estate is a piece of farmland, which he proposes to offer as the basis of his sister's dowry. He is unaware that his father, before going abroad on business, had buried a hoard of gold in the garden of their house and entrusted Callicles with the secret of the buried treasure and its safekeeping. After the young man's extravagant ways brought him to the brink of poverty, Callicles himself bought the house and took up residence there, with his wife and daughter; the merchant's son, Lesbonicus, moved out to the small house at the end of the garden, where he now lives with the family servant Stasimus.

After Callicles gets word of the marriage plans, he consults with another friend and together they invent the scheme to pretend that Lesbonicus's father, Charmides, has sent the letter of credit to Callicles in Athens—forging the letter and hiring the sycophant to deliver it. In fact, Callicles will dig up the buried treasure and take out a thousand gold pieces to give Lesbonicus for the dowry. But Charmides has now just arrived from abroad and as he approaches his house encounters the sycophant with the letter. In a scene of ironic interrogation Charmides eventually leads the sycophant into an admission that he didn't actually get the letter from Charmides, who is conducting this conversation. The sycophant leaves, having earned his fee for the day, and the family servant, Stasimus, appears, to

163

greet his master and tell him that this is no longer his house. Next
Callicles appears, wearing the working clothes he put on to dig up
the treasure hoard and rebury it, and assures Charmides that he will
clear up the confusion, as he invites him into "his" house.

In the last act of Plautus's modest morality play all the men are
comfortably reconciled to the turn of events. Only Megaronides,
initially critical of Callicles, then a sage adviser, then a shrewd de-
viser of the "three-dollar" plan, is at the end still somewhat grumpy
and dissatisfied with the idea that Lesbonicus does not have to suffer
for his ruinous misbehavior. Lesbonicus and his father Charmides
are affectionately reunited. A second marriage plan is broached, for
Lesbonicus to marry Callicles' daughter. The son accepts gladly:
he will marry her, and anyone else his father suggests. Meanwhile,
the original request that motivated the play's main action has been
cheerfully granted. Charmides' daughter is to marry her affluent
suitor, Lysiteles, to the latter's unbounded delight. Their wedding is
scheduled for the next day; Lesbonicus will marry Callicles' daughter two days hence.

In the prologue two allegorical figures appear to present this
play, Luxury and Poverty. Luxuria instructs her daughter, Inopia, to
take up residence with Lesbonicus, and as the daughter leaves,
Luxury addresses the audience to explain that Plautus has created
and named them, signifying that since the bankrupt young man has
nothing left to offer her, he must live with the lack of it. Luxury will
not summarize the plot of the play, which will unfold when the actors
start talking. She only says further that Plautus took the Greek comic
poet Philemon's play *Thensaurus* (*The Treasure*), translated it into a
foreign language, and gave it a new name, *Trinummus*, and asks that
it be allowed to retain this name.

> huic Grace nomen est Thensauro fabulae:
> Philemo scripsit, Plautus vertit barbare,
> nomen Trinummo fecit, nunc hoc vos rogat
> ut liceat possidere hanc nomen fabulam.
> [It comes from an old play called *Thensaurus*
> By the Greek playwright Philemon; Plautus
> Spun it into Latin, calling it *Trinummus*,
> And now I ask you to let it have this name]

(ll. 18–21)

This rare allegorical gesture on Plautus's part, together with his candor about his sources and his hopes for the successful survival of his own work, indicate his aims and working methods in the *Trinummus*.

Money is the measure of most things. Young Lesbonicus is embarrassed and ashamed of himself for having squandered his father's resources, but his pride and conscience impel him toward further ruin, the offer of the last piece of property left as his sister's dowry. Her suitor, Lesbonicus's staunch friend Lysiteles, wants to spare him additional loss and is more than willing to take a bride without a dowry; but this generous intention, socially deplorable as it is, only increases Lesbonicus's sense of moral chagrin. So the friends quarrel and can only resolve their dispute when Lysiteles persuades his father to present the proposal again on his son's behalf. And in the course of the conversation between this father and son, Plautus employs his moral vocabulary deftly:

> PHILTO: . . . Better to be the man you should be than
> You would be.
> LYSITELES: . ... There's no malice in him, so I'd like to help him
> In his need.
> PHILTO: . . . I warn you ahead of time to pity others
> In such a way that they will not pity you.
> LYSITELES: I'd be ashamed to abandon him, or fail
> To help him in his trouble.
> PHILTO: Shame is preferable
> To blame, even though each word has the same
> Numbers of letters, don't you see?

The sense of "shame" as "being sorry," distinguished from resentment or disgust, gleams brightly in Plautus's matching of his wits with his words:

> PHILTO: pol pudere quam pigere praestat, totidem litteris.
> [Shame is better than regret and has the same Number of letters,
> practically.]

> (l. 345)

The shame of incurring a bad reputation is again linked to the revulsion at such a status when the "good" young man Lysiteles again tries

to persuade the confessedly dissolute young Lesbonicus to accept
his offer for his sister's hand:

> LYSITELES: . . . I don't like to see my work go to waste
> And you not taking my words to heart.
> And besides,
> I'm embarrassed because you are not ashamed.

The cast of exclusively male characters in this play seem to be
rehearsing their ideas about human behavior in conventional society
constantly. Everyone moralizes, even the sycophant who has earned
his dishonest three pieces of money honestly, and who reminds
Charmides of his respectability: his tax payments are up to date. The
servant Stasimus has left his sodality ring behind in a tavern and
realizes that it's gone for good because his disreputable drinking
companions will simply lift it. He launches into an excited soliloquy
on the inferiority of modern behavior to the good old days when
traditional social standards prevailed. Now it is greed, self-interest,
and self-advancement that dominate men's minds. Referring to the
ancient device of adfixing rigorous laws in bronze to the walls above
the forum, Stasimus wishes that now modern modes of misconduct
could be pinned up similarly, but as a study in aberrance: "ut malos
mores adfigi nimio fuerat aequius" [much more becoming for bad
ways to be fixed up] (l. 1040). Such a fixation would be a better
measure of justice. The modern style is to get around the laws, to
take advantage of them and so control them—to an even greater
degree than children wield control over their parents, Stasimus
suggests. He has loaned a large sum of money (from his servant's
savings) to a friend and anticipates the difficulty of recovering it:

> If you lend someone money
> It's as good as lost. When you ask for it back again,
> You find that by your kindness you have made
> A friend an enemy . . . two choices then develop:
> You lose whatever you handed over in trust,
> Or you lose that friend.
>   (ll. 1051–54)

When Lysiteles approaches his father to ask that the money for
the dowry be waived, the father at first voices his disgust with the
slipshod morality of the times. He echoes the words of the two other

older men in the opening scenes of the play in which Megaronides, misunderstanding Callicles' intentions in buying Lesbonicus's house, takes his friend to task for apparently sharp money practices. As the misunderstanding is resolved both older men display an admirable, if somewhat self-righteous, commitment to virtue and reputation. And Lysiteles' father eventually yields to his son's "permissive" plea, after delivering himself of such maxims as the "shame and blame have the same number of letters" phrase cited above, and the Polonius-like injunction to his son:

> Better to be the man you should be, than the man
> You would be.
>
> (l. 309)

Both young men share and indeed revel in this moral fervor. Lesbonicus realizes how far wrong he has gone and is thoroughly ashamed of himself. He clings to his last vestige of self-respect by offering the farmland in lieu of a dowry for his sister, but his moral compunction is neutralized by Stasimus's persuasive words to the prospective father-in-law about how ruinous an investment this land would be. Money and respectability are repeatedly linked in the characters' minds.

The young lovers have learned to their cost how prohibitive the price of passion can be. Lysiteles in his opening soliloquy conducts a vigorous quarrel with himself on this subject and delineates Love as a crafty guide who entices men deeper and deeper into financial quicksand. Plautus's psychology also has Lysiteles probing in this speech into the socially demeaning dimensions of sexual indulgence. "Love leaves a bitter taste," Lysiteles discovers,[1] when a man is ashamed to be seen in public, and compromises his self-respect and his reputation among his friends. It takes effort, he concludes, to be good, but virtue rewards you with wealth (res, i.e., property, resources) and social esteem. Lesbonicus, on the other hand, in his dialogue with Stasimus, can only add up his losses; he is then taken

---

[1] "Amor amara dat tamen" (l. 259). A parallel play on the noun amor and the adjective amarus (from amaror, "bitterness") occurs at the end of Virgil's Third Eclogue, where the songs of the passionate shepherds are both thought worthy of the prize, as is "et quisquis amores aut metuet dulcis aut experietur amaros" ["anyone else who fears love's sweet rewards or knows its bitter consequences"] (ll. 109–10).

quite by surprise at the request that his sister be given to Lysiteles in marriage without having to provide a dowry. After hesitating and volunteering to make over the farmland for her portion, he accedes to the offer momentarily but later reverts to his stubborn insistence in supplying his sister with the resources conventionally conveyed in a marriage contract. The fiery debate between the two young men in the second scene of act 3 constitutes Plautus's last setting of the moralizing counterpoint in this drama, which so often takes on a serious tone of earnest self-examination and a search for the right choices in matters of conduct. Lysiteles sees the force and magnetism of passion as a threat to good sense and the power of reason. Love "mores hominum moros et morosos efficit" ["makes men moral morons / And morose"] (l. 668). He himself, of course, is passionately determined to marry Lysiteles' sister, so we must conclude that the conventional status of husband and wife is superior in status and mental clarity to "love," that man can progress from chaos to stability. Lesbonicus believes that to deny his sister the proper financial basis for marriage would erode even further his own all too evident desperate social standing: "is est honos homini pudico, meminisse officium suum" ["it's a matter of honor for an upright man / To remember his duty"] (l. 697).

Lysiteles considers the probability that Lesbonicus may go through with the marriage plans on his own terms and then go into exile, leaving everything behind him. In that case, he, Lysiteles, would be blamed for having ruined his friend. He will not let that happen. At this point, Stasimus, who has been standing by as a casual judge at the scene of the dialogue, applauds Lysiteles' resolve, and congratulates him on being the better actor: "facile palmam habes: hic victust, vicit tua comoedia" ["You win the first prize easily. / He's been beaten. Your comedy has won"] (l. 706). Like the director or the producer of this play, Stasimus judges Lysiteles to have had the better lines and to have spoken them better; he'll fine Lesbonicus for a poor performance! We suddenly sense how Plautus likes to manage his characters in their situations, when at a heavy moment in a tense moral duel he directs Stasimus to comment on these impersonations. And Stasimus seems to be right, for Lysiteles' final persuasive argument is simply that he knows Lesbonicus's true worth and that no matter what ensues he will always remain his firm

friend. Should Lesbonicus consent to the dowry-less marriage and
stay on, he will share his prosperity with him. Should he leave,
Lysiteles wishes him the best of luck. Meanwhile, Lesbonicus has
suggested that they continue the discussion indoors; they exit, and
the subject of the dowry—the stumbling block in the action and a
strain on their friendship—is dismissed from the play.

The four pairs of male characters complement each other quite
geometrically in Plautus's stagecraft. The four older men, experi-
enced, wise, sage in counsel, and married, have individual features.
Callicles is markedly thoughtful and concerned at all costs for the
young man left in his care. His caustic friend Megaronides stands
severely on principles, but when he realizes what Callicles has been
doing on behalf of his ward, he promptly sides with him to support
Lesbonicus's fragile condition, and cleverly proposes the plan of
action. At the end he is somewhat disgruntled by the good fortune
that rewards the spendthrift. Philto, like them, rails against the
falling off of high standards that threatens contemporary society, but
his affectionate and rueful response to his son Lysiteles' appreciable
intentions brings him down from his high horse. He is glad to take a
hand in the action after grousing about the situation in society in
general. A glimpse of his natural good will and common sense can be
caught in his remark as he concurs with his son's wishes:

> PHILTO: . . . a man who takes some thought
> For his son only in respect to his own self-interest
> Acts like a fool. He just makes himself more nervous
> And is in effect, ineffective. He's laying up
> A harder winter in store for his own old age
> If he stirs up a storm like that ahead of the season.
>
> (ll. 394–99)

When Charmides arrives home from abroad and encounters the
sycophant, his acumen enables him to outsmart the impostor; his
good mood is sustained further in the playful recognition scene with
Stasimus. Like Philto, Charmides is ultimately won over by his
affection for his son and is perfectly willing to underwrite the son's
future. "The treasure" has been saved, after all. Megaronides and
Callicles, like many husbands in Plautus's work, indulge briefly in
misogamy—if not misogyny. Yet all four older and wiser men pro-

mote the sons' marriages, which may presumably make them older
and wiser someday. All men are equal, as Philto suggests to the
suspiciously indignant young Lesbonicus in proposing the affluent
alliance with his sister:

> PHILTO: Homo ego sum [2] homo tu es: ita me amabit Iuppiter,
>   neque te derisum advenio.
>   [I am a man, And you are a man.
>   I haven't come here to mock you,
>   So love me Jove.]
>
> (ll. 447–48)

Some lines later, reflecting on the pursuit of wealth and status,
Philto again alludes to their common humanity as "mere men":

> The gods are rich;
> High rank and opulence are appropriate to them:
> But we are mere men, well . . . *homunculi sumus.*
> And once we have sent out our last little breath of life,
> The poor man is rated at just the same value
> As the rich, at the banks of Acheron
>
> (ll. 490–94)

The four other men square off in individual contrasts. The slave
Stasimus, unlike many such figures in Plautus, does not help his
young master out of his predicament. Instead of aiding and abetting
and outsmarting, as is often the case in other plays, the serving man
mainly rolls with the punches. He just keeps hoping. His "graphic"
description of the farmland as a hell hole is received with delight by
Philto, but the latter has already decided against it. Stasimus can
only hope for the best, and his hopes are fulfilled—except for having
lost his ring irretrievably and having made a bad loan. The perfect
impostor goes about his business jauntily and "graphically" (Plautus
prizes the Greek term *graphice*), and walks away with his three
pieces of money for a day's work he didn't even have to do. His
dialogue with Charmides produces a wild scenario of misremem-
bered names, false places, and a misrepresented document: when
Charmides calls his bluff, the sycophant is free to go back where he

---

[2] A casual forerunner of Terence's sonorous maxim: "Homo sum: nil humani alienum mihi
puto"—"I am a man; I think that nothing human is alien to me" (*The Self-Tormentor*,
l. 77).

came from, that is, out of nowhere. The earnest young lovers, Lesbonicus, the prodigal son, and Lysiteles, the faithful figure of filial piety, end up on the same high plane of character, both redeemed by their eloquently voiced sense of responsibility. They are as strong in their friendship as they are strenuous in their arguments.

Plautus is seldom at a loss for words, and in the *Trinummus* as elsewhere he invests recklessly in the Latin language he did so much to invigorate. As the characters savor their ideas about disreputable conduct, the common currency of moral convictions is embellished by such weighty contributions as Philto's

> The really good man regrets that he's not better,
> Even more moderate. The one who is complacent
> About himself is neither good nor moderate.
> Doing good needs to be roofed over
> With more good doing, to keep the rain at bay.
>
> (ll. 320–22)

This may sound ponderous as well as percussive in Plautus's pointed words:

> is probus est quem paenitet quam probus sit et frugi bonae;
> quis ipsus sibi satis placet, nec probus est nec frugi bonae
> bene facta bene factis aliis pertegito, ne perpluant.

Such a saying may be heavy, but it is also ponderable, as is the same man's insight into old age:

> . . . it's not years,
> It's character that confers wisdom. Age merely adds
> Spice to Wisdom. Wisdom nourishes age.
>
> (ll. 367–68)

The "sayings" flow freely and contribute to a fund of good sense throughout this serious comedy of manners and misdemeanors. An inventive vocabulary is also brought into play. Neptune is not only salt-powerful (*Salsipotens*) but a great fermenter, a powerful brewer of storms (*Mulsipotens*—l. 820); a sneak thief who operates at night is a "sleeper" (*dormitator*) or perhaps, a belt-slasher (*sector zonarius*—l. 862); money, in a Greek phrase, "runs out on you" (*argentum "oichetai"*—l. 419); the devouring gullet is a hard taskmaster, a trainer who keeps hungry mortals in shape ("gurguliost exercitor: is hunc hominem cursuram docet"—l. 1016).

To start the action Luxury had walked in on, and then out on Lesbonicus, leaving Poverty in residence. But his friend, his father's friends, and his father, in their strenuous and value-charged discussions, found the means of prying him loose from his predicament. He was not, after all, one of your modern unscrupulous profiteers, or, as Plautus coins the word for the thing, a "lowdown-lucre-lecher" (*turpilucricupidus*—l. 100)! Society offers room in the middle between these extremes. A treasure, the golden means, may help. Mutual trust, good-natured affection, reason, and coming to one's senses can be brought into play as the (golden?) rule in conventional society.

Palmer Bovie

10 characters
all male
interesting plot—bad end

THE THIRTY-DOLLAR DAY

CHARACTERS

LUXURY
WANT
MEGARONIDES, an old gentleman of Athens
CALLICLES, his friend
LYSITELES, a young Athenian
PHILTO, his father
LESBONICUS, a friend of Lysiteles
STASIMUS, a slave of Lesbonicus and Charmides
CHARMIDES father of Lesbonicus
A SWINDLER

SCENE: *Athens. The street where* CHARMIDES *and* MEGARONIDES *live.* PHILTO's *house is nearby. Between the houses is a lane from which one may enter a little annex in back of* CHARMIDES' *house.* LESBONICUS *has sold his father's house to* CALLICLES; *since then he has lived in this annex, while* CALLICLES *lives in the main part of the house.*

SITUATION

This tells how Charmides, going abroad,
Relegates his worldly affairs and fortune
In trust to his old friend Callicles.

173

Now, his son runs through the money, sells the house
Vide infra, to Callicles, leaving his poor sister
Minus her dowry at the altar. Callicles, wanting
Money he'd pledged for the bride to seem to come
Under Charmides' orders, hires this agent who
Shows up just as Father arrives for the wedding.

PROLOGUE

(*Enter* LUXURY, *richly dressed. Behind her comes* WANT, *dressed in
ragged clothing.*)

LUXURY: This way, my daughter, come along now.
　　It's time to get to work.

WANT: I'm coming, I'm coming. But I do wish
　　you'd tell me where we're going.

LUXURY: Here we are. Look, there's the house!
　　Go on, get in there, march!

(*Exit* WANT. *To audience.*)

Now, so that all of *you* know where we're going
let me put you on the right road
with a few clear directions. I'm at your service
if you'll be kind enough to lend me an ear.   10
You're probably wondering who I am, and who
was the lady that disappeared through the doorway.
Listen, and I'll tell you all you need to know.
First, about myself: The playwright has named me
Luxury. Second, the girl: it was his wish
she should be my daughter and she would be named
Want. Why did she enter this house at my bidding?

You'll find out soon enough if you will listen.
A young man lives there. With my help, the fellow
squandered his father's entire fortune.   20
Now he's no fun for me; he can't support Luxury
in the style to which I am accustomed. So
I'll give him my daughter, Want. He'll have to be
satisfied with her.
              Now I've given you plot enough
to see you on your way. Some fine old gentlemen
are waiting in the wings to act out the story.
It comes from an old play called *Thensaurus*
by the Greek playwright Philemon; Plautus spun it
into Latin, calling it *Trinummus*. Now Epstein has
dressed it up once again, in English verses, calling it
The Thirty-Dollar Day.   30

ACT I

(*Enter* MEGARONIDES, *perplexed and moody*)

MEGARONIDES: Of all the thankless duties, this is the worst:
    having to scold a friend who has done wrong.
    It's a thankless job, but someone has to do it.
    So here I am, a friend whose friend's offense
    deserves a good bawling out, without mincing words.
    A bitter business, but loyalty drives me to it.
    I tell you, a plague has settled on our city:
    a total collapse of morals. While morals languish,
    vice and ribaldry spring up all round,   40
    as rank as watered weeds. Vice is the only crop
    to come to market this year, the only thing
    one can buy cheap. Why, there's a certain crowd
    more interested in sucking up to power brokers
    than they are in the general welfare of the state!

It's obstructive and it's odious and it's wrong,
for all of us, as public citizens, private men.

(*Enter* CALLICLES *into his doorway*)

CALLICLES: (*To his wife within*)
Dearie! It's time to honor the Household God
with a garland. Make it a nice one. Pray he will bless
this house and make it lucky and pleasant and rich—   50
(*As she closes the door*)
and also to hasten the day I will see you buried.

MEGARONIDES: There he is, the man turned boy again in his
old age,
an old boy who needs a good scolding.

CALLICLES: Do I hear a voice? Who is it?

MEGARONIDES: One who wishes you well if you're the kind
of man
I'd like you to be. If not, I'll be a furious enemy.

CALLICLES: O Megaronides! My old friend! Good morning.
How are you?

MEGARONIDES: And a good morning to you, Callicles.

CALLICLES: How is it going? How's your health these days?   60

MEGARONIDES: Oh, all right. I'm feeling well enough.

CALLICLES: And the wife? Is she in good health?

MEGARONIDES: Better than I like.

CALLICLES: Ah, by Jove, it's a wonderful thing to have one's wife
alive and in good condition.

MEGARONIDES: And, by Jove, I think you delight in my
    misfortune.

CALLICLES: Now you know I want for my friends what I have
    myself . . .

MEGARONIDES: Ha, you rogue. Tell me, how is *your* wife?

CALLICLES: Immortal. She'll live forever, I'm sure.

MEGARONIDES: Good news, good news! I pray to God it
    should be   70
that way, that you'll die before her.

CALLICLES: That's just the way I'd like it—if I had *your* wife.

MEGARONIDES: I'll tell you what: we'll swap wives; give me yours
    and you take mine. Believe me, you wouldn't be
    running away with such a great bargain.

CALLICLES: Ha! You're just trying to soften me up for the kill.

MEGARONIDES: I'm telling you. You'd find out soon enough
    what you had won.

CALLICLES: A booby prize? Well, you know what they say:
    "Better
the familiar evil than the unknown." I've got no time
    anymore   80
for mysteries, especially women. I wouldn't know what to do.

MEGARONIDES: Now you're talking like the old philosopher: "A
    long life has taught us how
to live!" But enough of the small talk.
I'm here on serious business.

CALLICLES: What business?

MEGARONIDES: To give you a good old-fashioned tongue-lashing.

CALLICLES: Me?

MEGARONIDES: Do you see anyone else in the vicinity?

CALLICLES: No.

MEGARONIDES: Then who else would I be scolding? Myself?
    Listen to me. When a man's morals grow overripe,   90
    and then rotten in him, it's bad enough he becomes
    sick himself. But if he doesn't return to health,
    after a while, his friends suffer as well; his friends
    eventually can't stand the sight or smell
    of the rottenness in him.

CALLICLES: Why are you talking to me like this?

MEGARONIDES: As your friend, I am bound to remind you
    of the duty of every decent man and woman
    to remain absolutely free of suspicion and guilt.

CALLICLES: Nobody can remain free of both.   100

MEGARONIDES: Why not?

CALLICLES: Can you really wonder? Here I keep
    the key to my private thoughts, in a safe place
    where guilt can never enter. But suspicion?
    Suspicion is stored up in the minds of others.
    Right now I may suspect you, Megaronides, of stealing
    the crown from Jove's statue on top of the temple.
    Maybe you didn't do it, but if I want to
    suspect you of it I will and you can't stop me.
    Come now and tell me what's really troubling you.   110

MEGARONIDES: Do you have a friend with good common sense?

CALLICLES: Well, to be honest, there are some people I know
    to be friends, some I suspect of it, and others
    whose nature I don't know enough to say for certain
    if they are friends or foes. But of all these
    the one I am most sure is a friend is you, Megaronides.
    So, if you think I have done something stupid
    or dishonorable, and you, my best friend, won't tell me,
    then indeed you are the one who deserves a tongue-lashing.

MEGARONIDES: I understand. That's exactly why I'm here.   120

CALLICLES: So?

MEGARONIDES: First of all, they're saying terrible things
    about you all over town. They're calling you
    an omnivorous monster, a cormorant who'd gobble up
    anyone's fortune, a foreigner's treasure, or the gold
    stash of a fellow citizen, it's all the same.
    You know when I hear such talk it hurts me deeply.

CALLICLES: Now this is a matter mostly out of my hands,
    Megaronides. People will talk. I'm free to ignore them.

MEGARONIDES: This Charmides, he was a friend of yours,   130

CALLICLES: He was and he is. No one could doubt it. Why,
    when his son wrecked his estate and reduced him to poverty;
    when his wife died and his motherless daughter neared the age
    a maiden ought to be married—at this ominous time in his life
    he was called away to Seleucia. And he left me here
    to handle his affairs, the whole scramble: the spinster daughter,
    the business, the profligate son. Now if that isn't friendship
    I'd like to know what to call it. He sure trusted me.

MEGARONIDES: He trusted you. And what did you do with the
        young rascal in your care? Did
    you improve him? I don't think so.   140
    It was your job as his guardian to bring him up right,

to make a man of him. From what I've seen,
you've simply become a companion in his revels,
adding your own meat to his stew of degeneracy.

CALLICLES: What have I done?

MEGARONIDES: What only a scoundrel would do.

CALLICLES: But that's not my style.

MEGARONIDES: You bought this house from the boy, right?
And now you live in it yourself?

CALLICLES: Yes, yes. I paid a hundred thousand dollars for it, 150
and made out the check to the lad himself.

MEGARONIDES: You gave him the money, did you?

CALLICLES: I sure did, and I don't regret a penny of it.

MEGARONIDES: You don't! Good Lord, the treacherous hands
that boy was placed in! How could you do such a thing?
Might as well give him a sword to cut his throat.
Isn't that what you've done when you've handed over
that much cash to a skirt-mad, wild young libertine,
a grant for him to complete the structure of folly
and wickedness he started on his own?   160

CALLICLES: You think I shouldn't have paid him the money.

MEGARONIDES: No, I don't think you should have paid him the
    money.
You should have bought nothing, sold nothing to the boy,
nor supplied him with any tools he could use to make
himself worse than he is already. You're his guardian!
He was entrusted to your care, and what have you done?
You've bundled the whole family out of their home.

Haven't you now? A fine guardian you are. Oh, you can be
trusted indeed—to improve your own portfolio.

CALLICLES: Megaronides, this attack so surprises and
    overwhelms me   170
I hardly know what to say, except a thing I promised
to tell no one, a deep secret entrusted to me
in faith. Now I'm forced to entrust it to you.

MEGARONIDES: Whatever you trust to me you know is safe.

CALLICLES: Can anyone hear us? Look around for eavesdroppers.

MEGARONIDES: The coast is clear. Now will you tell me—

CALLICLES: Be quiet and I'll tell you. Just before Charmides
went abroad, he showed me, walled up in this very house
. . . a treasure . . . What was that?

MEGARONIDES: There's nobody.   180

CALLICLES: Some thirty thousand dollars in gold coins.
We talked together, he and I alone.
And I tell you, Megaronides, the man wept
as he begged me in the name of friendship and loyalty
never to tell his son about the gold,
never to tell anyone who might tell his son.
You see, if Charmides returns here safe,
I am to give him his money. If something happens
to him, I'll have the wherewithal to provide
a dowry for his daughter, my ward,   190
and see that she is suitably matched and married.

MEGARONIDES: Immortal gods! How quickly a few sentences
have spun me around and made me a different man
than when I arrived! But . . . you were saying . . .

CALLICLES: I was about to tell you how my friend's wisdom,
   my own loyalty, and thirty thousand dollars were
   damn near driven to ruin by that young rascal.

MEGARONIDES: No! How?

CALLICLES: I left for the country for six days.
   While I was gone he put the house up for sale—   200
   without a word of notice or consultation.

MEGARONIDES: Oh, the ravening wolf! I can see his fangs
   gleaming. He was waiting for the sheepdogs to doze,
   so he might gobble up the whole flock.

CALLICLES: And, by God, he would have done it, if this sly dog
   hadn't got wind of the beast and his desires.
   But now I'd like to ask you a thing or two.
   What was my duty exactly? Tell me now. Should I
   have told the young spendthrift about the treasure
   despite my vow of secrecy to his father?   210
   Should I let some stranger buy the family home?
   Would the hidden gold in the house belong to the man
   who bought it? Well? So I bought the house myself.
   I paid good money to keep my friend's treasure safe
   so it might return to him when he returns.
   I didn't buy the house to please myself.
   I bought it for my friend, and paid with money
   out of my own pocket. Those are the facts.
   Right or wrong, that's what I did, Megaronides.
   There's your monster of avarice, cormorant!   220
   There's the truth behind the scurrilous gossip.

MEGARONIDES: Enough! You've silenced this critic.
   I'm absolutely speechless.

CALLICLES: Can I count on your help?

MEGARONIDES: Anything you ask.

CALLICLES: Where can I reach you?

MEGARONIDES: At home.

(*About to go*)

CALLICLES: Is there anything else on your mind?

MEGARONIDES: Well . . . just try to be trustworthy.

CALLICLES: I'll do my best.   230

(*Going*)

MEGARONIDES: But wait!

CALLICLES: Yes?

MEGARONIDES: Where's our young gentleman living now?

CALLICLES: He's still in the house. I let him keep one room
    as part of the deal.

MEGARONIDES: Hm. Well enough. You can run along now. But
    wait!
    What about the girl? She's with you, I suppose?

CALLICLES: She is. And you can rest assured
    I treat her as I would my own daughter.

MEGARONIDES: Good, good.   240

CALLICLES: Anything else?

(*He exits*)

MEGARONIDES: Good bye! Surely there's nothing so stupid,
  so vapid and deceitful, so loudmouthed and perfidious
  as these streetcorner busybodies that call themselves
  "men of the world." Yes, and I suppose
  I have to count myself as one of them,
  swallowing that swill of lies from gossip-mongers,
  know-nothings who think they know it all.
  Why, they know what a man is thinking before he thinks;
  they know what the king is whispering to the queen;   250
  they know what Juno chats about with Jove.
  What never is or was or ever will be,
  they know that too! And as for whether or not
  the praise or blame they scatter abroad
  is fair or unfair, what do they care as long
  as the gossips know what they like to know!
  Everyone in town said Callicles was a disgrace,
  sharking that young man out of his house and land,
  a disgrace such a man was alive and breathing
  the air of his hometown. And I listened to them,   260
  and went after my friend without a thought
  he might be innocent. Oh, if we only looked
  for facts behind the rumors! If we only
  made these tattletales expose their sources,
  and fined or jailed the sleazy ones who wouldn't,
  what a service that would be to the public!
  Then, you can bet there wouldn't ever be
  so many people knowing what they don't know,
  and yammering on in the marketplace about it.

(*He exits into his house*)

ACT II

Scene 1

(LYSITELES *enters, nervous and upset*)

LYSITELES: Thoughts keep tumbling through my head,   270
   over and over until I think I'll go crazy!
   My brain is as worn out with thinking
   as my body would be if my boxing coach
   made me run all day. Yet with all this pondering
   I can't decide which is the best way for me
   to go in this life, which way leads
   to a firmer footing in the future.
   Should I concentrate on love affairs, or business?
   In the long run, which will bring me more happiness?
   The question is harder than it looks.   280
   In fact, I think I can do it justice
   only by calling up love and business success
   as two defendants in a court of law,
   myself serving as judge and counsel in the case.

   So. Let us begin with Art of Love. Ladies
   and Gentlemen of the Jury: What does Love
   hope to catch in his net? A certain species
   of man, quick and unruly in his desires.
   Such men Love contrives to wreck and ruin.
   He gives them bad advice; he is smooth-talking,   290
   affable, alluring, grasping, luxurious;
   Love is a plunderer, a gigolo
   who turns men into ghosts of the bawdy houses.
   When there's no other action he turns to blackmail.
   No sooner is a lover pierced by a blissful kiss
   than his property melts and soon starts dripping away.
   "O sweety, if you love me just give me this trinket!"
   "Darling, of course you shall have it,

one of *those* too!" says our poor saphead.
And when she's got him all tied up to be whipped,   300
she lays it on: asking for a little of this,
and some of that, no harm done yet, but a little
more cash for wine, for meat, for presents.
At last she lets him take her home for the night;
next day she moves in with him, her whole entourage:
the wardrobe mistress, the masseur, the accountant;
and of course the lady who cares for her fans,
another who cares for her sandals, and a soprano,
several errand boys, and a cashier
to work with the accountant, all of these people   310
eventually on the payroll of her host, the fortunate lover,
whose money is bound to run out before his affection.

Now, when I think this over, and consider
the sort of respect a poor man gets,
all I have to say is: Love, get lost!
I've got no use for you! From eating and drinking
you get at least a few hours of satisfaction—
but from love there's only this pain and wasting away.
The lover flies from the forum, rejects his family,
runs away from his own honest opinion of himself.   320
No man wants to be called his friend. No, Love,
you're a demon to be avoided by all means,
for any man who's fallen in love is in more trouble
than if he had thrown himself off a cliff.
Be gone, Love, take back your dowry!
Never call yourself a friend of mine! Go
nuzzle up to some other poor blockhead,
somebody who's already fallen under your spell.
Now that's all settled. Today I pledge myself
to practical pursuits, business affairs, work,   330
good clean honest effort. For there's nothing
a good man values as much as wealth and fame
and the confidence and esteem that go with them.
These are the prizes of integrity. Oh, give me a man

of integrity and I won't waste a minute more
with these smooth-talking rogues and rascals.

Scene 2

(PHILTO *enters*)

PHILTO: The boy just stepped out here a minute ago.
　　Now where has he gone?

LYSITELES: Here I am, Father, at your service. I'm not the kind
　　to keep you waiting, hiding in some nook or cranny.　　　　340

PHILTO: And that's just as it should be, just as I expect.
　　You have been and continue to be a model of filial duty.
　　Now, my son, during this current vogue of sodden morality
　　I wish you would refrain from all intercourse, verbal
　　and otherwise, with outlaws and degenerates,
　　in the streets, in the forum, and everywhere else.
　　An evil man wants company like himself, so he
　　works to infect the good man, making him wicked.
　　Just as bad money drives out the good,
　　bad men pull down standards to their level.　　　　　　350
　　That pack of wolves, greedy and envious,
　　regards the sacred as profane, private things
　　as public. This galls me. It so torments me
　　it keeps me awake nights, in terror my own son
　　might become one of their victims. Why, the only wrong
　　they acknowledge is trying to steal the things they can't!
　　As for everything else, it's fair game, snatch and bag it,
　　clear out and head for the hills! Oh, it's sad
　　to have lived so long as to see such a generation.

　　I'd almost rather go and join the dead.　　　　　　　　360
　　These living scoundrels praise the goodness of ancestors,
　　then defile their example with vile deeds.

You, my boy, must be the exception, free
of such habits, immune to the general contagion.
Let me serve as your model of the old ways,
the good old standards. Follow my example,
for I have no use for the filthy relativism
that has disgraced so many of our good men.
Follow my lead, take what I say to heart,
and countless blessings will come as your reward.   370

LYSITELES: Father, since I was a child I have taken
　　your words for law. Though I was born free,
　　my duty to you, as son to a wise father,
　　bound me to subject my passions to your guidance.

PHILTO: So much better to fight that battle when you're young!
　　Decide early if you are the sort of man
　　who pleases his passions or his family!
　　When passion wins, the man is lost, a slave
　　to the conqueror all his life. But a warrior
　　who defeats passion will be hailed   380
　　forever as the master of conquerors.
　　Rejoice, my son, if you've already
　　beaten down your vain hungers and lusts,
　　for it's better to be the man you ought to be
　　than the monkey your passions would like to make of you.
　　Once a man has conquered his baser desires,
　　he's known as a virtuous citizen ever after.

LYSITELES: I have made your principles the shelter
　　for my life. Hanging out in bars and gambling dens,
　　roaming the streets at night or taking what isn't mine—   390
　　being in any way a source of anguish to you, Father—
　　these are things I have studiously avoided.
　　My saintly self-control has kept pace with your program.

PHILTO: Come on, come on, it hasn't been so bad.
　　Your good behavior does more for you than for me.
　　My life is nearly over: you're the one who has to live

with the consequences of his actions.
The man who's truly virtuous seldom feels it,
while those who praise themselves as paragons,
often are neither virtuous nor praiseworthy.   400
Good deeds must be roofed over with more good deeds,
or the next rain will wash them all away.

LYSITELES: The reason I'm reminding you of my well-spent youth
   is that I'm hoping to win your trust and support
   in a certain matter . . .

PHILTO: Yes? You know I'm always eager to oblige.

LYSITELES: It concerns a certain young man in this city.
   He comes from a good family. He's a friend about my age.
   You see, Father, this young man has managed
   his business affairs . . . how shall I say . . . imprudently.   410
   With your permission, I'd like to help him out of a jam.

PHILTO: With your money?

LYSITELES: Why, yes. After all, what's mine is yours,
   and vice versa, right?

PHILTO: So what's his story. Is he flat broke?

LYSITELES: Yessir.

PHILTO: And he had a good deal of money?

LYSITELES: He did, at one time.

PHILTO: Well then, what happened to it? Did he pour it
   into one of those public bond issues, or a ship that sank
      at sea?   420
   Did he lose it in trade or the slave market?

LYSITELES: None of the above.

PHILTO: Then how did he lose it?

LYSITELES: First and foremost, Father, it was his open-hearted,
    generous good nature. And then I suppose he did
    let some of it slip away from him . . . by being too kind
    to his animal passions.

PHILTO: Aha! I like *that* piece of background! He lost his holdings
      in a wholly
    illegitimate manner, and now he's broke, is he?
    I'm not so sure I want such a man to be your friend.   430

LYSITELES: Really, Father, he has the best intentions.
    I just want to help him get back on his feet.

PHILTO: You can't help a beggar by giving him food and drink;
    it's a dead loss that only prolongs his wretched life.
    Now you know I'm willing to help you do what's right
    for others and yourself. But please, try to pity others
    in such a way that others will not take pity on you.

LYSITELES: But if I desert him now, I'll be disgraced.

PHILTO: Better to be disgraced than dragged through the mud.

LYSITELES: But Father, look: Thanks to God and our
      grandfathers   440
    and yourself, we are well off in the world, we have
    more than enough for our needs. If you have a chance
    to help a friend in trouble, and turn him down because
    his trouble offends your sense of propriety—
    that really *is* a disgrace, a sorry disgrace.

PHILTO: If you've got a million dollars and you give
    some of it away, is your money growing or shrinking?

LYSITELES: Shrinking, of course. But you know the old saying at
    the swap-meets:

Give only to get what you want
You cheap son-of-a-bitch;   450
Nothing you've ever given away
Would make a man envy the rich.

PHILTO: All right. I know there are misers in the world.
   But, believe me, the real outcast at the swap-meet is
   the poor bastard who's got nothing to give away.

LYSITELES: Thank God we have plenty for ourselves, and can
      afford
   to be generous to our friends.

PHILTO: Well, well. I guess you're not going to take no
   for an answer. So, who is it you want to rescue
   from the poorhouse? Speak freely.   460

LYSITELES: Charmides' son, young Lesbonicus. He lives right
      there.

PHILTO: That good-for-nothing rascal who consumed everything
   he had, and a good deal that he didn't have?

LYSITELES: Now, Father, don't jump to conclusions.
   A lot can happen to a man against his will.

PHILTO: That's a lie, and you're not a very good liar!
   You know very well that any man worth his salt
   will hammer up the house of his own good fortune.
   Not much happens to a wise man against his will
   —unless he's a lousy builder.   470

LYSITELES: To design an entire life would require
   a far-seeing architect, with a lot of experience,
   Father. And this fellow is still very young.

PHILTO: Wisdom comes of character, not age.
   Though wisdom is the hallmark of great age,

years only lend it a certain . . . distinction. But come now,
speak up. What do you want to give the rascal?

LYSITELES: Nothing. All I'm asking is that you not interfere
if he gives *me* something.

PHILTO: How are you going to relieve his poverty   480
by letting him give you things?

LYSITELES: I just will, that's all.

PHILTO: Boy, that's a trick I'd like to learn.

LYSITELES: Good. You know the family situation?

PHILTO: It's a good family.

LYSITELES: One sister, grown-up, marriageable. Now,
you see, Father, I would very much like to marry
this woman. But she doesn't have any dowry.

PHILTO: No dowry? A wife without a dowry?

LYSITELES: Yes. Can you imagine how grateful he would be
to us,   490
how he would honor you and me? For there's no better way
that we could help him. And it costs us . . . nothing.

PHILTO: What about the dowry you'd get if you married someone
else?

LYSITELES: Please, Father. I don't love anybody else. I love her.
And marrying the
sister of Lesbonicus, in her situation,
will bring a new luster to our family name.

PHILTO: Oh well. I guess I could speak platitudes
and spout good advice until I was blue in the face,

and it wouldn't make any difference. You've made up your
  mind.
You're bound to prove yourself as a loyal friend,   500
and bring honor to us by this selfless act—then go ahead,
with my blessings. Ask for her hand, and marry her at once.

LYSITELES: God bless you, Father! Can I ask you one more favor?

PHILTO: What is it?

LYSITELES: Just this: I'd appreciate it if you would broach the
  subject with
Lesbonicus. I want you to make the arrangements.

PHILTO: If that doesn't beat everything—

LYSITELES: For you it will be a cinch! Your actions in a situation
  like this will be definitive. One word from the father
  is worth a hundred from the son in these matters.   510

PHILTO: There's the thanks I get for being nice—
  you put me to work. Well, I suppose I can do it.

LYSITELES: Excellent! Lesbonicus lives in that house.
  Go to it, Father. I'll be waiting back at home.

(*He exits*)

Scene 3

PHILTO: Now this is not exactly the way I would choose
  to spend my morning, yet surely there are worse things
  I could be doing. One thought consoles me:
  I'm doing it for him. The father who sees his son
  and his son's happiness as no more than a footnote
  to his own welfare is brewing up rough weather   520

for his old age, a bitter winter. But the door is open!
There's Lesbonicus himself, with his servant.

(*Conceals himself around the corner*)

Scene 4

(*Enter* LESBONICUS *and* STASIMUS *into their doorway*)

LESBONICUS: No more than two weeks ago you received
    a hundred thousand dollars from Callicles in payment
    for the house. Is that right, Stasimus?

STASIMUS: Now that I look back on it, that sounds about right.

LESBONICUS: So where's the money?

STASIMUS: Some of it we ate up; some we drank up; some
    caught on fire and burned; some went down the sink hole
    in the baths. The fish man got away with some of it,   530
    the bakers, butchers, cooks, greengrocers, the poultrymen
    got theirs, and then there was the perfume salesman . . .
    I mean, it got away fast. My God, it vanished in all directions
    like poppy seeds thrown to the ants.

LESBONICUS: Oh come on, Stasimus.
    No more than ten thousand could have gone that way.

STASIMUS: Oh yeah? What about the whores?

LESBONICUS: I'm counting them too.

STASIMUS: What about the money I took off the top?

LESBONICUS: Ha! That's the biggest slice of the pie.   540

STASIMUS: Man, you're so busy spending money you can't
  possibly
see where it's going. Do you think your money is special,
a kind you can spend without having it get away from you?

PHILTO: (*Aside*) What a fool, trying to sort out his accounts
after the money is gone. He should have done it before.

LESBONICUS: I look at these figures and for the life of me
  I just don't get it.

STASIMUS: Oh you "get" the accounting; you just don't get the
  cash,
because it's *gone*. You got a hundred thousand from Callicles
and he got the title to your house, right? 550

LESBONICUS: Right.

PHILTO: (*Aside*) It seems our prospective in-law has sold his
  house.
When his father comes home from his travels
he can set up housekeeping under a bridge,
if he can't take his fortune out of his son's hide.

STASIMUS: Then you paid the banker Olympicus the twenty
  thousand
you owed him.

LESBONICUS: Twenty thousand dollars I advanced in security—

STASIMUS: Security bullshit! You borrowed money to help that kid
  you thought had resources— 560

LESBONICUS: That's true.

STASIMUS: And you'll never get a penny of it back.

LESBONICUS: Maybe not. But he was in such a bad way you had to
feel sorry for him.

STASIMUS: Not me, *you* had to feel sorry for him. You pity others
but you have no pity for yourself, no self-control.

PHILTO: Time to move in.

(*Stepping forward*)

LESBONICUS: Hey, isn't that Philto? The man himself.

STASIMUS: By God, I'd love to have him in my corner,
with that mountain of capital gains at his disposal.

PHILTO: Lesbonicus, Stasimus, a most excellent good
    morning   570
to both of you, master and slave, from yours truly, Philto.

LESBONICUS: Why, Philto, how nice! May God hear your prayers.
How's your son?

PHILTO: He sends you all his good wishes.

LESBONICUS: And I send him my good wishes.

STASIMUS: (*To the audience*) Good wishes, my eye. Wish in one
    hand, spit in the other,
see which fills up first.
I've got wishes enough to fill an hour of telling,
what good are they? I wish, just for one thing, that I were free.
My master, he wishes he was smart. It'll never happen.   580

PHILTO: I'm here on an errand for my son. It is his desire
that we unite our families in an honorable and harmonious
    bond—
in short, he wants to marry your sister, and I'm all for it.

LESBONICUS: Please, sir. Don't make fun of me. It's unbecoming
    in a man of your position.

PHILTO: I didn't come here to make fun of you. I came
    as one man to another, to tell you the plain truth:
    my son has begged me to ask on his behalf,
    if he can marry your sister.

LESBONICUS: It is my duty   590
    to inform you, in case you don't already know it,
    my family is *not* on an equal footing with yours.
    You'll have to look for someone of your own class.

STASIMUS: (*Aside to* LESBONICUS) What's gotten into you? Have
    you lost your mind? The man is offering you the chance of a
    lifetime!

LESBONICUS: Oh go to hell!

STASIMUS: I would, but you won't let me go anywhere.

LESBONICUS: So Philto, if that's the question, no is the answer.

PHILTO: Think it over, Lesbonicus; maybe tomorrow
    you'll think more kindly of me, maybe not.   600
    Playing hard to get will get you nowhere in this life;
    and playing the fool really doesn't become you.

STASIMUS: (*To* LESBONICUS) Listen to him! He's talking sense!

LESBONICUS: One more peep out of you and I'll poke your
    eye out.

STASIMUS: Then I'll talk with one eye instead of two.

PHILTO: Look, Lesbonicus. Do you really think your family
    is beneath mine in any way that matters?

LESBONICUS: I do.

PHILTO: Look at it this way. Suppose you were seated at a temple
     banquet,
   one of those where the public dines in common;
   and right next to you sat a billionaire whose friends   610
   kept passing him platters of the finest cuisine.
   Would you pass the plates without taking what you wanted?
   Sitting next to the billionaire, would you go hungry?

LESBONICUS: I would eat, unless the man had some objection.

STASIMUS: I would eat, by God, whether he objected or not!
   I'd stuff my face with both hands and fill my belly,
   gobbling first the food he liked the most! I wouldn't
   spare him a measly crumb of what I needed. No man on earth
   has the right to be selfish at the dinner table—
   when we dine together that may be the only time   620
   we share in a way both human and divine.

PHILTO: Wise words.

STASIMUS: Anywhere else I'd give the billionaire a wide berth—
   on the street, on the sidewalk, in public office—
   but when it comes to the dinner table I won't give him an inch,
   that is, unless he's quicker than me with his fists.
   The price of meat being what it is these days,
   a good meal is like an inheritance without taxes.

PHILTO: Remember, Lesbonicus, nothing is better than being
   the best sort of man; but if you can't be the best,
   keep company with the best, I always say. Now,   630
   this marriage I've proposed to you, Lesbonicus.
   I do wish you'd agree to it. As for any inequality
   between us, consider that we're just simple mortals.
   Only the gods are rich with a *real* difference.
   We come into this world naked, and after taking
   our little breaths of life we'll all go out the same way

to Acheron, beggar and billionaire, all with the same
credit rating. You can't take it with you.

STASIMUS: I thought that in your case they might make an
      exception,
so you might keep lending money at high interest in hell.   640

PHILTO: Just to show you I mean business, and that status
      and assets have absolutely nothing to do with this transaction,
      I insist that you give your sister to my son *without* a dowry.
      Okay? And may God shower the couple with His blessings.
      How do you like that? Well, aren't you going to say something?

STASIMUS: Ye gods! What a deal!

PHILTO: Come on, man! How about some enthusiasm!

STASIMUS: Damn it all. For weeks he's been saying yes
      to everybody, mostly when he should have said no.
      Now when he ought to say yes, he can't.   650

LESBONICUS: Philto, I must say that I'm grateful to all of you
      for considering me worthy of being a part of your family.
      Now I have made kind of a mess of things here in the city.
      But just outside of town we still own a farm.
      The farm shall be my sister's dowry.
      That's all I have left to offer—except my poor life.

PHILTO: I told you I don't want any dowry.

LESBONICUS: My sister shall have a dowry. I insist upon it—

STASIMUS: Master . . .
      (*Musically*)
      Do you want to bite the hand that wants to feed us?
      Really, do you like being hungry?   660

LESBONICUS: Pipe down! Who's the master here, you or me?

STASIMUS: If I don't come up with something, we're done for.
Philto, a word with you, sir.

(*Drawing him aside*)

PHILTO: Well, Stasimus, what is it?

STASIMUS: This way, sir.

PHILTO: Fine, fine.

STASIMUS: I'm telling you this in strictest confidence.
Don't tell him or anybody else.

PHILTO: You can trust me.

STASIMUS: I swear to you by God and my own mother,   670
you must never let that farm come into your possession.
I have my reasons for warning you thus.

PHILTO: Let me hear them!

STASIMUS: Well. First of all, after the first plowing every year
the oxen all fall dead in the fifth furrow.

PHILTO: No! It sounds like your farm is the mouth of hell.

STASIMUS: Then there's the grapes. The grapes hang
and go rotten before they ever get ripe.

LESBONICUS: Listen to him work on Philto. Old Stasimus
may be a devil, but he's a loyal devil.   680

STASIMUS: And that's not all: During harvest time
when all the farmers are giving thanks for a bumper crop,
that farm yields only a third of what was planted.

PHILTO: Ah! A perfect field where men can plant the seeds
   of wickedness, where they may die in the bud.

STASIMUS: I tell you, sir, there was never a man who owned that
      farm
   who had a moment's peace afterward: some ran away, some
      died,
   some hung themselves. Just look at the man who owns it now—
   you want to end up like him?

PHILTO: God save me from such a farm!   690

STASIMUS: Pray on, pray on. And you don't know the half of it.
   Listen to this: during storms every other tree
   gets struck by lightning. The pigs get tonsillitis,
   which kills off herds at a time. The sheep get the mange
   so most of them are as bald as the palm of my hand.
   And the slaves? There's not a breed that can survive the
      summer there—not
   even the Syrians—they all drop dead of malaria.

PHILTO: I've heard this new breed of slaves, the Campanians,
   is even heartier than the Syrian tribe. Maybe they would
   stick it out. Anyway, from what you've told me, this farm   700
   would make a perfect Siberia for libertines, something like
   the Isles of the Blessed where good folks go to their final
      reward.
   Likewise it seems fitting that our villains should all be
   rounded up on that farm—that is, if it's the hell you say it is.

STASIMUS: I'm telling you, it's Calamity Central. What more can
      I say?
   You want trouble? That's the place to find it.

PHILTO: Oh, I think you can find it wherever you go.

STASIMUS: Now please, sir. Don't breathe a word to anyone.

PHILTO: Your secret is safe with me.

STASIMUS: He'd love to unload the farm on someone,   710
    if he can just find the right sucker—

PHILTO: It won't be me, rest assured.

STASIMUS: Not while you're playing with a full deck.
    (*To the audience*)
    Well, I guess I scared the old man away from the farm. And a
    good thing, because that's all we have left!

PHILTO: Now, Lesbonicus, where were we?

LESBONICUS: Do you mind if I ask you what that was all about?

PHILTO: What else? Being a man, your slave wants to be a
    free man.
    But he's got no money.

LESBONICUS: And I want to be a rich man, but I've got the
    same problem.   720

STASIMUS: But you could have been rich if you'd really wanted it;
    you didn't want what you had and now you've got nothing to
    work with.

LESBONICUS: Lecturing me again, Stasimus?

STASIMUS: Just interpreting your own words: you'd be rich
    if you'd wanted it before; the ship sailed,
    and your ambition missed the ship.

PHILTO: Look, I'm going to leave this business of the dowry
    for you and my son to settle. All I want is the nod from you
    that you'll grant my boy your sister's hand in marriage.

And may heaven smile upon their union! Well? What do
   you say?   730
Still can't make up your mind?

LESBONICUS: Oh well, if that's the way you want it.
   God bless the match. I agree to it.

STASIMUS: Good Lord! I've been like a man waiting for his wife
   to deliver a baby, fretting over the birth of this agreement!
   I thought you'd never say yes! May you both prosper.

PHILTO: I hope so.

LESBONICUS: Stasimus, go to my sister at Callicles' and tell her
   the news.

STASIMUS: Pronto!

LESBONICUS: And congratulate her.   740

STASIMUS: Of course.

PHILTO: Come with me, Lesbonicus. Together we'll plan
   the wedding day, and put the finishing touches on our
   agreement.

(*He exits*)

LESBONICUS: Tell Callicles to meet me—

STASIMUS: Yes, yes—

LESBONICUS: —so we can decide about the dowry.

STASIMUS: But you should be going.

LESBONICUS: No dowry, no marriage, and that's final.

STASIMUS: Whatever you say. Get going!

LESBONICUS: Now I mean it! She's not going to suffer—   750

STASIMUS: The man is waiting!

LESBONICUS: —any more from my foolishness.

STASIMUS: She will if you don't *move!*

LESBONICUS: It's only fair that the punishment for my sins—

STASIMUS: Oh, for crying out loud.

LESBONICUS: —should be borne by me alone.

STASIMUS: Fine, fine. But get out of here!

LESBONICUS: O Father! Will I ever see your face again?

STASIMUS: Lesbonicus, clear out or you'll be seeing stars!

(LESBONICUS *exits*)

STASIMUS: Ugh! Finally. I thought he'd never stop   760
    whimpering and whining, and that Philto would leave him!
    Now it looks like our sad tale might have a happy ending
    if we can save the farm. But I'm not going to count on it
    quite yet. For me it'll be hell to pay if the farm is lost
    and my boss leaves town after the wedding. No doubt he'd go
    and join the foreign legion in Asia or Cilicia, some
    godforsaken place with me along as pack-mule, shield-bearer,
    and valet. Oh well, I guess I'll go wherever I'm told,
    as I always have. Come to think of it, I don't like it *here*
    very much either, particularly since Callicles took our
        house.   770

(*He exits*)

ACT III

Scene 1

(*Enter* CALLICLES *and* STASIMUS)

CALLICLES: What was that, Stasimus? Did I hear you right?

STASIMUS: Our young master Lesbonicus has betrothed his sister.
That's the long and the short of it.

CALLICLES: Whom is she to marry?

STASIMUS: Lysiteles, Philto's son. Without a dowry.

CALLICLES: Oh, come now, Stasimus. How could she marry
into all that money without a dowry? You're losing
your credit with me.

STASIMUS: Credit? Credit? You never give anybody credit.
But if you don't credit this, you can take your credit and—   780

CALLICLES: —and do what with it?

STASIMUS: Oh . . . buy me some new sandals?

CALLICLES: When did this happen? Where did it happen?

STASIMUS: Right here, in front of this door. Or, "hereabouts,"
as they say in the country.

CALLICLES: Well, it sounds like Lesbonicus flat broke
is a lot shrewder than Lesbonicus wealthy.

STASIMUS: What's amazing is that Philto himself came here
to make the proposal on his son's behalf.

CALLICLES: If that doesn't beat everything!   790
  It'll be a scandal if the dowry doesn't go along with the girl. I
    see I'm
  going to get mixed up in this, for better or worse.
  Now if I can just find that paragon of common sense and
    sanctity,
  my old friend, Megaronides, he'll know just how to advise me.

(*He exits into* MEGARONIDES' *house*)

STASIMUS: Seems to me there can only be one reason why
  he's in such a hurry—that's to bamboozle us out of the farm
  just the way he bamboozled us out of the house. O Charmides,
  my poor master! While you're gone your estate is crumbling!
  I'd give anything to see you safe at home
  with a chance to get revenge on your enemies   800
  and reward the man who's been forever true. Me!
  A man who truly deserves to be called a man, a man
  you can trust with everything you own, and then
  lie down and sleep at night without a care!
  You may search the world over and never find another . . .
  But wait—here comes our son-in-law with his new relative.
  They're walking fast, my master leading and Lysiteles coming
  right behind him, clutching his cloak. It looks to me
  like things aren't going so very well between them . . .
  there, they've stopped. I'll just stand here out of the way   810
  so I don't distract them and . . . I'd love to hear their
    oratory . . .

Scene 2

(LESBONICUS *enters,* LYSITELES *clinging to him*)

LYSITELES: Stand still a minute. You keep turning away and
  hiding your face—

LESBONICUS: I just want to go about my business.

LYSITELES: If your business was prospering, Lesbonicus,
    if it were either honorable or reputable, I'd let you go.

LESBONICUS: Oh, what you're doing is so *easy.*

LYSITELES: What's that?

LESBONICUS: Hurting me. It's easy to hurt a friend.

LYSITELES: But that's not my nature, and it's not my training.

LESBONICUS: Then you're a brilliant amateur. Imagine   820
    how much damage you might do if you were trained.
    Lysiteles, here you are pretending to do me a favor
    and what you're really doing is screwing me
    and giving me bad advice on top of that.

LYSITELES: Me?

LESBONICUS: Yeah, you.

LYSITELES: I'm screwing you? How do you figure?

LESBONICUS: The very thing I don't want to do you want me
    to do.

LYSITELES: I'm only thinking of your best interests.

LESBONICUS: Oh, you're going to treat me better than I treat
    myself?   830
    At least give me the credit of knowing what's best for me.

LYSITELES: But this is crazy, running from a friend who wants to
    do you a favor!

LESBONICUS: It's not a favor if it doesn't please the man you're
    doing it for.
I know my duty and have the means to accomplish it;
I haven't lost my wits, and a lot of smooth talking
is never going to distract me from what's right
and honorable in the eyes of the world.

LYSITELES: So that's how you see it? Then, my friend,
    you give me no choice but to say what's on my mind.
    What do you suppose your ancestors would think,   840
    your father and your grandfathers and mothers,
    if they could see you now—broke and ridiculous?
    Do you think they passed on the great name you bear
    so that in one atrocious orgy you could lose
    all their labors had taken centuries to build?
    What do you think? They gave you the chance to carry on
    their tradition, and be an example to your children;
    they made the path to honor level and smooth for you.
    And you made it hard with your weakness and laziness,
    your stupid antics. You put love affairs ahead of work.   850
    And now a friend comes to you with a proposal
    to set you on track again. And it's not good enough?
    You can't tell right from wrong anymore! Come on,
    Lesbonicus, wake up and get in the game!
    Leave the women in bed and join your friends in the forum.
    Where the farm's concerned I only have one motive:
    I want you to keep it, so while you're working your way
    back to solvency you won't be a total pauper, subject
    to the sneers and jibes of men who never liked you.

LESBONICUS: I know and understand all that you're saying   860
    and I set my seal to it. The glory of the family name
    and my father's trust and fortune, I've lost it all.
    I knew better, but I couldn't do what was right,
    poor wretch that I am. I got caught in that sweet,
    slick embrace of Venus; I became her slave.
    Now I am past rescue, sure as hell. But really
    I do thank you for your efforts to save me.

LYSITELES: Hold on a minute. You're not just going to dismiss
my efforts and my counsel with that kind of contempt.
Where are your manners? Where is your sense of shame?   870
I'm afraid if you don't start listening to good advice
your better self may sink so low that honor will never
retrieve it; the good you are hiding will never come to light.
Lesbonicus, I know the goodness that is in you,
your true nobility; I know you didn't mean to get in trouble.
But Love got in your way, clouded your vision.
I know how that is. Love comes like the bolt
a catapult shoots from afar; there's nothing
so sudden and rapid in its flight. Love changes our ways,
scatters our wits, and makes us headstrong, crazy.   880
Love makes us lust for what's forbidden, shun what's allowed.
You want the rare thing, and never what's plentiful.
Oh, it's a long hard night a man spends in Cupid's Hotel.
Lesbonicus, think twice before you do something stupid.
If you carry out that plan of yours as I understand it
you may as well burn your relatives at the stake.
You'll be crying for water, and with a lover's luck
find enough to drown flames and kin at once.
There won't be a spark left to light the family name.

LESBONICUS: That's easily fixed. I'm sure you'd give us
a light.   890
Even my enemies wouldn't deny that. But really, Lysiteles,
your preaching only drives me off the road,
off one bad road and onto a path that's worse.
You beg me to let you marry my sister without a dowry.
Right! Wouldn't that be exemplary behavior on my part,
after I've squandered the entire family fortune—
wouldn't it be gracious of me to live comfortably
as a gentleman farmer, having left her with nothing?
She'd hate me, and with good reason. So would everyone.
The man who earns no respect in his own house   900
will get none in town. I will do what I said.
And now I wish you would mind your own business.

LYSITELES: You think it's better for you to be a pauper
　for your sister's sake—while I take the farm—
　than for you to have some means of paying your bills?

LESBONICUS: You keep harping on this idea of saving me
　from the poorhouse, without ever considering that I'll be
　not only broke, but a joke, if I take your advice.
　Everybody would be gabbing about how Lesbonicus
　gave away his own sister, like a concubine,   910
　without even granting her a dowry! Why, I'd be
　ranked with the greatest scoundrels of our time.
　You take her without a dowry, and the gossips will
　glorify you and dump on me; you'll get the glory
　and I'll get nothing but what they throw at me.

LYSITELES: So what do you expect? Do you think you can
　give me the farm and somehow keep the upper hand?

LESBONICUS: I don't expect it or wish it or even dream of it.
　But even a man who's sunk as low as I
　can find some dignity in remembering his duty . . .   920

LYSITELES: Now I'm beginning to see what's on your mind,
　a little light, a glimmer—I get it. Here's the plan:
　once you've got our two families tied together,
　and you've given up the farm, and nothing is left you here
　to keep you going, then . . . then you'll flee the city,
　a desperado. That's it. After the wedding
　you'll walk into the sunset, a poor tragic figure,
　abandoning his country, his family, and his friends.
　And they'll all turn to me and point their fingers,
　saying it was I, I the selfish miser Lysiteles,   930
　who forced dear Lesbonicus into exile. Well, dream on, my
　　friend, it'll never
　happen. I won't let it happen.

STASIMUS: (Applauding) Bravo, bravo, Lysiteles. Encore!
　You take the prize for best actor. Such intelligence,

such phrasing! Why, Lesbonicus, you never had a chance.
In fact the drama critics are fining you a hundred bucks
for overacting, and another hundred for . . . stupidity.

LESBONICUS: What? What are you saying? What on earth
    brought you
into the arena of our discussion?

STASIMUS: (*Pointing to his feet*) Feet. Feets brought me in,   940
and feets gone take me away again . . .

(*Running from* LESBONICUS)

LESBONICUS: Come on, Lysiteles. Let's go to my house where we
    can talk in peace.

LYSITELES: No. We'll have our conversation here in the open.
    Here's how I feel, straight from the heart: you give me
    your sister's hand in marriage, under the proper conditions—
    that is, without a dowry—and if you don't head for the hills
        then we will
    live like brothers. What is mine will be yours.
    Of course, if this doesn't suit you, you can go your own way,
    and I wish you luck. But not as a friend. If you want
    my friendship, then you'll have to see it my way.   950
    That's it, and that's my final word in the matter.

(LESBONICUS *exits, then* LYSITELES)

STASIMUS: Already gone? Hey, Lysiteles! Wait a minute! He's
    gone too.
    Well, Stasimus, now you're on your own. What'll I do now?
    Might as well shoulder the knapsack, sling the shield
    on my rear end, and pull on the combat boots. I'll be
    in the army before you know it, a beast of burden.
    The boss will be living high on some king's commission;
    and they'll be calling him the best soldier since Achilles
    (though he's only the best at running, running *away*).

Oh, the treasures, the glory, the spoils of war! 960
(Especially to the soldier that fights my master.)
As for me, put a bow in my hand, a quiver of sharp arrows
on my back, a helmet on my head, and I'm ready . . .
ready for a nice quiet snooze in my tent.
Meanwhile I have an engagement in the forum.
Six days ago I lent this guy a thousand dollars.
Now I'll ask him to give it back, so
I'll have a little something for traveling expenses.

(*He exits*)

Scene 3

(*Enter* MEGARONIDES *and* CALLICLES)

MEGARONIDES: From all you've told me, Callicles, the girl
   has to have a dowry, no two ways about it. 970

CALLICLES: Absolutely. I can't allow her to go without,
   when I know there's all that money of hers right here
   in the house, within easy reach. The hidden gold.

MEGARONIDES: You could use that. Or you could let her brother
   have his way and marry her off without it, then tell Philto
   that you'll provide the dowry as a token of friendship
   to her father, and out of the goodness of your heart.
   Only one problem: nobody will believe it.
   People will think you have ulterior motives.
   They'll say her father gave you money for her dowry 980
   and that you've been spending it, living high off the hog,
   and only gave her the scraps that were left over. Anyway
   you can't wait forever for Charmides to come home.
   You've got to do something. That young man
   will grow old and lose his desire to marry the girl.
   You can't let that happen. It's far too good a match.

CALLICLES: All this has occurred to me. Don't you think
   it might be more practical and wise in the long run
   to open up to Lesbonicus and explain the whole situation . . .
   What am I saying? Tell that juvenile delinquent   990
   about a hidden treasure in gold, when his first thought
   will be how fast he can spend it on wine and women?
   He'll gobble up the treasure and the house
   where it's hidden, before I can even turn around!
   If he hears me digging for it the young vulture
   will smell the money for sure—if he's heard of the dowry.

MEGARONIDES: Isn't there some way to move the
   money . . . under the table?

CALLICLES: With a little luck I might find a friend who would
   lend it.

MEGARONIDES: Don't you have a friend who could be persuaded?

CALLICLES: I sure do.   1000

MEGARONIDES: You wish! Your friend will give you the old
   brush-off:
   "Me? Get serious, I don't have a dime to lend!"

CALLICLES: *You* get serious, my friend! Deny me the loan, but
   don't lie to me.

MEGARONIDES: I've got a better idea.

CALLICLES: Now what?

MEGARONIDES: This one's a masterpiece.

CALLICLES: I bet.

MEGARONIDES: Right now, this afternoon, we hire a stranger,
    somebody really foreign-looking,
    a con artist with a lot of tricks and flim-flam.   1010

CALLICLES: So he can swindle us?

MEGARONIDES: We get him a good tailor to make him up
    like a real foreign emissary . . . from Seleucia. He'll go
    to young Lesbonicus, bringing his father's greetings,
    tell him that Charmides is in good health, his business
    is going splendidly. Everything is great and he'll be back soon.
    We'll have our man present two letters that we'll write
    ourselves. One will be for the boy, and one for you.

CALLICLES: What next?

MEGARONIDES: He'll tell Lesbonicus he's brought an
        allotment   1020
    of gold from his father for the girl's dowry.
    The old man has ordered him to deliver the gold . . .
    to you alone. You get it?

CALLICLES: I like what I'm getting.

MEGARONIDES: Then you'll give the gold
    to the bridegroom after the wedding.

CALLICLES: It sounds foolproof.

MEGARONIDES: So the young spendthrift won't have his ear to the
        ground
    while you're digging up the treasure; he'll think the pile of gold
        came from
    abroad, while you're hauling it up from the cellar.   1030

CALLICLES: That really is ingenious. First-rate, though at my age
    I wish I didn't have to resort to such smoke and mirrors.
    Now wait. When the letters come to the boy, all sealed,

don't you think he'll miss his father's signet ring,
its mark on the wax?

MEGARONIDES: Don't fuss over details!
   There are any number of possible excuses—he lost his ring
   and got a new one—or we can even deliver the letters
   unsealed, and say they were opened at the customhouse.
   But enough talking. We have a job to do.
   We can't waste all day worrying over trifles   1040
   when there's never an end to worry. Now go and see
   to the treasure, go about it quickly and quietly.
   Get your slaves out of the way first. And one more thing.

CALLICLES: What?

MEGARONIDES: Your wife. You've got to keep her in the dark as
      well.
   She can't keep quiet for the life of her. Now
   what are you doing, standing here like a statue?
   Snap out of it! Go dig up the gold, grab what we need,
   and cover up the rest as fast as you can—
   but do it quietly, like I told you, and remember: 1050
   get everybody out of the house first.

CALLICLES: It's as good as done.

MEGARONIDES: It's *not* as good as done while we stand here
   running our mouths, wasting daylight when we ought to be
   getting to work! Don't worry about the seal. Trust me.
   That's a good excuse, the one about the letters being opened
   at the customhouse. Besides, look what time of day it is.
   What sort of shape do you suppose our boy is in,
   with the sun that low in the sky? He's probably been drunk
   for several hours now. He'll believe anything we tell
      him—   1060
   especially when he hears our man announce his business
   and the news that he's come to *deliver,* not collect.

CALLICLES: That's bound to get him.

MEGARONIDES: Now just let me find some proper sneak-thief at
      the forum
   and make him an offer that he can't refuse.
   I'll brief him, dress him up, write the two letters, then
   point him in Lesbonicus's direction. We'll be in business.

CALLICLES: I'll act my part well if you'll direct the rest.

MEGARONIDES: I'll show you stage direction at its best.

ACT IV

Scene 1

CHARMIDES: Lord Neptune, brother of Jove and Nereus,   1070
      Commander of the salt waves, the briny deep,
   I thank you with all my heart. Thanks to the waves
      who held me gently, bore me and my cargo
   home safely from the endless, alien sea
      to my own kind and peaceable country.
   You, Neptune, above all other gods deserve
      my deepest thanks, enduring gratitude.
   Men call you savage and severe. Some say
      that you are all-devouring, odious, mad,
   and cruel. But not to me. All the while   1080
      I rode upon the deep, I found you fair and gentle,
   as good and kind as ever I could have wished.
      So much for the old adage that Neptune
   was honored most among men for chastening
      the rich and powerful, while sparing the poor.
   It's not so! I offer you my praises,

    for you know how to treat a man like me
according to his just deserts. You have given
    me fit treatment, and this befits a god.
Men call you faithless. But you were faithful to me: 1090
    if it weren't for you, I believe your deputies,
the four winds, and their furious hurricanes
    would have blown me and my ships and their cargo
to hell across the blue wastes of the ocean.
    Just yesterday the winds swirled 'round my ship
like dogs howling and biting, rain and billows
    made ready to snap the mast, tear up the sails,
and mangle the yards. If you had not appeared,
    noble and omnipotent, to quell the riot and save us . . .
Enough! It's over now. I have no more ambition   1100
    except to lead the quiet life at home.
Thanks to this last adventure I have enough
    in land and gold to guarantee the fortune
will satisfy my children, and their children.
    But what's this? Who is this character
in the funny clothes, coming down the street,
    looking at me like he would serve me papers,
though I'm just off the boat? Good God,
    as much as I want to get home to my own house,
I think I'll take a little detour here   1110
    until I figure out what's on his mind.
(*Hiding around the corner*)

Scene 2

(*The* SWINDLER *enters*)

SWINDLER: This looks to me like a thirty-dollar day,
    no more or less, thirty dollars is all I'll get
    for my expertise. I just blew in from, let's see now,
Seleucia, Macedonia, Asia, Arabia? I've never set my eye
or foot on any of those places. A rotten job this is,

but what's a poor man to do? I'll get thirty bucks for lying,
   telling somebody
I received these letters from a man
I don't know or care about—maybe he was never even born.

CHARMIDES: Look at the hat! Is this guy all head, or what?   1120
   He must be some species of mushroom! I know, he's from the
      west.
   You can tell 'em a mile away.

SWINDLER: So this old guy approaches me, takes me to his house,
   explains the deal from start to finish, the way everything
   is supposed to be handled. Any little frills I add may get me
   a bonus, or at least I'll be giving him his money's worth.
   He takes me to the costumer's and gets me duded up like this.
   See what a little cash will do for the old figure?
   I'm supposed to return the suit. But, hey, what do they expect?
   Do they call me a swindler for nothing? How do I look?   1130

CHARMIDES: The more I see of this guy the less I like his looks.
   I'll be hanged if he isn't some kind of a mugger or cat burglar.
   Casing the neighborhood, checking out the doorways and
      windows.
   By God, I think he's inspecting the area with a view
   to robbing my house later. I'll keep an eye on him.

SWINDLER: This is the neighborhood I'm supposed to come to.
   Right there is the house where I'll earn my fee.
   Enough dawdling. I'll just go up and knock on the door.

CHARMIDES: He's going right for my house! Can you believe it?
   No sooner do I get home than I have to do sentry duty.   1140

SWINDLER: Hey there! Anybody home? Hello? Is there a porter
   here
   or a watchman?

CHARMIDES: Beg your pardon, young man. What can I do
    for you?
  Do you have any business here?

SWINDLER: Old man, when my taxes were due
  I filed my returns *on time*. Nobody had any questions. Okay?
  Maybe you could tell me where to find the residence
  of a young man named Lesbonicus. Also an old geezer
  with white hair like yours. The man who gave me these letters
  told me the old fellow's name was . . . Callicles.   1150

CHARMIDES: (*Aside*) He must be looking for my son Lesbonicus;
  and the old man is my friend, Callicles, the one
  I put in charge of my children and my finances.

SWINDLER: So where do they live, dad?

CHARMIDES: What is it to you? Who the hell are you, anyway,
  and where are you from?

SWINDLER: No fair. That's too many questions all at once.
  I don't know what to answer first. If you'll calm down
  and ask me one thing at a time, perhaps then I may
  begin to tell you something about my career   1160
  and the roundabout journey of my life.

CHARMIDES: All right then. First tell me your name.

SWINDLER: My name! Why we hardly know each other.
  You ask too much.

CHARMIDES: What do you mean?

SWINDLER: My name, dad, is so long that if you started out
  before dawn to say the first part, you would be traveling
  all day until bedtime before you got to the end of it.

CHARMIDES: I see. If what you say is true I'd have to apply
for a traveling fellowship to tour that name of yours.   1170

SWINDLER: Lucky for you, I've got this little portable name,
kind of like a hip flask.

CHARMIDES: Oh good. What is it?

SWINDLER: Zero. That's what my friends call me. Zero.

CHARMIDES: I love it! A charming little name. It's like
a little black hole into which things disappear. Zero.
I give you something and quickly it comes to nothing.
(*Aside*)
This guy is a con man if ever I've seen one.
(*Aloud*)
Now look here, young man—

SWINDLER: I'm looking, but I don't see much.   1180

CHARMIDES: I can tell.
Tell me, what do you want with the men you mentioned?

SWINDLER: The young fellow, Lesbonicus—his father
gave me these letters. He's a friend of mine.

CHARMIDES: (*Aside*) Now I've got him dead to rights.
He says I gave him the letters. I'll turn the tables on him.

SWINDLER: I'm not saying another word if you don't stop
talking to yourself, and pay attention.

CHARMIDES: Okay, okay. I'm all ears.

SWINDLER: He told me to give this letter to his son,
Lesbonicus. The other letter goes to his friend, Callicles.   1190

CHARMIDES: (*Aside*) Yessir, it's time for the con man to swallow
  some of his own medicine.
  (*Aloud*)
  So you got these
  from the boy's father in person, did you . . .

SWINDLER: He put them right into my hands.

CHARMIDES: What does he look like, your friend?

SWINDLER: Tall, very tall. A foot and a half taller than you.

CHARMIDES: Makes me uncomfortable, being so much
      shorter now
  than when I'm absent. Hey, are you sure you know this man?

SWINDLER: That's a stupid question. We eat lunch together—

CHARMIDES: What's his name?   1200

SWINDLER: Oh, it's an excellent name, for an excellent fellow . . .

CHARMIDES: I'd love to hear it.

SWINDLER: What is it with you and names? Well, if you have to
      know, it's . . . it's . . .

(*Choking*)

CHARMIDES: What is it, man?

SWINDLER: I . . . I swallowed it. I just swallowed the man's
      name.

CHARMIDES: What do you mean, you swallowed it? What kind of
      a man
  keeps his friends caged up behind his teeth?

SWINDLER: I was just rolling it around in my mouth, savoring it,
and it slipped—

CHARMIDES: Now I've got this sneak-thief just where I
want him.   1210

SWINDLER: (*Still holding his throat*)
I'm afraid he's got me.

CHARMIDES: Well? Have you brought it up again? His name?

SWINDLER: God in heaven, I'm so embarrassed.

CHARMIDES: I see how well you know the man.

SWINDLER: As well as I know myself. Isn't it always the way—
you're looking all around you for the thing
that's right under your nose. Now I know I can put it together
from the letters. His name begins with a C.

CHARMIDES: Callias?

SWINDLER: No.   1220

CHARMIDES: Callipus?

SWINDLER: No.

CHARMIDES: Callidemides?

SWINDLER: Too long.

CHARMIDES: Callinicus.

SWINDLER: Not that, either.

CHARMIDES: Callimarchus.

SWINDLER: Oh, it's no use. I was never any good with names.
What does it matter as long as I can remember
what I need to remember? 1230

CHARMIDES: Ah, but the street is teeming with
Lesbonicuses. So if you don't know his father's name,
I can't help; you find the men you're looking for.
Let's get back to the sound of the name. Guess. Come on.

SWINDLER: It reminds me a little of . . . Cha . . .

CHARMIDES: Is it Char . . . Chares . . . Charmides?

SWINDLER: Charmides! That's it! Charmides. I knew
I would remember his name goddamn him. Now, as I was
saying—

CHARMIDES: It would behoove you to speak kindly of your friend.

SWINDLER: When the son-of-a-bitch slipped down my throat 1240
and nearly strangled me?

CHARMIDES: Now, now, don't talk like that behind his back.

SWINDLER: I'd just like to know why Charmides was hiding
from me.

CHARMIDES: He would have come if you'd only called his name.
Where do you suppose he is now?

SWINDLER: Why the last time I saw him . . . it must have
been . . .
at the illustrious court of Rhadamas . . . on the fabled Isle of
Cecropia . . .

CHARMIDES: (Aside) I don't know which of us looks sillier,
me asking him my own whereabouts, or this jackass
telling lies. I'll play along with him.

(*Aloud*)
Hey,   1250
tell me this: Where have you sailed? I bet you and Charmides
have been all over the world by now.

SWINDLER: Incredible places. Why, you wouldn't believe it.

CHARMIDES: Oh, do tell me. If it's not too much trouble.

SWINDLER: I'm dying to tell you. Are you comfortable? Good.
  (CHARMIDES *reclines*, SWINDLER *beside him*)
  Now, we set out for the ports of Pontus on the coast of Arabie.

CHARMIDES: I thought Pontus was in the other direction.

SWINDLER: No, that's *another* Pontus. This isn't the land
  where grows the precious frankincense, but the Pontus where
  they make absinthe and the gallinaceous origanum.   1260

CHARMIDES: Right.
  (*Aside*)
  This guy is so full of it.
  But I guess I'm as big a fool as he, to sit here asking him
  about my own travels, when I know what I did
  and he doesn't know. Where will it all end, I wonder?
  (*Aloud*)
  Then where did you go, you and your dear friend?

SWINDLER: If you will listen without talking to yourself,
  then you shall hear, and know all.
  (*With sensual rapture*)
  He'd gone to the country to feed the slaves. Anyway, we rowed
  away out of heaven, and after that . . .

CHARMIDES: After that, I don't want to hear any more of
    your crazy lies.   1270

SWINDLER: But I was just getting to the good parts—

CHARMIDES: Any more and I'm warning you, I'm gone. Really, Zero,
a man's journey from earth to heaven, as I understand it,
is never a fit topic for conversation among gentlemen.

SWINDLER: All right. Just tell me where I can find these two men, so I can deliver the
letters and collect my thirty bucks.

CHARMIDES: If this man Charmides, the man who gave you the letters,
walked by us right now, would you know him if you saw him?

SWINDLER: Would I know him? Would I? You must take me for
a complete meathead, if you don't think I would recognize   1280
a man I've known all my life. And what kind of dummy
do you think he is, trusting me with two hundred thousand dollars in gold for
his son and his friend Callicles who is managing
his affairs? Do you think he would trust me with all of that
if he didn't know me through and through? Come on.

CHARMIDES: (Aside) Boy, would I love to trick this trickster here and now.
If there was only some way I could fake him out of all that gold
he says I gave him! I, who don't know him and never saw him before today!
Trust him with gold? I wouldn't trust him with a lead nickel.
But easy, easy . . . I must go to work on him carefully.   1290
(Aloud)
Oh, Zero! Can I have a word with you?

SWINDLER: I thought you'd never ask.

CHARMIDES: You say that Charmides gave you some gold.

SWINDLER: Two hundred thousand dollars' worth of solid gold
    coins,
  counted out at the banker's from his hand into mine.

CHARMIDES: Charmides himself gave it to you?

SWINDLER: What do you think, that I got it from his dead
    grandfather,
  or his great-grandfather, who's even more dead?

CHARMIDES: Now listen here, you young punk, hand over the
    gold to me
  right now.   1300

SWINDLER: What gold am I supposed to give you?

CHARMIDES: The gold you say you got from me.

SWINDLER: From you?

CHARMIDES: Yes, me.

SWINDLER: Who in the hell are you?

CHARMIDES: I'm Charmides, the man who gave you the two
    hundred thousand.

SWINDLER: Damn it all, you're not and you never will be,
  at least not as far as this gold is concerned. Buzz off,
  you cheap chiseller. You're trying to flim-flam a professional.

CHARMIDES: I really am Charmides.   1310

SWINDLER: You may be, but it won't do you any good, because
  I really don't have any gold. Ha, Ha! Oh, you're a slick one,
  showing up here in the right place at the right time;
  you hear me mention gold and suddenly, presto! You're
    Charmides!

You weren't Charmides until you heard the word *gold*. Sorry,
but it doesn't work like that. Now, the same way you got
Charmidized, you can go and get yourself *un*-Charmidized
    again.

CHARMIDES: But who am I, if I'm not who I am?

SWINDLER: What do I care? You can be anyone you like
    as far as I'm concerned, so long as you're not somebody   1320
    I object to. A little while ago you weren't who you were,
    and now you've become somebody you've never been
        before . . .

CHARMIDES: Do what's right.

SWINDLER: What's that?

CHARMIDES: Give back the gold.

SWINDLER: Old man, you must be dreaming.

CHARMIDES: You said that Charmides gave it to you.

SWINDLER: Well, on paper . . .

CHARMIDES: Listen to me, you cat burglar. If you're not out
    of this neighborhood by the time I count to ten,   1330
    I'll have you beaten into hamburger.

SWINDLER: What for?

CHARMIDES: For fraud! The very man you've been talking about,
    making up the most outrageous lies about, that man is me,
    I'm Charmides, the man you say gave you the letters—

SWINDLER: Oh my dear! Are you really the very man?

CHARMIDES: I sure as hell am.

SWINDLER: You don't mean . . . you're Charmides himself?

CHARMIDES: You heard me.

SWINDLER: Himself is . . . yourself?   1340

CHARMIDES: I myself am Charmides, I tell you!

SWINDLER: Therefore you are yourself.

CHARMIDES: Myself is my very own self! Get out of here!

SWINDLER: We ought to honor your arrival with . . .
    a public whipping! When my arm gets tired
    I'll let the police take over.

CHARMIDES: Now, don't get rough with me!

SWINDLER: I wouldn't waste my time. You know,
    it would've been all the same to me if you'd drowned
    on the way home. I've been paid already for my labor,   1350
    and you can go to hell. What do I care who you are
    or who you aren't? I'm going to tell the man who paid me
    my thirty bucks, that he wasted his money.
    Bad luck to you, and sickness too! May the gods
    who brought you home safe, now strike you dead in the street,
    Charmides, or whoever the hell you are!

(*He exits*)

CHARMIDES: Whew! Good riddance. Now I can speak freely.
    All this time I've been on pins and needles, wondering
    what he was up to, here in front of my house.
    The letter he mentions calls up a battalion of fears   1360
    in my heart. What about all that gold? Let me tell you,
    where there's smoke there's fire, and the alarm bell
    never goes off of its own accord. But wait!

Who's coming, running down the street? Let's see
what he's up to. I'll just step back out of the way.

(*He withdraws*)

Scene 3

(*Enter* STASIMUS, *jogging unsteadily*)

STASIMUS: Come on, Stasimus, shake a leg, get on home to
    Master.
  Come on, you don't want to put your shoulder blades
  in the way of the whip, stupid, so put on the steam,
  make a dash for it! You've been away from home a long time
  and the longer the master misses you the more delight   1370
  he takes in the music he makes with the rawhide
  on your rear end. So keep running, running . . . whoa!
  What have you done, you fool? You've gone and left
  your slave ring in the tavern, after scalding your belly
  with cheap booze. Now there's nothing to do but run back
  or crawl back, and get it before somebody else does.

CHARMIDES: Well, whoever this man is, he's certainly in training.
  Hard drinking has made quite a runner of him.

STASIMUS: Really! Aren't you ashamed of yourself, you worthless
    fellow?
  Losing your memory after no more than three pitchers!   1380
  Well, after all, I was in excellent company,
  such honest upright gentlemen as would find it easy
  to keep their hands off other people's property . . .
  I mean, men like Jack Sharper, and Jack Badger, and Bobby
    Thug;
  then there was Louie Gypster, Louie Shyster, and Sammy
    Stickup . . .
  My God! These are jailbirds so moldy from prison,

they limp around like they're still wearing leg irons!
How in the world am I ever going to get my slave ring back
from a gang like that? Any one of them can swipe the sole
off a runner's shoe while he's still running full speed.   1390

CHARMIDES: God help me! It's another prince of thieves.

STASIMUS: Well, what's the use of chasing after what's gone?
    I'd just be adding labor hours to my loss, as the only bonus.
    No use crying over spilled milk. Bring her about and back
      home
    to master.

CHARMIDES: It's no runaway slave. He's thinking of home.

STASIMUS: Oh for the good old days on the plantation
    when right was right, and good old-fashioned thrift
    was a way of life, instead of this damned obstacle course
    of manners and policy and protocol.

CHARMIDES: Good God, do you hear that? The slave's
      discoursing   1400
    on the state of society. He wants the old order; you can tell
    he loves the old-fashioned ways just as his ancestors did.

STASIMUS: These days it's proper manners to do what's easy
    and pleasant rather than the thing that's right.
    And devious ways are sanctioned by other manners,
    policy and fine print in the contracts. There's etiquette
    to defend all sorts of evil—dropping your shield
    and fleeing the enemy might be seen by some as mannerly,
    so cowards and renegades attain high office.

CHARMIDES: Oh dreadful policy!   1410

STASIMUS: Dreadful policy indeed, the policy
    of passing over stout-hearted men for polite loafers.

CHARMIDES: Outrageous!

STASIMUS: "Policy" has usurped our precious laws,
    and rules them like some tyrannical child rules his parents.
    Our poor old laws are strung up on the walls and nailed there
    while it's "policy" I'd like to see nailed through the heart!

CHARMIDES: I'd like to hail him and applaud.
    But I like it even better to listen to this,
    and if I break in he might change the subject.   1420

STASIMUS: Nothing is safe from policy, nothing is sacred,
    not even the law; policy sweeps everything out of its path,
    regardless of its religious or civic sanctity.

CHARMIDES: Gracious! This "policy" deserves the maximum
    sentence!

STASIMUS: And the government does nothing to stop it.
    These men, who are no better than public enemies,
    wreck the fabric of society. Their treachery
    makes us distrust honest men, who begin to judge
    their own character by the false standards of the wicked.
    Now, you might ask, what has brought me to this
        dim view   1430
    of our world? No more than my own sad experience.
    Lend a man something, anything, and you'll see,
    it's soon no longer lent, but lost forever.
    Ask for it and you'll see how fast your kindness
    has turned your friend into an enemy. Ask him again
    and you'll find yourself confronting a sorry choice:
    of bidding farewell to your friend or your property.

CHARMIDES: By God, that's my own servant, Stasimus!

STASIMUS: It's like this: I lent a friend a thousand dollars—
    for that price I bought an enemy, sold a friend.   1440
    But what a dimwit I was, going far out of my way

to solve other people's problems when I should have been
covering my own ass, which is right behind me! I'm going
home.

CHARMIDES: Hey you! Stop where you are, and listen!

STASIMUS: Hey yourself. I'm not stopping for anybody.

CHARMIDES: I want you—

STASIMUS: So what if I don't want you to want me?

CHARMIDES: Now Stasimus, come down off your high horse.

STASIMUS: If you want a slave, go and pay for one.

CHARMIDES: Dammit, I did buy one and paid cash for him!   1450
But what good is that if he won't come when I call him?
What am I to do, huh?

STASIMUS: Take it out of his hide.

CHARMIDES: Now there's a thought. I'll get started . . .

STASIMUS: I mean, unless he's got something on you.

CHARMIDES: If you're a good servant, you'll have your influence;
if not, I'll follow the advice you just gave me, and show no
mercy.

STASIMUS: Are most of your servants bad?
What are the odds you'll be punishing a good one?

CHARMIDES: None of you is wholly good or wicked.   1460

STASIMUS: Well, I'll make you a free gift of the wickedness in me
and keep the good, so you may not tire yourself in
whipping me.

CHARMIDES: Fair enough, if you're mostly good. Now,
    turn around, you fool, and look at me. I am Charmides.

STASIMUS: What? What? Who, of all men alive on this earth,
    has been honored as the finest gentleman of all?

CHARMIDES: The finest of all living men, in the flesh.

STASIMUS: O Sea and Earth under Heaven! O gods above!
    Is it true what I'm seeing with these eyes? Is this
    the man himself or an apparition? It is, surely, it is he!   1470
    O my master, how I've prayed for this moment,
    when I'd see you come home safe and sound.

CHARMIDES: It's nice to see you too, Stasimus.

STASIMUS: I'm *so* glad you're safe, safe in the peaceful harbor—

CHARMIDES: Yes, yes. I get it. I believe you. Enough!
    Now tell me: how are the dear ones I left behind,
    my son and daughter?

STASIMUS: Alive and well.

CHARMIDES: Both?

STASIMUS: Both.   1480

CHARMIDES: Then I have truly arrived safely, thanks be to the
    gods.
    The rest of my questions can wait. Let's step inside.

STASIMUS: Uh . . . where are you going?

CHARMIDES: Into my house, of course.

STASIMUS: You think that's where we're living.

CHARMIDES: Where else would we be living?

STASIMUS: Well—

CHARMIDES: Well, what?

STASIMUS: This isn't our house.

CHARMIDES: Is something wrong with my hearing?   1490

STASIMUS: Your son sold the house.

CHARMIDES: Good God!

STASIMUS: He got cash for it, good money.

CHARMIDES: How much money?

STASIMUS: A hundred thousand.

CHARMIDES: Dammit. Who bought it?

STASIMUS: Callicles, the man you trusted with your affairs;
    he took over the house and threw us out.

CHARMIDES: Where is my son living now?

STASIMUS: Here in a little annex.   1500

CHARMIDES: Stasimus, this is a disaster.

STASIMUS: I was afraid you'd take it like this.

CHARMIDES: Can't you see, I risked everything, suffered the
        worst
    tedium on the sea, survived cold, sickness, and pirates
    to return in one piece, so I can be torn apart at home
    by my own family, the loved ones for whom I have worn out

my poor old life to tatters. It's a bitter blow, Stasimus,
that takes my very breath away. Help me.

STASIMUS: How about some water, sir?

CHARMIDES: They should have watered my estate when it
    was burning.   1510

Scene 4

CALLICLES: What's all this racket going on outside my door?

CHARMIDES: O Callicles, Callicles, Callicles! What kind of a
    friend
    did I trust with all my worldly goods?

CALLICLES: A wise friend, and loyal, and true. Welcome!
    I'm so glad to see you're home again, safe and sound!

CHARMIDES: And I'd like to believe you. Why are you dressed
    like a ditch-digger?

CALLICLES: You, I can tell. I was digging up the treasure
    so your daughter could have a dowry for her wedding—
    but I'll explain all of that, and some other matters too,
    after we go inside. Come on!   1520

CHARMIDES: Stasimus!

STASIMUS: Yessir.

CHARMIDES: I want you to run down to the Piraeus, full-speed.
    There you'll find the ship we came in on.
    Tell Sangario to see that everything I ordered gets unloaded.
    Don't take your eyes off him! All the duties have been paid

at the customhouse, so there shouldn't be any delay.
Go on, now. Step lively, and come right back.

STASIMUS: I'm gone and come back already, Boss!

CALLICLES: Now, come on inside.   1530

CHARMIDES: After you.

(*They exit*)

STASIMUS: There's the one man in the world
   who's been loyal to Master through thick and thin,
   the only man whose faith has never faltered.
   At least, I think his faith has never faltered.
   Now we'll see if his loyalty was worth the trouble.

ACT V

Scene 1

(*A few minutes later*)

LYSITELES: I'd like you to meet the happiest man alive,
   a man whose joy and delight are beyond compare.
   Lysiteles! How perfectly your heart's desire
   answered your call, and all that you longed for   1540
   now clambers to serve you, crowding around,
   joy treading upon the heels of joy! Just now
   Stasimus, Lesbonicus's servant, knocks on my door
   to tell me Charmides is home from his travels.
   I'll introduce myself as soon as I can; one way to win
   the son's confidence is to get the father's blessing. And

the sooner, the better. But wait! I hear a noise
at the door, somebody's there, dammit! What terrible timing.

Scene 2

(*Enter* CHARMIDES *and* CALLICLES)

CHARMIDES: There never was or will be or could be
    another man on earth whose loyalty   1550
    and faithfulness to a friend could match your own.
    Were it not for you, my son would have lost our home.

CALLICLES: If I have helped my friend or served his interests,
    this doesn't call for praise; I'm pleased enough to know
    as time passes I can't be blamed for anything.

CHARMIDES: Whatever. But really, Callicles, this is marvelous,
    that my son has betrothed his sister to such a gentleman
    from such a noble family.

CALLICLES: Indeed, to Lysiteles, Philto's son.

LYSITELES: Aha, he's calling my name!   1560

CHARMIDES: He couldn't have picked a better family.

LYSITELES: How shall I approach them? Not yet;
    I'll let him go on like this a while.

CHARMIDES: Hmmm . . .

CALLICLES: What is it?

CHARMIDES: There's something I was about to tell you

a minute ago, inside, it slipped my mind. When I arrived here
some loafer accosted me—I mean a real dyed-in-the-wool
     swindler.
He said he was bringing you and my son Lesbonicus two
     hundred thousand
dollars in gold that I had given to him. I had no idea   1570
who the fellow was. I'd never laid eyes on him before.
Why are you laughing?

CALLICLES: Because I hired him.
He was supposed to pretend he was bringing me gold
from you, to use for your daughter's dowry.
Your son was to think, as I handed her the money,
it had come from you—he'd never guess the truth.
I was afraid if he found out I had your treasure,
he'd sue me for it as part of his patrimony.

CHARMIDES: A stroke of genius!

CALLICLES: Really, it was our friend Megaronides who
     dreamed it up.   1580

CHARMIDES: In any case I applaud it!

LYSITELES: Why am I standing here like a dummy, afraid of
     interrupting
the conversation, when I mean to talk to both of them?

CHARMIDES: Who's this, coming toward us?

LYSITELES: Charmides, I am your new son-in-law, Lysiteles.

CHARMIDES: May the gods grant your every wish, Lysiteles!

CALLICLES: And what about me?

LYSITELES: Of course, Callicles, my warmest greetings! But you understand, this is the gentleman, the kinsman who must come first, "as the shirt goes on before the coat." 1590

CALLICLES: May the gods bless all of your plans, and make your wishes come true!

CHARMIDES: I hear my daughter is promised to you.

LYSITELES: If you have no objections, sir.

CHARMIDES: Oh no, I have no objections.

LYSITELES: Then you promise me your daughter's hand in marriage?

CHARMIDES: I promise her hand, her arm, and two hundred thousand dollars
for a dowry.

LYSITELES: Oh, I don't care about the dowry.

CHARMIDES: Well, if you're going to be pleased with her, you'll have to learn to be pleased with the money too. 1600
In other words, you won't be getting what you want unless you also take what you don't want.

CALLICLES: His plea is just.

LYSITELES: And with you as judge and jury, he'll win his case. Well then. Those are your final terms?

CHARMIDES: On those terms I promise you my daughter.

CALLICLES: And I'll second his promise with my own.

LYSITELES: Then, God bless you both, my dear family!

CHARMIDES: Now wait a minute. I still have a bone to pick with
    you . . .

LYSITELES: What did I do?   1610

CHARMIDES: You corrupted my son.

LYSITELES: Now just a minute. If I had anything to do with that
    you'd have every right to be furious with me. But,
    all joking aside, sir, I want to ask you a favor.

CHARMIDES: What?

LYSITELES: Just this: if the boy did some foolish things,
    it's water under the bridge. He's young, forget it.
    Why are you shaking your head?

CHARMIDES: Well, I'm torn, between anguish and anxiety.

LYSITELES: I'm not sure what you mean.   1620

CHARMIDES: Anguish that my son has become what I don't ever
    want him to be; and anxiety that if I deny your request,
    my future son-in-law might think I don't take him seriously.
    Oh well, I won't be pig-headed. I'll do as you wish.

LYSITELES: Great! I'll go and get him.

CHARMIDES: It's a sad state of affairs,
    when bad behavior can't be punished as it should be.

LYSITELES: Open up, open this door right now and call
        Lesbonicus,
    if he's home! I want to see him right away. It's important!

(Enter LESBONICUS into the doorway, angrily)

LESBONICUS: Who's the man that's made such a glorious
   racket   1630
   just to get me outside?

LYSITELES: Your friend, a good friend if you ever had one—

LESBONICUS: You are, are you? Tell me about it.

LYSITELES: A true friend who's truly happy to have your father
   safe at home after his voyages—

LESBONICUS: My father? Who says so?

LYSITELES: I do!

LESBONICUS: You've seen him?

LYSITELES: You can see him yourself.

LESBONICUS: O Father, my father, God bless you!   1640

CHARMIDES: (*Embracing*) And you, my son, my dear son.

LESBONICUS: If I've caused you any trouble, Papa—

CHARMIDES: Nothing, nothing at all, don't worry about it.
   I've done well in my business and now I'm home.
   And I'll consider myself truly blessed if you'll settle down
   and begin to make something of yourself. Now
   to get you going, we've found a wife for you,
   the daughter of our friend, Callicles.

LESBONICUS: Whatever you say, Father. I'll marry her,
   and anybody else you have in mind.   1650

CHARMIDES: No. I may have been angry at you, but not *that*
   angry.
   One wife is punishment enough for any man.

CALLICLES: Not for him! A hundred wives would never be
    enough
  to pay for all *his* sins.

LESBONICUS: From now on, I'll keep myself in line.

CHARMIDES: You've said it—now just keep your word.

LYSITELES: Is there any reason why I can't get married
  first thing tomorrow?

CHARMIDES: None that I can think of. And you, my son,
  prepare for your own wedding the day after.   1660

STAGE MUSICIAN: (*stepping forward*) Your applause, please!

EPIDICUS

Translated by Constance Carrier

INTRODUCTION

If plot is the soul of drama, as Aristotle suggested, it is little wonder that Plautus loved the *Epidicus* "as well as his own self."[1] The masterful slave Epidicus improvises plot after plot in this comedy, involving himself and his fellow actors in so many intricate moves that it is a wonder that they finally escape into the unencumbered truth about themselves. But their success is also the result of Epidicus's tireless inventions.

The comedy of intrigue that Plautus loved "as well as his own self" swirls in the wake of Epidicus's sailing on ahead through crisis after crisis. The main actor is like a dramatist imagining how to maneuver his characters into situations that compound their anxiety but ultimately combine and free them to enjoy their lives all the more. It is as if Epidicus were putting on a play: if plot is the soul of drama, Epidicus's resourcefulness helps that soul conduct its energetic search for its true destiny.

As the loyal family slave of Periphanes, Epidicus means to meet the demands of both masters, the father Periphanes and the son Stratippocles. When Stratippocles went off to war against Thebes, he charged the slave to acquire for him a girl he was fond of, named Acropolistis, and as the play opens just after the conclusion of the local war with a victory of Athens over Thebes, Epidicus proudly informs Thesprio, Stratippocles' orderly, that he has accomplished the mission assigned him by his young master. Thesprio jolts Epidicus with the news that Stratippocles has, as it were, gone over to the enemy: he has purchased a young female captive Theban; when he arrives in Athens, Stratippocles intends to stay at his friend Chaeribulus's house next door and not show up at home until he has

---

[1] Plautus, *Bacchides*, l. 214: "Epidicum quam ego fabulam aeque ac me ipsum amo."

245

found the money needed to pay back to the moneylender who advanced the price for the Theban captive.

When Epidicus first bought Acropolistis he had persuaded Periphanes to advance the money for her purchase and accept her into the family home by convincing Periphanes that this girl was in fact his real daughter by a liaison Periphanes had had years ago with a woman of Epidaurus. But now Epidicus must ponder how to undo this mischief and raise the cash due to the moneylender. His soliloquy here is the first of the many arguments he has with himself during the course of the play as the action keeps taking its turns for the worse:

> Look the facts in the eye: time's running out
> If you can't summon up sufficient strength
> To face it. There's a sort of rock that's balanced,
> Barely, above your head. Prop it up somehow
> And somehow keep your footing, or you'll slip
> And the whole wretched weight come down to crush you. . . .
>   What shall I do?
> Don't ask, or don't ask me. To think that I
> Used to give good advice to other people!
> Well, somewhere there's a plan, if I can find it.
>
>   (ll. 82–100)

He listens from a doorway as Stratippocles and Chaeribulus enter in conversation. Stratippocles is at odds with his friend, for he assumes that it is Chaeribulus's natural duty as a friend to supply the cash to pay the moneylender, but Chaeribulus does not have the money to advance to him. All Chaeribulus can offer is words of congratulation for having found so exemplary a girl, and words of consolation for being at a loss for the money.

When Epidicus comes forward to greet Stratippocles and take credit for having obtained the wrong girl, Stratippocles tells him about his change of heart and obstinately commissions Epidicus to find the money for the new girl. Epidicus promptly reassures Stratippocles that he has a plan in mind and will take the responsibility for bringing it off. Stratippocles hails the slave as his true friend, and a genius as well. Luckily, a rich captain from Euboea has had his eye on Acropolistis for some time: Epidicus has to find a way to substitute Stratippocles' new love for his former one, and have the

captain pick up the bill and the girl. In a short speech he calls a
meeting of the senate in his brain to work out the details: "iam
senatum convocabo in corde consiliarium." He will have to work fast
and storm the castle (Periphanes).

The older men in the play make their entrance, conversing
about Periphanes' intention, as a widower, now that he has discovered his daughter, to find and marry the girl's mother. His friend
Apoecides applauds Periphanes' motives: the wife had been a trial to
live with, a harder test of nerve than the Sixth Labor of Hercules (the
stealing of Hippolyta's Girdle), and Periphanes need not be ashamed
of desiring a woman of good character, however poor, who is their
daughter's mother. Apoecides can only compliment his friend Periphanes on his modest and virtuous behavior. But Periphanes is
troubled by what his son may think of the father's amatory adventure
late in life.

This conversation between the two older men bears a curious
resemblance to the conversation between the two young men that
preceded it in the play, as if the audience were hearing the same
amicable but anxious tones an octave lower. And when Epidicus
returns to the scene and overhears the two older men's antiphonal
talk, a new scheme comes to his mind. Periphanes has said that the
best thing would be to have Stratippocles marry at once, for he has
heard that his son is infatuated with a music-girl (the "Acropolistis"
Epidicus had inveigled Periphanes into sequestering). Epidicus
pretends to rush past the two old men without seeing them on a
frantic search for Periphanes and when they accost him, spins a yarn
about the courtesans in Athens who went down to meet the returning soldiers. He says he overheard them saying how lucky it was for
one of them, a dazzling specimen, that Stratippocles was now back
and would buy her freedom. When the two friends ask Epidicus for
advice on how to proceed he at first demurs, then produces his latest
improvisation: let Periphanes pretend that it is he who wants to buy
the girl's freedom, and so preempt his son's (alleged) intention and
send the girl out of the city before Stratippocles can marry her.
Epidicus explains how the money invested will soon be returned to
Periphanes because the captain is eager to have the girl and will buy
her from the new owner at a higher price.

The old men like the idea. Periphanes steps inside to get the

money, while Apoecides heads for the forum to meet Epidicus and
serve as the go-between in the transaction. As Epidicus is left alone
on the stage he savors the moment for indulging in some self-
congratulation. It looks like he is harvesting a rich crop of cash from
this field. Puzzling out the next move, he remembers that Periphanes had asked him to hire a music-girl that very day, to come to
the house and provide the music during the sacrifice Periphanes will
conduct to celebrate his son's safe return from the war. This is the
girl he can now acquire and instruct in a supporting role. So, as he
gives the new sum of money, gotten from Periphanes under false
pretenses, to Stratippocles, Epidicus explains his plan to have the
music-girl play the part of Stratippocles' alleged mistress.

When Apoecides eventually appears with the music-girl, she is
taken into the house and Periphanes is temporarily taken in by the
trick. But when the captain comes along and makes his request for
"Acropolistis" and the music-girl is produced, Periphanes sees that
he has been duped. This point in the play marks the first phase of the
denouement; the music-girl in a sharp exchange with Periphanes
informs him that "Acropolistis" has been in fact bought and set
free by Stratippocles. Temporarily, Periphanes assigns his trouble to
the muddling of his friend and agent Apoecides, a blocking idea
that again resembles Stratippocles' earlier disgust with his friend
Chaeribulus.

The next phase of the denouement unfolds after the entrance of
Philippa, Periphanes' quondam mistress from Epidaurus, anxiously
inquiring for her captive daughter Telestis. She and Periphanes
recognize each other and he assures her happily that her daughter is
in fact in his house. But when he brings out Acropolistis (the girl
Epidicus originally fobbed off on him as Telestis) Philippa is aghast
and Periphanes beside himself with rage at the extent to which he
has been deceived; he is determined to punish Epidicus.

The final denouement arises from the identity of the Theban
captive Stratippocles acquires by paying the required sum to the
moneylender. Staring hard at her, Epidicus recognizes her as Telestis, the true natural daughter of Periphanes. He can congratulate
Stratippocles on not pursuing a liaison with his half-sister and console him with the thought that Acropolistis is still at hand. Stratippocles seems to be somewhat dazed by his escape from the clutches of

his various fates. But Epidicus can now savor the triumph he anticipates and proudly stands his ground:

> . . . Can't make my exit now,
> Since I've decided to stay home. Nobody's
> Going to say I took to my heels and challenged
> Him to catch me. I'd better get on inside:
> I'm talking too much out here.
>
> (ll. 664–65)

He goes into Chaeribulus's house to explain the new situation to
Stratippocles; when Periphanes and Apoecides return Epidicus confronts them and demands that they tie him up and conduct their
inquisition. The sparring dialogue gradually reveals the whole truth.
Epidicus gains his freedom and a humble apology from Periphanes.
Epidicus pardons his former master for having tied him up and
interrogated him and graciously lets Periphanes undo his bonds, as
the author of this play steps out to deliver the two-line epilogue:

> POETA: Hic is homo est qui libertatem malitia invenit sua.
> Plaudite et valete. Lumbos porgite atque exsurgite.
> AUTHOR: [Here is a scamp who rose above his station
> And, by his mother-wit, went free. Give us applause,
> Then stretch your legs, stand up—and so, farewell!]
>
> (ll. 732–33)

As Epidicus's bonds are undone, an unspoken thought may also
occur to the spectators: his plots released the others from their
wrong impulses and uncertainties.

The forward motion of Epidicus's intrigue involving Acropolistis, the hired music-girl, and Telestis is matched by the three
phases of the denouement. His deception of Periphanes is counter-
balanced first by the captain's initial unmasking of the music-girl,
then reinforced by the mother's rejection of Acropolistis as her alleged daughter, and crowned by the fortunate discovery of Telestis'
identity. Flung into the air at the opening by Thesprio's melodrama-
tic news, Epidicus lands triumphantly at the end, thanks to the good
news conveyed undramatically in person by Telestis.

The several characters balance and oppose one another. The
two older men want to cooperate and connive, but they diverge. The
two young men are friends who differ. The four women display equal

nerve and energy and prove capable of storming back at the men who offer them bland assurances. Telestis' calm embodiment of the truth hands the situation back to Epidicus just when he seems to have finally lost all control of it. While the women occupy a comparatively small space in the play, their jaunty logic and sharp words form a strong antidote to the male characters' colorful profusions. And although Plautus as usual makes room for the common criticisms of women men indulge in—expensive to clothe, at the whim of fashion, a Herculean labor to live with—an impetuous young man vulnerable to feminine beauty loses his heart twice, in rapid succession. His father, yearning to have his own daughter back again, is easily tricked by Epidicus's deception, and spiritedly decides to try and find his former mistress and marry her.

The interlocking steps in this drama set us to thinking about the not exclusively comic predicament of loving passionately, of marriage as conflict, of renewed respect for womankind. But above all and in charge of all the recognizable good intentions and characteristic misapprehensions is Epidicus, alone and unmatched, who sees his passengers safely through the difficulties ahead of them. He even manages to create some of these complications and can make others' anger flare up and provoke their instincts for revenge. But his lowly existence finds gratification in its own designs, and his cheerful temperament proclaims him as an artist in comedy. Plautus had good reason to love this play "as well as his own self." All those involved in it were trying to perform sensible and natural actions without causing harm or distress to any of the others. To create such intricate circumstances and make them come out right would surely entitle a master craftsman to his freedom.

Palmer Bovie

EPIDICUS

CHARACTERS

EPIDICUS, slave of Periphanes
THESPRIO, orderly to Stratippocles
STRATIPPOCLES, son of Periphanes
CHAERIBULUS, a young man of Athens and friend of Periphanes
PERIPHANES, an old gentleman of Athens and a widower
APOECIDES, an old gentleman and friend of Periphanes
A MUSIC-GIRL
A SLAVE
A CAPTAIN
PHILIPPA, a woman of Epidaurus
ACROPOLISTIS, a music-girl
A USURER, of Thebes
TELESTIS, daughter of Philippa and Periphanes

SCENE: *A street in Athens on which stand the adjoining houses of* PERIPHANES *and* CHAERIBULUS.

ACT I

Scene 1

(*Enter* THESPRIO, *followed by* EPIDICUS)

EPIDICUS: Say there, young man!

THESPRIO: Who's got hold of my cloak?
   Who's trying to stop me?

EPIDICUS: One of your family.

THESPRIO: You'd bother me less if you were less familiar.

EPIDICUS: Just look around.

THESPRIO: Oh, it's Epidicus I see.

EPIDICUS: That's twenty-twenty vision.

THESPRIO: Well, good morning.

EPIDICUS: Thanks for your wishes. Good to see you back.

THESPRIO: What's new?

EPIDICUS: The usual thing, a dinner in your honor.

THESPRIO: I promise—   10

EPIDICUS: What?

THESPRIO: To come, if you invite me.

EPIDICUS: And what's with you? You're well? No doubt of that—
    I can see for myself you're good and husky.

THESPRIO: Thanks to a good left hand.

EPIDICUS: You should have cured that
    Long since.

THESPRIO: I'm less light-fingered now.

EPIDICUS: How so?

THESPRIO: Just holdups now.

EPIDICUS: Indeed? The devil take you,
    What strides you're making in your chosen field!
    When I first saw you at the port, I chased you
    But never did catch up until just now.

THESPRIO: You're just a city slicker.

EPIDICUS: Whereas you   20
    Are a real military man.

THESPRIO: Say that again.
    Oh well, what's new? Your health—

EPIDICUS: Is up and down.

THESPRIO: I hate that phrase. It makes me think of beasts
    Whose backs are ribbed with the long welts of whippings.

EPIDICUS: I'm telling you the truth. Now what's with you?
    Come clean now.

THESPRIO: All okay.

EPIDICUS: What's with our master?

THESPRIO: A top-notch soldier and a fine athlete.

EPIDICUS: I couldn't ask for better news. Where is he?   30

THESPRIO: We came together.

EPIDICUS: Well, where is he, then?
    Stowed in your wallet? In your knapsack, maybe?

THESPRIO: Oh shut up, you.

EPIDICUS: And you—give out. Look here:
    Do me a favor; get one in return.

THESPRIO: You're talking like a judge.

EPIDICUS: And very fitting.

THESPRIO: You've been elected praetor, I suppose?

EPIDICUS: Does Athens have a better candidate?

THESPRIO: Two things you don't have that a praetor's got.

EPIDICUS: So?   40

THESPRIO: Lictors and the rods they use for whips.

EPIDICUS: To hell with you. But I must say—

THESPRIO: Speak out.

EPIDICUS: Where is Stratippocles? Where are his arms?

THESPRIO: His arms? Gone over to the enemy.

EPIDICUS: You mean it?

THESPRIO: Yes, and in a hurry, too.

EPIDICUS: Seriously?

THESPRIO: Seriously. The enemy's got them.

EPIDICUS: Why, that's disgraceful!

THESPRIO: Well, it's not the first time,
   And he'll come out of it with honor.

EPIDICUS: What do you mean?

THESPRIO: It's happened before this. If Stratippocles
   Used weapons forged by Vulcan, they were magic—   50
   So were Achilles'—and flew to the enemy.

EPIDICUS: Well, let the son of Thetis lose them;
   The Nereids will keep him well-supplied.
   He'd best provide the shield-makers with metal
   If he keeps giving spoils to his opponents.

THESPRIO: That's quite enough of that.

EPIDICUS: Well, knock it off then.

THESPRIO: You and your questions—

EPIDICUS: Where's Stratippocles?

THESPRIO: Because of certain causes, he was afraid
   To come with me.

EPIDICUS: Afraid? What do you mean?

THESPRIO: He doesn't want to see his father now.   60

EPIDICUS: Why?

THESPRIO: Sure you want to know? Well, from the loot
   They took, he bought a pretty, well-bred girl.

EPIDICUS: He *what?* What's this you're telling me?

THESPRIO: My story.

EPIDICUS: Why did he buy her?

THESPRIO: Lost his heart.

EPIDICUS: Come on.
   How many hearts has he? Before he left
   To join the army, he commissioned me
   To bargain with a pimp for a music-girl
   He thought he was in love with, and I did it.

THESPRIO: Good sailors trim their sails to the wind.

EPIDICUS: Oh dammit,
   A dirty trick he's played—

THESPRIO: Now what's the matter?   70

EPIDICUS: The girl that he's just bought—what did she cost him?

THESPRIO: She was a bargain.

EPIDICUS: That's no answer.

THESPRIO: So?

EPIDICUS: How much in dollars?

THESPRIO: Say eight hundred bucks—
   Cash that he borrowed from a moneylender
   At Thebes—with daily interest 2 percent.

EPIDICUS: Wow!

THESPRIO: The moneylender's here now for his cash.

EPIDICUS: Lord help us, that's the final blow for me.

THESPRIO: What do you mean, Epidicus? What's wrong?

EPIDICUS: He's done me in.

THESPRIO: Who? How?

EPIDICUS: The man who lost   80
  His weapons.

THESPRIO: What's all this?

EPIDICUS: He used to write me
  While he was in the army, every day—
  But that's enough. I'd better shut my mouth.
  Better to know too much than talk too much.
  That's wisdom for a slave.

THESPRIO: Epidicus,
  You're so scared that you're shaking—I don't know
  The reason, but to judge by your expression
  You've got into a jam while I've been gone.

EPIDICUS: If you could manage not to be a nuisance—

THESPRIO: That's it. I'm leaving.

EPIDICUS: Wait. You mustn't go—   90

THESPRIO: No? Try and stop me.

EPIDICUS: Does he love that slave?

THESPRIO: Love her? He's mad for her.

EPIDICUS: God, I'll be skinned
  Alive.

THESPRIO: He never loved you half as much.

EPIDICUS: Shut up!

THESPRIO: Let go. He told me, "Don't go home;
  Stay with Chaeribulus, next door to here,
  And wait there till I come." That's what he said.

EPIDICUS: Why?

THESPRIO: Can't you guess? He doesn't want his father
  Around until the girl is his and paid for.

EPIDICUS: This is the worst mess that I've ever seen.

THESPRIO: I've had enough of all this. Let me go.   100

EPIDICUS: When the old man gets wind of this, it means
  I'll be sunk stern-first—wait and see. Just wait.

THESPRIO: What do I care whether it's stern or bow?

EPIDICUS: You'd better care; I don't propose to sink
  Alone. We'll go together, friend.

THESPRIO: Shut up and go to hell with your proposals.

EPIDICUS: If you're in such a hurry, go along.

THESPRIO: I never met a guy I left more gladly.

(*He exits*)

EPIDICUS: He's gone and you're alone, Epidicus.
   Look the facts in the eye: time's running out   110
   If you can't summon up sufficient strength
   To face it. There's a sort of rock that's balanced,
   Barely, above your head. Prop it up somehow
   And somehow keep your footing, or you'll slip
   And the whole wretched weight will come down to crush you.
   How can I turn the tide before it drowns me?
   Fool that I am, I've made the old man certain
   He's buying his own daughter. What he bought—
   Bought for his son—that was the music-girl
   My master loved and left in my protection.   120
   Now that he's left the army, has he brought
   A new wench who has caught his eye? If so,
   No hope for me. Let the old man find out
   That he's been tricked, he's going to have my hide.
   All you can do is watch and wait, my boy.
   All you can do, indeed—you know that's nothing,
   Epidicus, you addled idiot.
   What do you think you gain, bad-talking yourself?
   You know damned well you're lost.
                          What shall I do?
   Don't ask, or don't ask me. To think that I   130
   Used to give good advice to other people!
   Well, somewhere there's a plan, if I can find it.
   Now I must meet my young man and find out
   What's going on. Oh, there he is! Good Lord,
   How glum he looks! A crippled snail could beat him,
   Walking along there, with Chaeribulus.
   I'll duck into this doorway and give ear.

Scene 2

STRATIPPOCLES: Well now, Chaeribulus, you've heard my story—
   How much I love, how much I stand to lose.

CHAERIBULUS: Look here, Stratippocles, you're even
dumber   140
   Than anyone so young and brave should be.
   What are you squirming over? Having bought
   A well-born captive wench, part of the booty?
   Who in the world could blacklist you for that?

STRATIPPOCLES: Who? Every man made envious by that action—
   And yet I've never forced myself upon her.

CHAERIBULUS: More credit to you, since you love her so.

STRATIPPOCLES: You can't console a man in my position
   With words; a friend in need needs deeds.

CHAERIBULUS: What kind?

STRATIPPOCLES: Well, you could lend me cash to pay
    my debt   150
   And get that moneylender off my back.

CHAERIBULUS: You know that if I had that kind of money—

STRATIPPOCLES: Oh, what's the use of offers you can't fill?

CHAERIBULUS: You know damned well I'm dodging bill collectors.

STRATIPPOCLES: I'd rather see such friends in an oven than
    bankrupt.
   Epidicus—what I'd give for his help!
   I'll have that fellow whipped until he's sodden
   Down at the mill, unless he gets my money
   Before I finish saying *eight hundred dollars*.

EPIDICUS: (*Aside*) I'm safe; an easy job, and his word's
    good—   160
   Blows ready for my shoulders, free of charge.
   I'll speak to him.

(*Aloud*)
                              Master Stratippocles,
Epidicus your servant bids you welcome
On your return.

STRATIPPOCLES: (*Looking around*) Epidicus? Where is he?

EPIDICUS: Right here, sir. Now that you've returned, and safely—

STRATIPPOCLES: I believe you as I'd believe myself.

EPIDICUS: You have been well?

STRATIPPOCLES: In body, not in mind.

EPIDICUS: Oh no more worry, sir; that's taken care of—
   I carried out your orders, and the girl
   You wrote me of so often—she's been purchased.   170

STRATIPPOCLES: It was all done in vain.

EPIDICUS: In vain, sir? Why?

STRATIPPOCLES: I'm not in love with her. She doesn't suit me.

EPIDICUS: Then why all those directions, all those letters?

STRATIPPOCLES: I loved her then; now someone lovelier
   Weighs down my heart.

EPIDICUS: Well, I must say it's hard
   To get no thanks for doing a good turn.
   The good turn's soured with your changing desire.

STRATIPPOCLES: Out of my mind, I was, sending those letters.

EPIDICUS: If you're a fool, why should I be your victim?
   Why should my back be punished for your folly?   180

STRATIPPOCLES: Oh, knock it off. Words get us nowhere fast.
  I need my money now, hot off the griddle
  And soon, to pay my moneylender.

EPIDICUS: Sure;
  Just tell me where to get it. Choose your banker.

STRATIPPOCLES: Go choose your own, but get the cash by sunset,
  Or find my door locked to you. Off to the mill.

EPIDICUS: Easy enough for you to talk—you're safe,
  Nothing to worry you. But thrashings hurt—
  I know too well.

STRATIPPOCLES: What's left for me to do?
  Kill myself?

EPIDICUS: No, no. I'll take the risk—I've got the
    nerve—   190

STRATIPPOCLES: Now that's a real friend, that's the way to act!

EPIDICUS: I'll take the whole responsibility.

STRATIPPOCLES: What do we do about the music-girl?

EPIDICUS: We'll find a way. I'll get us out of this.
  Don't worry, pal; I've got a thousand plans.

STRATIPPOCLES: A genius, you are—as I've always known.

EPIDICUS: A wealthy captain's here, straight from Euboea.
  Just let him learn you've bought the music-girl,
  And brought the other girl along besides—
  He's going to come and beg you for the first one.   200
  But where's the second?

STRATIPPOCLES: She'll be here, I swear it.

EPIDICUS: What do we do now?

STRATIPPOCLES: Go and celebrate.

EPIDICUS: (*As they go*) You go in. I'll call a little meeting
Here in my head to work out the details—
Like who it is we're going to lay siege to
For money. But watch out now—this is sudden
And serious; it needs to be approached
With caution, but you mustn't dawdle, either.
Ready? We'll storm the old man, no holds barred.
Come on, inside the house. Warn your young master   210
Not to walk out in case the old man meets him.

ACT II

Scene 1

APOECIDES: Too many men suffer embarrassment
When there's no cause, but never feel a qualm
Though they've done something that should give them shame.
You're one of these, my friend. Why so defensive?
You're marrying a woman poor but well-born—
And further, as you've said, your daughter's mother.

PERIPHANES: My son—it is his feelings that alarm me.

APOECIDES: Oh come now! Not regard for your dead wife?
You're always leaving offerings at her tomb—   220
And just as well: you've outlived her so long.

PERIPHANES: While she was living I was Hercules.
His tasks were less than those she set for me.

APOECIDES: A generous dowry is a pretty thing—

PERIPHANES: Especially if it comes without the wife.

Scene 2

(EPIDICUS *at* CHAERIBULUS's *house*)

EPIDICUS: (*To* STRATIPPOCLES *and* CHAERIBULUS *inside*)
   Quiet, now. Keep your spirits up. I'm leaving
   Under a lucky sign—a bird at my left.
   My knife is sharp to slit the old man's purse strings.
   Oh, oh—he's standing there before his house
   With Apoecides—just the old pair   230
   I want. Excuse me while I turn into a leech
   And suck some so-called senatorial blood.

APOECIDES: He's got to wed at once.

PERIPHANES: How right you are!
   I've heard he's mixed up with some music-girl,
   And the mere rumor gives me palpitations.

EPIDICUS: (*Aside*) The gods are on my side—see how they
     love me?
   These gaffers—why, they're outlining directions
   For me to get their money. Come on now,
   Get set, Epidicus; put your collar up
   And act as though you'd spent the whole day hunting   240
   The man all through the city. Now right on!
   (*Steps out of doorway. Aloud.*)
   If only Periphanes is at home—
   I'm all worn out trying to track him down.
   I've asked for him in the doctors' offices,
   At barbershops, in the gymnasium,
   Down in the public square, at the perfumer's—

Even at the bank and in the butcher's place.
I'm hoarse and almost ready to collapse.

PERIPHANES: Epidicus!

EPIDICUS: Who's calling me?

PERIPHANES: I am,
Periphanes.

APOECIDES: And I've been calling you, too. I   250
Am Apoecides.

EPIDICUS: And I'm Epidicus.
Master, what luck to come across you here!

PERIPHANES: What do you mean?

EPIDICUS: Wait—let me catch my breath.

PERIPHANES: Take a real rest.

EPIDICUS: I'm faint.

APOECIDES: Get your wind back.

PERIPHANES: Easy now; just relax.

EPIDICUS: Okay, sir. Now
Listen: the army's coming back from Thebes.

APOECIDES: Who says so?

EPIDICUS: I do.

PERIPHANES: It's the truth?

EPIDICUS: It is.

PERIPHANES: What makes you sure?

EPIDICUS: I saw them in the streets,
   Carrying arms and leading beasts of burden.

PERIPHANES: What better news?

EPIDICUS: And the captives! Boys and girls,
   Two or three apiece, and one has five.   260
   No street that isn't mobbed—the whole town's out
   To see their heroes.

PERIPHANES: This is a real triumph.

EPIDICUS: And the courtesans, every last one of them,
   All decked out in their best, came running out,
   Each looking for the lover she laid claim to.
   Why did I notice this particularly?
   I saw that they had nets under their clothing.
   And when I got to the gate, why, there she was,
   Waiting, I swear, and four flute-girls beside her.

PERIPHANES: Her? Who, Epidicus?

EPIDICUS: Why sir, the one   270
   Your son has been so mad about for years,
   The one he'd wreck his reputation for,
   Give up his wealth, his life—and yours!—to win.
   There she was, waiting at the gate.

PERIPHANES: You see
   Why, she's a murderess!

EPIDICUS: But attractive, sir—
   Her dress, her jewels—the last word in good taste.

PERIPHANES: Indeed? What was she—beggar maid or princess?

EPIDICUS: She wore the style that women call the Skylight.

PERIPHANES: What in the world?

EPIDICUS: Oh sir, that's not so strange.
    What woman won't parade her lover's fortune?—   280
    Fortunes the men are slow to pay a tax on,
    Though they pay up all that their whores demand.
    The adjectives they find for each new fashion!
    Thin-woven, closely textured, azure-linen,
    Lined, bordered, saffron, buttercup, shift (or shiftless),
    Veiled, regal, imported, sea-blue, or *embroidered,*
    Shell-shaped, wax-colored—none of them makes sense.
    They even use a dog's name.

PERIPHANES: Good Lord, what?

EPIDICUS: *Laconian,* Hound's Tooth. They use that for a tunic.
    No wonder that they leave their husbands bankrupt.   290

PERIPHANES: No doubt, no doubt, but go on with your story.

EPIDICUS: In back of me two women started talking.
    I wandered off a little, not too far
    To overhear their talk without their guessing.
    I missed a little, but I caught a lot.

PERIPHANES: I'd like to have you share it.

EPIDICUS: One of them
    Said to the other—

PERIPHANES: What?

EPIDICUS: Don't be impatient.
    Don't interrupt, sir. One said (and this was
    After they saw the girl your son's so mad for),
    "Shameful how things are always going her way—   300

Her lover even wants to set her free!"
"Her lover? Who?" the other asks. The answer?
"Stratippocles, son of Periphanes."

PERIPHANES: Damn everything—what's this?

EPIDICUS: The truth, sir, truly.
  After I heard their words, I backed up toward them
  To make it seem as though the crowd was pushing
  And shoving me (against my will that way).

PERIPHANES: Yes, yes—go on!

EPIDICUS: And then I heard the second
  Asking her friend, "You're sure? Who told you so?"
  The other says, "Why, just today a letter   310
  Came to her from Stratippocles himself,
  Saying he'd borrowed money there at Thebes—
  He had it with him and was bringing it."

PERIPHANES: Better that I were dead!

EPIDICUS: Those were her words.
  She knew it from the girl and from the letter.

PERIPHANES: What now? Advise me, Apoecides.

APOECIDES: Something hot off the griddle's what we need—
  The young man's either here or will be soon.

EPIDICUS: Would it be impudent for me to offer
  A plan that's pretty shrewd for your approval?   320
  I think you both—

PERIPHANES: Come to the point. Your plan?

EPIDICUS: —Would find it workable, I really do.

APOECIDES: What's all this hesitation?

EPIDICUS:								You're so wise—
  You should speak first. Then I'd be glad to follow.

PERIPHANES: Oh, don't be foolish. What's this plan of yours?

EPIDICUS: You'll just make fun of me.

APOECIDES:								No, no; don't worry.

EPIDICUS: Well, if you like it, use it; if you don't
  Think up a better. I'm not going to reap
  The harvest of my sowing; what I want
  Is what you want.

PERIPHANES:			You have my grateful thanks.				330
  Let's share your wisdom.

EPIDICUS:						Marry off your son
  At once, sir—and that music-girl of his,
  The one he plans to free, who'll be his ruin—
  Give her the punishment that she deserves
  And let her stay a slave until she dies.

APOECIDES: Exactly what I'd counsel.

PERIPHANES:						Do as you say,
  If we can bring it off.

EPIDICUS:				Our chance is now,
  Before he gets to town—and that's tomorrow,
  And not today, you understand.

PERIPHANES:						You're sure?

EPIDICUS: I am indeed. Further, another man					340
  Gave me his word he'd get here in the morning.

PERIPHANES: Go on. What should we do?

EPIDICUS: Well sir, I think
   You ought to act as though you'd like to free
   The music-girl to be yours—make it seem
   As though you've gone quite crazy for her.

PERIPHANES: Why?
   There can't be any point to that.

EPIDICUS: No point?
   The point is that, before your son comes home,
   You will have bought her, and can say to him
   It was to set her free—

PERIPHANES: I understand.

EPIDICUS: And once the sale is made, get her away   350
   Out of the city. Or what would you suggest?

PERIPHANES: Certainly nothing else.

EPIDICUS: (To APOECIDES)   And your view, sir?

APOECIDES: What can I say except that I approve?

EPIDICUS: Then he won't have to worry any longer
   About his marriage and your disapproval,
   And he'll obey your wishes.

PERIPHANES: You're a genius.

EPIDICUS: The only thing is, sir, we've got to hurry.

PERIPHANES: Of course.

EPIDICUS: And I can keep you from suspicion.

PERIPHANES: Speak out.

EPIDICUS: I shall, sir.

APOECIDES: Lord above, what brilliance!

EPIDICUS: The purchase money for the music-girl—   360
  Someone will have to take it to her master.
  It can't be you, sir—there's no need of that.

PERIPHANES: What do you mean?

EPIDICUS: Her master mustn't guess
  You're doing this to save your son—

PERIPHANES: Of course!

EPIDICUS: —From her. We don't want any complications,
  So we won't let that notion cross his mind.

PERIPHANES: Whom can we trust with such an errand?

EPIDICUS: (*Pointing to* APOECIDES)   Him.
  Who could be better? He'll be the soul of caution,
  And he knows every word in every lawbook.   370

PERIPHANES: (*To* APOECIDES) You should be grateful for those
    words of praise.

EPIDICUS: And I'll do everything I can, sir, trust me.
  I'll find her master and arrange a meeting
  Between him and this gentleman. I'll even
  Carry the money.

PERIPHANES: What's the least she'll go for?

EPIDICUS: Oh, at least eight hundred, that's my guess, sir,
    But if you give me more, I'll bring the rest back.
    Don't worry: there's no catch in this. Besides,
    You'll have your money back in ten days' time.

PERIPHANES: What do you mean by that?

EPIDICUS: Why, just by luck, sir,   380
    I know that there's another man who loves her—
    Young, and a millionaire from Rhodes, a soldier,
    A hero in the field, covered with glory.
    He'll buy her and he'll pay in solid gold.
    Just follow my advice; you'll strike it rich.

PERIPHANES: Pray heaven you're right.

EPIDICUS: The gods will prove I am.

APOECIDES: (*To* PERIPHANES) Go in, why not, and get the money
    for him.
    I'll walk around the square—Epidicus,
    Meet me down there.

EPIDICUS: Wait till I come. Don't leave.   390

APOECIDES: Till then.

(*He exits*)

PERIPHANES: (*Entering house*) Come in.

EPIDICUS: You go, sir; count it out.

(PERIPHANES *exits*)

Scene 3

EPIDICUS: I don't believe another field in Greece
    Could give as rich returns as Periphanes.
    He can shut up his money chest and seal it,
    But I'll shake out whatever cash I want.
    That's not to say that if he learned about it
    He wouldn't whip me till the switches clung
    Like leeches to my back and showed the bone.
    What really bothers me is something else, though—
    What music-girl—a hired one?—I show   400
    To Apoecides. That should work out, though.
    This very day the old man ordered me
    To hire a music-girl for him who'll come
    And play while he is offering sacrifice.
    Oh, I'll hire one, all right, and show her clearly
    Just how to pull the wool over his eyes.
    Now I'll go in and get the old fool's cash.

(*He exits*)

ACT III

Scene 1

(STRATIPPOCLES *and* CHAERIBULUS *enter from* CHAERIBULUS's
house)

STRATIPPOCLES: It's tearing out my very guts, this waiting
    To find what good I'll get from that smooth-tongued
    Epidicus. This torture has to end—   410
    Lord, let it end soon, whether I win or lose.

CHAERIBULUS: You expect help from him? Look somewhere
      else—
   Anywhere else. I knew from the beginning
   Whatever trust you put in him was lost.

STRATIPPOCLES: Oh, this is more than mortal man can bear!

CHAERIBULUS: Don't take on so; that's foolish. When I catch him
   That slave will find nobody goes unpunished
   Who tries to make fools out of you and me.

STRATIPPOCLES: What would you have him do, when you refuse
   To help your friends, or give a pal a loan?   420

CHAERIBULUS: You know damned well I'd lend it if I could.
   Oh well, you've got some chance of getting it
   Somehow, somewhere, from somebody, no doubt.

STRATIPPOCLES: The devil take you, chickening out again!

CHAERIBULUS: I wonder—do you *like* abusing me?

STRATIPPOCLES: What do you think?—blathering about
      something
   Somehow, somewhere, somebody—none of it
   Worth a man's breath—and being no more help
   To me in my trouble than a babe unborn.

                         Scene 2

(*Enter* EPIDICUS *from* PERIPHANES' *house, with money*)

EPIDICUS: I'll do my part, sir, just as you've done yours.   430
   Let your mind be at rest concerning this
   (*Door closes*)
   For it's all over; don't hope to get it back;

The whole thing's dead and buried. Just have faith—
I'm following my family's tradition.
The gods have given me a day of days,
And all so easy and so effortless!
But why am I stalling so? I've got to migrate,
Get these goods to some colony by myself;
I'm wasting my own time, hanging around here.
But now what's this? Look at them there, my master   440
Next to Chaeribulus at the front gate.
(*Approaching*)
What are you doing here?
(*Giving the bag*)
                              Please take this, sirs.

STRATIPPOCLES: How much is in it?

EPIDICUS: More than you will need.
   A hundred more than you owe the moneylender.
   If I can satisfy you, why, that's all
   I care for; never mind about my back.

STRATIPPOCLES: What do mean?

EPIDICUS: I'm going to change your father
   To a parenticide.

STRATIPPOCLES: What in the world—?

EPIDICUS: None of your cheap one-syllable words for me.
   Most father killers are dragged off in a sack.   450
   This one is going in a money bag.
   The pimp has got his payment for the girl—
   Got it in full. I counted it myself.
   Your father thinks the music-girl's his daughter.
   As if that weren't enough, there's one more chance
   To make a fool of him and help you out.
   I got him to agree—it took some talking—
   That he should buy the girl you aimed at freeing

To make it seem he set her free himself
And so, when you return, to keep you parted.   460

STRATIPPOCLES: Wonderful!

EPIDICUS: Now a new girl for your father
   To stand in for the one you used to love.
   The first girl's at the house now and pretending
   That she's his daughter.

STRATIPPOCLES: Oh, I see. Indeed!

EPIDICUS: He's naming Apoecides as director,
   Or overseer, or whatnot, at the sale,
   To keep an eye on me. I'm meeting him
   Down at the forum.

STRATIPPOCLES: Pretty good, I'd say.

EPIDICUS: And watch that very guardian being tricked.
   Your father hung this wallet around my neck,   470
   And he's at home preparing for your wedding.

STRATIPPOCLES: There's no way he can force me into marriage
   Unless Death steals the girl I brought with me!

EPIDICUS: Listen now, here's my plan. I'm going down
   To the pimp's house alone, to make it clear
   That he should say, in case I drop in on him,
   The music-girl's been paid for and he's got
   All of his money—as a matter of fact
   I gave it to him myself two days ago.
   That was to pay for that old girl of yours,   480
   The one your father's certain is his daughter.
   So then the pimp, not knowing what he's doing,
   Will swear it's true by all that he holds holy—
   And anyone would say he'd got the cash for
   The girl that you have brought along just now.

CHAERIBULUS: You can spin faster than a potter's wheel.

EPIDICUS: Now I'll go find a clever music-girl,
  Not too expensive, who'll swear she's been bought—
  That way we'll gull the two old guys completely.
  Then Apoecides takes her to your father.   490

STRATIPPOCLES: You're a real ball of fire!

EPIDICUS: I promise you,
  The girl I send to him will know her part,
  Ready to carry out the part I've taught her.
  But no more talk. We're behind time already.
  You know what to expect. I'm off.

STRATIPPOCLES: Good luck, then!

CHAERIBULUS: He's better to have with you than against you.

STRATIPPOCLES: God knows he's saved me time and time again.

CHAERIBULUS: We might as well go in.

STRATIPPOCLES: More happily
  By a long shot than I came out. Epidicus,
  Thanks to your courage and your watchfulness,   500
  I'm coming back to camp weighed down with loot.

(*They exit*)

Scene 3

PERIPHANES: There's not a man who shouldn't have a mirror,
  Not just to show his face, but, more important,
  To let him scan the heart of what seems wisdom;
  Then, having studied that, he might go on

To view the life he'd led since his young manhood.
Take me, for instance—I'd begun to worry
A while ago about my boy, to feel
He had offended me, as if I'd not
Been guilty as a youth of far worse faults.   510
Well, all old men go daft, no doubt, at times.
But here comes Apoecides himself
Bringing the booty.
(APOECIDES *approaches with music-girl*)
                    I'm glad to see the sale
Went through. All's well?

APOECIDES: The gods are on your side.

PERIPHANES: A lucky omen.

APOECIDES: True, and with it luck
    Is omnipresent. Now, I beg of you,
    See that the girl is taken indoors.

PERIPHANES: (*Calling*)   Come here!

SLAVE: Yes, sir?

PERIPHANES: Take her inside. And wait—

SLAVE: Sir?

PERIPHANES: See that she doesn't meet my daughter,   520
    Or come in sight of her. Is that quite clear?
    She's to stay in that separate small room.
    What does a mistress know of a virgin's world?

APOECIDES: You put it well. No man can be too careful
    To keep his daughter pure.
    (*Slave and girl exit*)

                                    So we've outwitted
Your son, I think, and in the nick of time,
By purchasing the girl.

PERIPHANES: What do you mean?

APOECIDES: Well, I've been told your son was seen in town
Not long ago, ready to buy that girl.

PERIPHANES: You put it on the line.

APOECIDES: You've got a slave   530
Who's worth his weight in gold, I'll swear to that.
He never let the music-girl suspect
That she was being bought for you. I tell you,
She was a cheerful sight when he brought her here.

PERIPHANES: Now that surprises me.

APOECIDES: You said you planned
To sacrifice at home in celebration
Of your son's safe return from Thebes.

PERIPHANES: That's right.

APOECIDES: Why, he's even told the pimp the music-girl
Was hired to assist you at the altar.
You should have seen the face I put on for them—   540
You would have taken me for a real numskull.

PERIPHANES: Ah! Very fitting!

APOECIDES: I must go along—
A friend of mine has most important business
Down at the forum. I've got to help him out.

PERIPHANES: But do come back as promptly as you can.

APOECIDES: Yes, yes, of course.

(*He exits*)

PERIPHANES: A friend in need's a friend
  Beyond all argument. You're not required to do
  A thing, and yet you'll get all that you want.
  Supposing in this business I had used
  A man less artful and expedient.   550
  I'd have lost everything, been made a fool of,
  And seen my son showing his fine white teeth
  In a wide gloating laugh—and I'd deserve it.
  But who's this coming on with such a stride
  His cloak is rippling like a wave? A stranger—

                    Scene 4

(*Enter* CAPTAIN *and slave*)

CAPTAIN: (*To slave, sternly*) Now pay attention. Do not miss a
      house—
  Ask at each one where Periphanes lives,
  And don't come back to me till you've found out.

PERIPHANES: Suppose, young man, I found that man for you.
  Would you consider that a favor done?   560

CAPTAIN: A man of arms like me, thanks to his courage,
  Is guaranteed the gratitude of all.

PERIPHANES: This is a place less peaceful than you'd hoped for
  To throw your martial weight around in.
  Let a bad soldier boast about his exploits;
  To a real hero, those exploits grow dim.
  But I am Periphanes, at your service.

CAPTAIN: (*Abashed*) The one they say who served with kings
    when young
  And made his fortune by his fame in war?

PERIPHANES: Man, if you knew the story of my battles,   570
  You would light out for home with your arms flailing.

CAPTAIN: I'm looking for a man to praise *my* triumphs,
  Not one to bend my ear with tales of his.

PERIPHANES: This is no place for you, sir; someone else
  May take more pleasure in your patched-up tales.
  (*Aside*)
  And yet it isn't really sensible
  To fault him when he does what I would do
  When I was his age and a soldier—Lord,
  How I'd wear down men's patience with my boasting!

CAPTAIN: Listen, sir, if you please, and hear the reason   580
  Why I am here. You, sir, have bought my mistress.

PERIPHANES: (*Aside*) Well well well well—so now I know who
    he is:
  The one Epidicus spoke of.
  (*Aloud*)
                  Yes, quite so.

CAPTAIN: I think this needs discussion, sir. Objections?

PERIPHANES: I don't know whether there will be or not
  Until you tell me what you have in mind.

CAPTAIN: And that is this: for you to hand her over—
  Oh, I shall pay; you see the money here.
  I don't see why I shouldn't be quite open:
  I want to give her liberty at once   590
  And take her for my mistress.

PERIPHANES: That's soon settled.
She cost eight hundred. Add another forty—
And she'll be yours to brighten up your lifetime—
On one condition. Get her out of here.

CAPTAIN: If I agree, she's mine?

PERIPHANES: She is.

CAPTAIN: A bargain!

PERIPHANES: (*Calling*) Hey, in there! Bring that music-girl
You took inside!
(*To* CAPTAIN)
                    I'll even add the lute
That she was playing, at no extra charge.
(*Enter slaves with girl*)
Come now, sir, take her, as you said you would.

CAPTAIN: Out of your mind, you are—what kind of tricks   600
Do you think you're playing? Come now, I say: order
The music-girl brought out.

PERIPHANES: This *is* the girl.
Nobody else is here.

CAPTAIN: What are you up to?
Bring out Acropolistis.

PERIPHANES: There she is.

CAPTAIN: There she is not—wouldn't I recognize
My mistress?

PERIPHANES: This is the girl my son adored.

CAPTAIN: She's the wrong one.

PERIPHANES: Wrong one?

CAPTAIN: Wrong one indeed.

PERIPHANES: Who is she, then, for God's sake? Where's she
    from?
  What have I paid for, if she's not the one?

CAPTAIN: You didn't get whoever it was you paid for—   610
  A splendid mess you've made of everything.

PERIPHANES: Look here, she *is* the one. My son's own servant
  I sent to buy her. She's the one he bought.

CAPTAIN: You have been had, sir—taken joint by joint
  Like Pelias—and by that selfsame servant.

PERIPHANES: How *had?*

CAPTAIN: The girl's some sort of substitute,
  Like the fawn for Iphigenia. He's palmed her off
  For reasons I can't guess. Yes, you've been taken.
  And now excuse me. I must go and find her.

(CAPTAIN *and servants exit*)

PERIPHANES: Captain indeed! Good riddance! Epidicus,   620
  You soul of honor, you best of all possible slaves,
  You're a real man to cheat me in my dotage!
  (*To the girl*)
  Tell me, did Apoecides buy you, then,
  From the pimp this morning?

GIRL: I'd never heard of him
  Until today—and nobody could buy me
  At any price. For five years I've been free.

PERIPHANES: What are you doing in my house, then?

GIRL: Listen.
   He hired me to sing and play the lute
   While an old man was sacrificing here.

PERIPHANES: There's no fool like an old fool, and I'm
     that—   630
   The laughing-stock of Athens. But do you know
   The girl Acropolistis?

GIRL: Sure I do.

PERIPHANES: Where does she live?

GIRL: I'm not sure, now she's free.

PERIPHANES: Free? What do you mean, she's free? Who freed
     her?

GIRL: I'll tell you what I've heard. Stratippocles,
   The son of Periphanes, bought her freedom
   While he was somewhere else.

PERIPHANES: (*Aside*)   This is too much—
   Supposing that it's true. That slave has robbed me
   Of my last cent.

GIRL: I've told you what I heard.   640
   You're sure you don't want anything else of me?

PERIPHANES: Get out of my sight, hear? And go hang yourself.

GIRL: My lute. I want it back.

PERIPHANES: No lutes, no flutes.
   Get out now, if you know what's good for you.

GIRL: (*Contemptuously*) I'll go, all right, but wait, I'll get that lute
   Later on, when the scandal really breaks.

(*She exits*)

PERIPHANES: What next? How can a man like me, whose name
    Has been so often honored in the senate,
    Be made a fool of, and so publicly?
    (Should she go scot-free? No, a hundred times!   650
    And even if I lost the same again,
    I'd rather lose it than be mocked and scorned
    As one whom swindlers find an easy mark.)
    And yet I'm no worse off than he who's hailed
    As having had a hand in all our laws!
    And how he did go on about his shrewdness!
    A hammer without a handle has more brains.

ACT IV

Scene 1

(*Enter* PHILIPPA, *in distress*)

PHILIPPA: If you are wretched enough to earn men's pity,
    Then you are wretched indeed. And so I am,
    Beset on all sides, troubles pouring down   660
    Upon me, beating at my heart—unending,
    How they besiege me! Poverty and fright
    Possess my mind in terror; I can find
    No refuge now for hope. And oh my daughter—
    Vanished, and fallen into enemy hands!

PERIPHANES: (*Aside*) Who is this woman, coming in such a state
    From God knows where, weeping and moaning so?

PHILIPPA: (*Scanning houses*) They said that Periphanes lives near
    here.

PERIPHANES: (*Aside*) That was my name she spoke then. Should I
    offer
This roof as shelter?

PHILIPPA: I'd bless anyone   670
    Who'd point him out, or show me where he lives.

PERIPHANES: (*Aside*) I've seen her somewhere, if I could
    remember.
    I almost recognize her—is she the one
    I've a half-notion that she is, or not?

PHILIPPA: (*Startled, hearing*) Now heaven help me, do I know
    that face?

PERIPHANES: Yes, yes, she is the one I loved and left
    In Epidaurus, all those years ago.

PHILIPPA: (*Aside*) Is this the man who slept with me and left me?

PERIPHANES: (*Aside*) The one who's mother to that very daughter
    There in my house! Should I step up and ask—   680

PHILIPPA: (*Aside*) What should I do? Should I go up to him?

PERIPHANES: (*Aside*)—Is she the same one?

PHILIPPA: (*Aside*)   If he is the man—
    And after all these years who can be sure?

PERIPHANES: (*Aside*) How can I judge now, after twenty years?
    But if she is—I'm half-convinced already—
    I'll go up carefully.

PHILIPPA: (*Aside*)   My intuition—
    I must depend on that.

PERIPHANES: (*Aside*)   I'll say good morning.

PHILIPPA: (*Aside*) I'll have to watch my words.

PERIPHANES: (*Stepping up*)   Good-morning, madam.

PHILIPPA: I thank you for your wishes, sir.

PERIPHANES: What more?

PHILIPPA: Good-day to you, sir—so we come out even.   690

PERIPHANES: I wouldn't doubt it. Could it be we've met?

PHILIPPA: If I know you, why then, you must know me.

PERIPHANES: Where was it, then?

PHILIPPA: Oh sir, you're most unfair.

PERIPHANES: I? How?

PHILIPPA: Expecting me to jog your memory.

PERIPHANES: You have a point.

PHILIPPA: To think that you'd admit it!

PERIPHANES: I do remember you—

PHILIPPA: Ah, that's more like it!

PERIPHANES: Do you remember—

PHILIPPA: Yes, what I remember.

PERIPHANES: In Epidaurus—

PHILIPPA: You cool my burning heart.

PERIPHANES: —A penniless girl and her mother. Can you
    forget   700
The help I brought you in your poverty?

PHILIPPA: The grief you brought me by your self-indulgence?

PERIPHANES: More shame to me. God bless you.

PHILIPPA: So He has,
    Finding you safe.

PERIPHANES: Give me your hand.

PHILIPPA: Here, take it,
    Though it's the hand of one worn down by sorrow.

PERIPHANES: What grieves you so?

PHILIPPA: The daughter that you fathered—

PERIPHANES: Yes? Yes?

PHILIPPA: I reared her lovingly, and lost her.
    Some enemy has her now.

PERIPHANES: Be calm and listen—
    She's in my house, there; nothing's come to harm her.   710
    The moment that my slave said she'd been captured,
    I sent him off to buy her. This he did
    With great good sense, though he's a rascal often.

PHILIPPA: Oh let me see whether she's mine, and safe—

PERIPHANES: (*Calling*) Canthara, come—bring out my child
    Telestis
To see her mother.

PHILIPPA: My heart revives at last.

Scene 2

(*Enter* ACROPOLISTIS)

ACROPOLISTIS: Why did you want me, Father?

PERIPHANES: Your mother's come.
  Go up and greet her. Give her a kiss.

ACROPOLISTIS: My mother?

PERIPHANES: (*Pointing*) The one who's spent her life in search
  of you.

PHILIPPA: (*To* PERIPHANES) Who is this girl you're ordering
  to kiss me?   720

PERIPHANES: Your child.

PHILIPPA: What? That one?

PERIPHANES: Yes.

PHILIPPA: Why should I kiss her?

PERIPHANES: Well, she's your daughter.

PHILIPPA: You're out of your mind.

PERIPHANES: I? Mad?

PHILIPPA: Yes, you.

PERIPHANES: Why so?

PHILIPPA: Because she's no one
  I ever saw. I don't know who she is.

PERIPHANES: I think I see why you're confused—because
   She's changed her dress, her hair-do—

PHILIPPA: Don't be silly.
   You can tell pigs from puppies by the smell.
   I swear I've no idea who this girl is.   730

PERIPHANES: Good God, tell me—what am I, then—
   A procurer, with a houseful of strange girls
   And money spilling out of doors and windows?
   (To ACROPOLISTIS)
   Come here, you young bitch! Calling me your father,
   Kissing me—why do you stand there, dumb as an ox?

ACROPOLISTIS: (Pertly) What should I say?

PERIPHANES: You understand, this lady
   Denied that she's your mother.

ACROPOLISTIS: Well, why not?
   If that's the way she wants it. Even so,
   Whatever she says I'm still my mother's daughter.
   It's not my place to say that she's my mother   740
   If she's against it.

PERIPHANES: Then why call me father?

ACROPOLISTIS: What can I call you else? You call me daughter.
   And if this lady spoke of me as hers,
   I'd call her mother. If I'm not the child,
   She's not the parent. What I mean to say
   Is this: I'm not to blame. I've just repeated
   The lesson that Epidicus has taught me.

PERIPHANES: Oh Lord, there goes the applecart.

ACROPOLISTIS: Why, Father,
   Have I done anything I shouldn't have?

PERIPHANES: (*Snort of rage*) Confound you—call me father
    once again,   750
  I'll tear you limb from limb.

ACROPOLISTIS: (*Pathetically*) Whatever you say.
  Be or don't be my father, as you choose.

PHILIPPA: Well, if you bought her, thinking her your daughter,
  What did you have for her identification?

PERIPHANES: I had none. None at all.

PHILIPPA: What made you certain
  She was our daughter?

PERIPHANES: The slave Epidicus.

PHILIPPA: Even if he thought so, couldn't you tell she wasn't?

PERIPHANES: Damn it, I saw her only once.

PHILIPPA: Oh horrors!

PERIPHANES: Don't cry, my dear. Go in. I'll find our girl.

PHILIPPA: Someone from here it was, they say, who bought
  her—   760
  A young Athenian.

PERIPHANES: Hush, I'll find her. Now
  Go in and watch this one, as much an orphan
  As Circe was, this daughter of the Sun.
  And as for me, I'll hunt Epidicus,
  And when he's found I'll send him to perdition.

ACT V

Scene 1

(*Several hours later*)

STRATIPPOCLES: (*Enters from* CHAERIBULUS's *house*)
    That moneylender—what a businessman!
    He hasn't come to me to get his money
    Nor brought the girl he purchased from the loot.
    Here comes Epidicus at a snail's pace—
    Why does he look so glowering, I wonder?   770

EPIDICUS: (*Disgusted*) Even if Jupiter and his eleven stalwarts
    Came down especially, they couldn't save me.
    Torture is right around the bend, Periphanes
    Is buying straps, and Apoecides
    Is with him; I suppose they're on my trail
    This very minute. Well, the jig is up—
    They know that they've been had. And had by me.

STRATIPPOCLES: How goes it, Father Time?

EPIDICUS: The way it goes
    With everybody. Badly.

STRATIPPOCLES: Why, what's wrong?

EPIDICUS: Come on: make me a loan and save my hide.   780
    Two men who've lost their own are hunting for me,
    Each with a length of rope to hang me.

STRATIPPOCLES: Come,
    Keep your chin up.

EPIDICUS: As if I had my freedom?

STRATIPPOCLES: I'll take care of you.

EPIDICUS: No thanks, they'll do that
   Better than you, once they catch up with me.
   But who's that young girl coming down the street
   With the grey-headed man?

STRATIPPOCLES: The moneylender,
   That's who he is, and she's the girl I bought
   Out of the loot.

EPIDICUS: (*Staring at* TELESTIS) So she's the one, is she?

STRATIPPOCLES: She is, believe me. Isn't she all I said?   790
   Oh, look her over, man; don't miss a thing—
   She's prettier than any picture painted.

EPIDICUS: Painted—that's what I'm going to be. In stripes,
   By Zeuxis and Apelles, with elm-pigment.

(*Enter usurer and* TELESTIS)

STRATIPPOCLES: Lord help us all, is this the way I told you
   To get here? Even a man with leaden feet
   Would have made it sooner.

USURER: Don't blame me, sir. *She*
   Is the one who held us up.

STRATIPPOCLES: (*Admiring* TELESTIS) If you went slow
   To please her, why, you're far ahead of time.

USURER: Never mind that, sir. Now I want my money.   800
   Count it out now; my friends are waiting for me.

STRATIPPOCLES: It's ready.

USURER: Here's a bag to put it in.

STRATIPPOCLES: What a go-getter! Wait till I bring it out.

USURER: Get going.

STRATIPPOCLES: It's in the house.

(*He exits*)

EPIDICUS: (*Looking at* TELESTIS) Should I be trusting
My eyes or not? Can this girl be Telestis,
Philippa's daughter, Periphanes' child,
Conceived in Epidaurus, born in Thebes?

TELESTIS: How does it happen, sir, you know our names,
My parents' and my own?

EPIDICUS: You don't know me?   810

TELESTIS: I'm sorry, but I don't remember—

EPIDICUS: Really?
Think of the man who bought you a gold crescent
Once for your birthday, and a finger-ring.

TELESTIS: Oh, now I do recall—what a nice man
He was! And he was you?

EPIDICUS: He was, be certain.
And you've been purchased, if you will believe it,
By your half-brother—part of your family,
But by a different mother.

TELESTIS: And our father?
What about him? Oh, is he still alive?

EPIDICUS: Don't be upset, child. Just be calm. Relax.   820

TELESTIS: It must be that the gods decided it—
    That I be found at last. Can I believe you?

EPIDICUS: My dear young lady, would I lie to you?

(*Reenter* STRATIPPOCLES)

STRATIPPOCLES: Here's what you're waiting for, my man. Come,
    count it—
Eight hundred forty dollars. Counterfeits
I will redeem.

USURER: (*Taking and counting money*)
    That's fine, sir. Now good-bye,
And lots of luck.

(*He exits*)

STRATIPPOCLES: (*To* TELESTIS) My dear, at last you're mine!

TELESTIS: Indeed I am—you've found your long lost sister,
    If you know what I know.

STRATIPPOCLES: (*To* EPIDICUS) Can she be sane?

EPIDICUS: Why yes, if she is speaking to her brother.   830

STRATIPPOCLES: What's this? I was her lover, and yet now,
    Between my going-in and coming-out
    We're siblings!

EPIDICUS: Look, don't crowd your luck.

STRATIPPOCLES: Sister, you've lost and found me in a breath.

EPIDICUS: Good Lord, you've got no sense at all—you still
    Have somebody to love: the music-girl.

And I've arranged it so that she's at home
Waiting, just as your sister's free at last.

STRATIPPOCLES: Epidicus, I must say—

EPIDICUS: Look, sir, go in
And have some water heated for this lady.   840
When things calm down, I'll explain everything.

STRATIPPOCLES: (*Toward house*) Sister, come with me.

EPIDICUS: I'll tell Thesprio
To come here too. If the old men make trouble,
It's me your sister and yourself should help.

STRATIPPOCLES: We will.

(*They exit*)

EPIDICUS: (*Calling at* CHAERIBULUS's *door*)
Go out through the garden, Thesprio;
Back me up at home.
(*Soliloquizes*)
                    The old guys trouble me much less.
I'll go and meet the guests as they arrive
And at the same time brief Stratippocles
On what I know. Can't make my exit now,
Since I've decided to stay on. Nobody's   850
Going to say I took to my heels and challenged
Him to catch me. I'd better get on inside:
I'm talking too much out here.

(*He exits*)

Scene 2

(*Enter* PERIPHANES, *furious, and* APOECIDES, *weary*)

PERIPHANES: That knave is making us fair game, is he?

APOECIDES: Oh heavens, no—it's you who make me wretched—
    You and this wretched business.

PERIPHANES: Oh be still!
    If I could only lay my hands on him—

APOECIDES: I've got a bit of news for you. Supposing
    You want a friend beside you, go and find one—
    I'm leaving. All this trailing you around   860
    Has left my legs swollen from knee to ankle.

PERIPHANES: That blackguard—fifty times he's made us goats,
    Both of us in one day, and robbed me blind!

APOECIDES: I've had my fill of him. His father's Vulcan,
    I swear—Vulcan at his most violent.
    Whatever he touches disappears in smoke,
    And even standing near him makes you sweat.

(*Enter* EPIDICUS, *unseen in doorway*)

EPIDICUS: I've got them all on my side—Jupiter
    And all his cohorts are my henchmen now.
    Have I done wrong in the past? It doesn't matter.   870
    I know my strength. I kick my foes away.

PERIPHANES: Where should I go to look for him?

APOECIDES: Anywhere,
    So long as you go without me. Try the ocean
    For all I care.

EPIDICUS: (*Stepping out*) Why gentlemen, can it be
  You look for me? No further problem, sirs,
  You see me here. I haven't run away,
  Have I? Left home? Escaped your eyes? No, no!
  What's more, I needn't kneel to you—if you
  Would tie my hands, I hold them out. I watched
  While you bought straps. Now use them. Don't be shy.   880

PERIPHANES: What can I do? He's even offering
  His own recognizance.

EPIDICUS: Well, bind me, then.

APOECIDES: A shameful property!

EPIDICUS: Why, Apoecides,
  I'd not expected you to intercede!

APOECIDES: Your expectations, sir, will be fulfilled.

EPIDICUS: (*To* PERIPHANES) Come on, do something.

PERIPHANES: Something
  you'd like me to?

EPIDICUS: Exactly that, and not because you choose.
  Fasten these hands of mine, I tell you.

PERIPHANES: (*Puzzled*)   No,
  I will not. It is not my wish.

APOECIDES: (*To* PERIPHANES) Watch out—
  He's going to attack; he's got some weapon.   890

EPIDICUS: (*To* PERIPHANES) You're wasting time, letting me stand
  here.
  Quick, tie me up!

PERIPHANES: No. I'll quiz you as you are.

EPIDICUS: I'll tell you nothing.

PERIPHANES: (*To* APOECIDES) How do I deal with this?

APOECIDES: You let him do as he wants.

EPIDICUS: Now that's discretion.

PERIPHANES: Stretch out your hands, then.

EPIDICUS: See how they obey!
  Tie the rope tighter—

PERIPHANES: In short order. So.

EPIDICUS: Oh, you're too gentle.

PERIPHANES: Judge me when I'm done.

EPIDICUS: Ah now, that's fine. Now grill me as you wish.

PERIPHANES: What right had you to tell me that the girl—
  The one bought at the sale two days ago—   900
  Was my own daughter?

EPIDICUS: Merely that it pleased me.
  That was my right.

PERIPHANES: It gave you pleasure, did it?

EPIDICUS: You bet it did. Come on now, make a bet
  She's not a
  (*Slurring the "a"*)
              daughter.

PERIPHANES: When her mother even,
  Says that she's never seen her?

EPIDICUS: Make your bet—
  Two hundred bucks to twenty cents—that she
  Is not her mother's daughter.

PERIPHANES: Oho, a trick!
  Who is this woman?

EPIDICUS: Mistress of your son,
  Since you'd know everything.

PERIPHANES: Epidicus,
  I gave you money for my daughter's purchase.   910
  Do you deny it?

EPIDICUS: Certainly not. I took it
  And bought that music-girl, your own son's mistress—
  Bought her and not your daughter. And I robbed you
  Of your eight hundred dollars in the sale.

PERIPHANES: The same way that you tricked me with the girl
  You hired to play the lute?

EPIDICUS: Quite right, quite right,
  And a good job I did, in my opinion.

PERIPHANES: Where is the money that I gave you last?

EPIDICUS: It was no good-for-nothing that I gave it to—
  It was Stratippocles.

PERIPHANES: How did you dare—   920

EPIDICUS: It pleased me to.

PERIPHANES: My God, what impudence!

EPIDICUS: You're treating me as if I were a slave.

PERIPHANES: You have your freedom, then? That's news to me.

EPIDICUS: I deserve freedom.

PERIPHANES: Free? The likes of you?

EPIDICUS: You will agree once you have looked inside.

PERIPHANES: What are you saying?

EPIDICUS: The facts will speak for me.
   Go look inside.

APOECIDES: Yes, do; I think he means it.

PERIPHANES: All right, but watch him, Apoecides.

(*He exits*)

APOECIDES: What is this all about, Epidicus?

EPIDICUS: What kind of justice keeps me standing here,   930
   My hands bound like a criminal's, when through me
   And by my efforts, he has found his daughter?

APOECIDES: You are the one who found her? *You* are?

EPIDICUS: Yes.
   I found her, and she's back at home, right here.
   It isn't easy, though, to be rewarded
   With scorn and hatred when you've done a good deed.

APOECIDES: You mean the girl we've worn ourselves to shreds
   Trying to find a trace of, all day long?

EPIDICUS: If you're worn down, it's just from hunting her.
    In my case, it's from finding.

(*Enter* PERIPHANES)

PERIPHANES: (*To* STRATIPPOCLES *and* TELESTIS *inside*)
    Tell me this: 940
    What good is all this begging on your part?
    I see it's I who'll have to do the begging—
    To be allowed to do what he deserves.
    (*To* EPIDICUS)
    Come on now, let me untie your hands.

EPIDICUS: No sir.
    Don't touch it.

PERIPHANES: Come, hold out your hands.

EPIDICUS: No sir.

PERIPHANES: You should play fair.

EPIDICUS: Play fair? I'll give my oath
    To keep these bonds till you apologize.

PERIPHANES: That's fair enough. Look, you shall have new shoes,
    A tunic, and a cloak.

EPIDICUS: And then what else?

PERIPHANES: Your freedom.

EPIDICUS: And what else? For a man who's just been freed   950
    Will need some wherewithal.

PERIPHANES: You'll get your food.

EPIDICUS: (*Sulking*) I swear you'll never set me loose until
  You eat your share of humble pie.

PERIPHANES: (*Humbly*)   I do.
  I ask forgiveness if I've done you ill.
  Your liberty should be enough to win it.

EPIDICUS: (*Loftily*) It's hard to pardon your offense, or you,
  Under the circumstances—but oh well,
  Loosen my bonds now, if it gives you pleasure.

EPILOGUE

(*Spoken by the author*)

  Here is a scamp who rose above his station
  And, by his mother-wit, went free. Give us applause,   960
  Then stretch your legs, stand up—and so, farewell!

THE HAUNTED
HOUSE

(MOSTELLARIA)

Translated by Palmer Bovie

INTRODUCTION

The *Mostellaria* has always been one of Plautus's more popular comedies, valued as an amusing and tightly constructed play. It influenced English and European playwrights in the seventeenth and eighteenth centuries, and with the *Menaechmi, Amphitryo, Rudens,* and *Miles Gloriosus* belongs to the group of Roman comedies most often read and appreciated by students of Latin and by general readers today.

Shakespeare, who had read the play in Latin (as he had others of Plautus), named two waiting-men in *The Taming of the Shrew* Grumio and Tranio, after two characters in the *Mostellaria,* and assigned a similar role to his Tranio, the mischievous accomplice and ostensible guardian of Lucentio. Although not directly indebted to this play, the musical comedy *A Funny Thing Happened on the Way to the Forum* (1962) by Shevelove and Sondheim happily has provided one of the most accomplished actors on our stage with a superb comic role as the leading character, in the role of the manipulating slave Pseudolus. Like Tranio, he rides out the storms and controls the crazy crises of his drama with gigantic aplomb and brazen inventions drawn from a hundred different plot elements in Plautus and Terence. The marvelous performance of Zero Mostel in the main part has been the most hilarious evidence our stage has yet seen of what Plautus was capable of creating over two thousand years ago when he defined this type of role. For one of the very successful features of the *Mostellaria* is the masterful daring of its star. Tranio begins, continues, and ends as the master of the situation. Of course he is its lock as well as its key, a heady developer of difficulties and a compounder of intricate maneuvers that would trip up any but the most accomplished escape artist.

When the father of the young man Tranio has been assigned to

307

protect and guide suddenly appears at the harbor after three years' absence, the son Philolaches is frantic. As a young man about town he has lavished money sumptuously on feasting and entertainment and borrowed heavily to buy the freedom of his mistress slave girl Philematium. The first act of the *Mostellaria* arrays the characters so as to give a candid but sympathetic exposition of this state of affairs, from the ferocious opening debate between Grumio the good country slave and Tranio the bad town slave, through the soliloquy of Philolaches on his abandonment to pleasure, and the worldly scene between Philematium and her older attendant Scapha, to the romantic encounter between Philolaches and Philematium and the subsequent beginning of another of their never-ending round of parties. As their friends appear to join in the festivities, and the stage is set once more in this last scene of the first act for a cheerful day of pleasure, we see how this whole first act is virtually a play before the play, a brightly sketched view of how the young people acted in the absence of the censorious father. It sparkles with joyous abandon, but at intervening moments, like the soliloquy of the young man, or Scapha's worldly interview with her young charge, expresses worry and self-criticism and betrays a haunting concern with the perishability of pleasure.

When the hour of reckoning arrives, it provides Tranio with an opportunity to show what a lightning calculator he is. He takes command and begins to invent the "plot" from which the play is named, the *mostellaria fabula* or "little monster" story (*mostellaria* is the diminutive adjective formed from *monstrum*). Hiding the nervous Philolaches and his group in the house behind barred and locked doors, Tranio boldly greets the father Theopropides with the news that his house is haunted. They discovered the ghost, oh, some six or seven months before, and of course no one lives there now. Has Theopropides by any chance disturbed the spooky spirit on the premises, the ghost of a murdered man, by rattling at the doors and pounding on them for admission? Horrors! Theopropides is quickly enough persuaded to withdraw from the scene with his head covered up in his cloak.

The remainder of the second and third acts is built on a series of natural, unpredictable interruptions that keep Tranio hopping as a master improviser. A moneylender appears to ask about the interest

on his loan; Theopropides returns from his interview with the former owner of the "haunted house." Hearing snatches of the argument between Tranio and the moneylender, Theopropides asks
Tranio what the money was for and what it amounts to. Tranio names
the sum promptly and says that Philolaches used it to buy another
house. Theopropides is pleased that his son was capable of investing
the money so wisely. "Going into business, is he?" Theopropides
remarks delightedly. "He takes after his father!" (*Patrissat*). The
second invention of Tranio has explained the money very neatly: and
it rids the stage of the moneylender whose demands Theopropides
promises to satisfy on the following day. The inevitable question
"What house?" now makes Tranio take the third step in his creative
thinking. "This house right here, next door to ours," he decides, as
the next natural interruption in the form of the neighbor himself,
Simo, is seen coming out the front door of the house in question.

Here in the third act in the central scenes of the play Tranio's
wits are doubly sharpened by the need to play Theopropides and
Simo off against one another. Approaching Simo on the pretext of
asking permission to look over the house, he wins a promise from his
new victim not to tell Theopropides about Philolaches' reckless behavior and then gains the permission sought on the pretext that
Theopropides wants to use Simo's house as a model for some building plans of his own. Bringing the two oldsters together Tranio
insulates the conversation dexterously and has a little fun of his own
at their expense. The act ends with Tranio triumphantly escorting
Theopropides over the threshold of the new house, stepping briskly
over a sleeping dog, while Simo strolls off to the forum.

The stage is now clear for the entrance of two slaves of Philolaches' friend Callidamates who have come to escort their master
home from the party. Finding the "haunted house" locked and apparently unoccupied they flutter about discussing the predicaments
of good and bad slaves in general and of themselves in particular.
Soon Theopropides and Tranio reappear from the inspection of
Simo's house, and Tranio is dispatched to bring Philolaches from the
country to receive his father's congratulations. Theopropides then
sees the slaves at the other side of the stage and accosts them.
Without revealing his identity he soon has more answers to his
questions than he had anticipated, for they spill the beans by re-

counting what has been going on in the "haunted house" these many months. When they leave to search for Callidamates elsewhere, Theopropides is reeling under the new information but is still not aware of how utterly he has been the dupe of Tranio until Simo returns from the forum in the next scene and disposes of the story of the alleged purchase of the house. Theopropides asks him for the loan of a pair of heavy-handed slaves to help in subduing Tranio.

At the beginning of the fifth act Tranio blithely saunters back, meditating on how to stave off still further the inevitable, for now Philolaches has had enough of his help and wants to confess all to Theopropides. Overhearing Theopropides' instructions to the strong-arm slaves (the Latin designation for them is simply *Lorarii*, "Floggers"), Tranio confronts the father, who asks him to account for Simo's denial of the house purchase. The dialogue continues as Theopropides stalls, waiting for the right moment to order the *lorarii* to pounce on the intractable Tranio, but Tranio meanwhile has edged nearer and nearer the altar standing in front of Simo's house. Suddenly he reaches it and vaults up onto it. Here, where he is immune from violent seizure, Tranio holds up his end of the dire conversation with Theopropides in a fine, fresh, supremely self-confident vein. The last scene of the play brings in Callidamates, who successfully pleads with the father to pardon Philolaches' youthful excesses, and promises to defray the total cost of their extravagance. He proceeds to ask for forgiveness for Tranio. At first Theopropides stubbornly refuses to spare Tranio, but ultimately he yields to Callidamates' appeal, reminded at the end by Tranio that tomorrow will find the slave in just as much trouble, some other trouble. So why not wait and punish him then for both times together?

Like all of Plautus's works, this comedy was drawn from a Greek original, the *Phasma*, or *Ghost*, perhaps of Philemon. It is a translation into Latin verse of the Greek text, one that doubtless represents an extensive reworking and adaptation. Certainly it has its own style and character, and sounds like Plautus at the height of his powers, agile and confident in the expression of its lively and lilting Latin verses, robust in situation, sly and occasionally arresting in thought. Against the fundamental currents of spoken verse in long lines of iambic or trochaic measures are set the lyric measures variously contained in the monologue passages (Philolaches' entering song, Callidamates' stagger scene, Simo's lament, Phaniscus's soliloquy). The jokes, turns, buffets, thrusts, ripostes are there for all to see and hear with their appropriate sound effects.

In translating the *Mostellaria* I have attempted to use long iambic and anapestic lines to reflect the fundamental meters of the dialogue, generally in an iambic scheme. For the lyrics I have changed the meter and introduced more definite rhyme patterns, to set these *cantica* in the niches where they separately belong. Throughout I have tried to incorporate alliteration, assonance, and rhyme freely enough to convey in English the equivalent effect of Plautus's love of alliteration and his abundant interest in words, and the sounds ideas make when they are pronounced on the stage.

Palmer Bovie

THE HAUNTED HOUSE

CHARACTERS

TRANIO and GRUMIO, slaves of Theopropides
PHILOLACHES, son of Theopropides
PHILEMATIUM, mistress of Philolaches
SCAPHA, her maid
CALLIDAMATES, a young man and friend of Philolaches
DELPHIUM, mistress of Callidamates
SPHAERIO, slave of Theopropides
THEOPROPIDES, father of Philolaches
MISARGYRIDES, a moneylender
SIMO, an old man
PHANISCUS and PINACIUM, slave escort of Callidamates
LORARII, whipsters

SCENE: *A street in Athens. The houses of* THEOPROPIDES *and* SIMO *at either end of the stage in the rear are separated by a narrow back street. The side entrances lead (left) to the harbor and (right) to the forum or countryside.*

313

ACT I

Scene 1

GRUMIO: Come out of the kitchen! Out here this instant, you lash,
    Giving me the smart side of your smooth tongue in the middle
      of those saucepans.
    Out of the house, you wreck of your master's existence!
    I'll pay you back in the country with interest, for sure.
    Out of the pantry, you stinker. Why hide in there?

TRANIO: What's all this noise out in front of the house? What's
    cooking?
    Think you're out in the sticks? Lay off the town house,
    You hick! Off to the field with you; stop thrashing around
    On our threshold.
    (*Cuffs* GRUMIO)
    That what you thought you had coming?

GRUMIO: Ouch! That hurt! Why throw those punches at me?   10

TRANIO: Because you're alive, that's why.

GRUMIO: All right. I'll endure
    It a little while longer. But just let the master come back,
    Just let him come back home safe, the one you're devouring
    In his absence.

TRANIO: That's illogical as well as unlikely, to speak of
    devouring
    Someone who's not there.

GRUMIO: Smooth-talking bum about town,
    Oh, they love you in Athens! And you throw the country at me?
    But I think I know why: in the back of your mind you're aware
    You're headed straight for the mill, to slave away there.

Time's almost up, season's finished, old Tranio;
You'll soon be a countryman too, rural yokels union
   of iron—   20
Workers, slaves who clank chains and grind daily bread in the
   mills.
Make hay in town while the sun shines, my boy: drink and
   spend,
Ruin that wonderful lad with your dissolute ways;
Drink day and night, live for pleasure like a Greek;
Buy up the girls, set them free, buy the meals
For your freeloading friends, spend like a god let loose
On earth with a credit card. Were those the instructions our
   master
Left, when he left? Is this how he told you to act
As the person in charge of affairs? Do you think that a slave
Has a duty to go through his master's estate   30
And ruin his son? And it's *ruin* what he's busy doing:
A lad who up to this time was the best you could find
In all Attica, thrifty and self-contained—
But now takes the prize for excellence in self-indulgence,
Thanks to your teaching and superb abandoned example.

TRANIO: Why should you care about me or what I do,
   Potato-face? You've got cattle to tend in the country.
   I like to drink and make love and go out with girls
   And I risk my own back in living it up, not yours.

GRUMIO: Cool! I say "you're a fool," yours drooly, Grumio.   40

TRANIO: Why don't you go up in smoke? I'll see you inhale first,
   You halitosis garlic-green rotten excuse for a rustic
   Retreat, with goat-goo on your feet. I repeat:
   You whiff of damp air, what's it like down there in your pigsty?
   Whew! What a combination of nanny goat and mongrel bitch!

GRUMIO: Oh, does your highness object? What did he expect?
   We can't all reek of Greek perfoom, though God knows you
   do—

Whew—We can't all sit above the lord at the head of the table,
Or live in the elegant style apparently you're able.
I'll take my food cooked in garlic. You can have your
    pigeons   50
En casserole, your fish and your fricasseed thrush.
No thanks, very mush. You're very well off; I'm poor;
And, ah, these things we must *endure,* at least till the day
Of RE-TRI-BU-TION: the wages of sin then will pay
You off with interest in evil, but decency won't leave me at bay.

TRANIO: All very moral, I must say. But Grumio, I assume you are
    Holding it against me that I'm in good shape and you're not.
    That's all very normal. It suits me, this passionate life
    With lasses to love at my liking. You're good at milking
    And mucking around in the mire. I live rather higher,   60
    You rather lower; my desires are gratified, your cows are
        satisfied.

GRUMIO: Oh, you crucified crookshanks, as I believe you will be!
    How the crucifiers will drill you as you carry your cross
    At the side of the road, when old Master comes home again.

TRANIO: How do you know that won't happen to you before me?

GRUMIO: For the simple reason that I've never deserved it, and
    don't
    Deserve it at present; you always have and you do.

TRANIO: Oh, save your hot air for some future inflation, deposit
    it—
    If you don't want your ribs in the red from the ruin I'll rain
    on you.

GRUMIO: Anything further? How about the fodder for my
    cattle?   70

If you're handing it over, come across; if you're not, just keep
    going
The way you've started; keep slinking around like a Greek
And drinking and stuffing your gluttonous sackful of guts.

TRANIO: Oh, hang up and head for the sticks. I'm off to the
    harbor
To find some nice fresh fish for our suppertime dish.
Tomorrow I'll have someone fetch that vetch fodder further
Out to the villa. What are you staring at, jailbird?

GRUMIO: That pen name will suit you sooner than me, that's what
    I think.

TRANIO: "Sooner," who cares, when the present's so particularly
    pleasant?

GRUMIO: Is *that* so? Here's one thing *you* ought to know:
    the bad   80
Comes along much sooner than you wish it had.

TRANIO: Well, let's not you be my bad news at present, you
    goose:
Flap off to your pen, get out from under my feet.
I repeat: *Shooo!*

(*He exits*)

GRUMIO: What? Whoosh! Well, he's beat a hasty retreat.
And he doesn't seem to care one frit for all that I've said.
O ye immortal gods, I'll apply then, instead,
To your holy powers. Bring my master back home from abroad
As soon as you can, perhaps even sooner, while the lord
Still has a home and a farm to be lord of. Three years   90
He's been gone and what's left of his property here
Will last about three more months at the most.
I'm off to the country. Here comes our host,

The master's son, once by far the best
Of all young men, now as ruined as the rest.

(*He exits*)

Scene 2

(*Enter* PHILOLACHES)

PHILOLACHES: I have thought about this, and pondered it deep in
    my heart:
  What is a man? And what is he like from the start?
  And I think I've discovered the answer—so let me disguise
  Man's likeness in an image you're likely to recognize.
  From the moment he's born, a man is just like a house!   100
  And I'll prove this, once and for all, so conclusively
  That all of you listening out there will agree inclusively
  As soon as you've heard my words. "Why, of course,"
  You'll admit. "That's it, to a *T*. That's us."
  So listen closely as I set about proving my case:
  I want you as cleverly informed by the portrait I trace
  As I am. When the house is finished and ready for its residents
  Beautifully built and cannily constructed, a precedent's
  Established in other people's minds. They envy the
    establishment
  And congratulate the carpenter. Ambitious for such
    embellishments,   110
  They take this house for a model and spare no labor or cost
  To create a copy of the house they admire the most.

  And then the new owner moves in, with his whole sloppy
    family
  And is lazy and disorderly and shiftless and worthless and
    shambly.
  So the house develops flaws because a good place is badly
    looked after.

And what often happens? A high wind exposes a rafter
By tearing some tiles from the roof or gouging the gutters
While the unindustrious lord and master hardly flutters
To replace the tiles or plug the holes. Then it rains cats and
    dogs
And the walls are lashed by the downpour and then
    waterlogged.   120
The wet rots the beams and undoes the intricate schemes
Of the carpenter-architect-maker. There go his dreams
Of a dwelling that's useful and good. Damp, rotten wood.
The place, much the worse for wear, becomes of less use.
Of course it's not the builder's fault. But there's no excuse
For the way owners generally act in a crisis like this.
They could patch the damage for a drachma but they will insist
On stalling around, not getting to it: they don't do it,
Until finally the walls come falling down to the ground
And the whole building has to be built up all over again.   130
Well, this is the case I've constructed for buildings. Now then,
I want you to think how like are these dwellings and men.

The children are the parents' building: as its architect,
The parents lay the foundation and on it erect
The framework, firm on a stable, reliable base.
They don't count the cost of materials, or in fact
Feel apprehensive because it's expensive to build a child
Who will grow to be useful and good and present a fine face
To the world. They are eager to drive other parents wild
With the wish to produce children exactly like those.   140
When the boys enlist in the army along with them goes
An older cousin or uncle to see them through the first throes
Of being on their own. Just so far are they allowed to stray
From the builders' hands. Duty done, they collect one
    year's pay
And go free. And this is the time to inspect the sample to see
What kind of a combination
Comes of all this edification.

Well, for a sample,
Just look at me, the perfect example.
Up until the time my military service was ended   150
I was as good as could be, while I still depended
On the power of my makers. I was worthy and wise.
But then I moved into the house of my natural guise
And wrecked the builders' work from the roof to the ground.
Laziness dropped in: this was my high wind, I found,
When it tore off my self-control and innate sense of shame.
It unroofed them, but I was the one most to blame
For not replacing those tiles. I put it off too long.
And soon enough, like the rain love came along,
Drenching by body and seeping down into my chest   160
And soaking my heart through and through. Dispossessed
Am I now of money and credit and reputation, all of them fled,
Like my good character and sense of honor: they've left me for
   dead.
No Excuse: Worse for Wear, I've Become of Less Use.
Lord! How these timbers are crumbling with rot! I'll never
Be able to prop up my house. It'll tumble right over
Since the dampness has seeped inside. And no one outside
Can help me stave off this inner collapse, my soul-slide.

How my heart aches to think of myself, so far gone
In ruin from the young man I was, the paragon   170
Of young animals. With a healthy interest in strength
And sports, I lived for the daily delight of more length
With the discus, or javelin; in footrace, in parries and feints
With the broadsword; in gymnastics, in horsemanship trials,
I was a lesson to others in the manly art of self-denial
And austerity. All the best young men were inspired
By the example I set. And now, when I've virtually expired,
And dwindled down to nothing, I've learned to make sense
Of the truth by the simple exercise of my own intelligence.

Scene 3

(*Enter* PHILEMATIUM, SCAPHA. PHILOLACHES *withdraws to far right of stage.*)

PHILEMATIUM: Heavens! That lovely cold bath was
    marvelous.   180
  I've never felt better inside and out, Scapha dear,
  So clean and fresh.

SCAPHA: With some end in view,
  I do hope, some successful solution from all these ablutions.
  After all, there's been a very happy harvest this year.

PHILEMATIUM: But what has a harvest to do with my taking a
    bath?

SCAPHA: Nothing more than your bathing has to do with a
    harvest, my dear.

PHILOLACHES: (*Aside*) Lovely Love Herself! That's my heavenly
    hurricane,
  Who unroofed the top from the whole sphere of self-control
  I'd been housed in. Exposed as I was and then doused
  When love and desire rained down hard and flooded
    my heart,   190
  I can never put the roof on again. The walls of my heart
  Are all soaking wet. My dwelling is falling apart.

PHILEMATIUM: Tell me now, Scapha, my love: Does this dress do
    me justice?
  I want to look nice for the apple of my eye, that wonderful guy
  Who possesses me, my dear Philolaches.

SCAPHA: Really, Philematium,
  You're superbly presentable, you with your adorable ways,

Just because you're so lovely. Men in love aren't in love
With what their women wear but with what they find there.

PHILOLACHES: (*Aside*) Ye gods! That Scapha knows lovers inside
     out,
How they really feel, and just what they're thinking about.   200

PHILEMATIUM: Now how's this?

SCAPHA: How's what?

PHILEMATIUM: Oh, please, take a look
     And tell me now how you like this on me.

SCAPHA: It so happens,
     Thanks to the fact that you're very beautiful, anything
     Looks good on you.

PHILOLACHES: (*Aside*) For these kind words, Scapha you scamp,
     I'll see that you're given a generous . . . something or other
     Today. That is, it won't be gratis or complimentary
     That you are gracious to this girl who is so very dear to me.

PHILEMATIUM: Oh, but I don't agree.

SCAPHA: Come now, how dumb can
     the lady be?
     You wouldn't rather have me criticize you falsely than praise
     You honestly, would you? I'd rather be praised unduly   210
     Than be criticized truly or have others laugh at my looks.

PHILEMATIUM: I cherish the truth and I want you to tell me the
     truth.
     I can't abide lying.

SCAPHA: Well, so help me then, and on a stack of
     drachmas,
     Philolaches adores you, as much as you are adorable.

PHILOLACHES: (*Aside*) What's that you say, you devil? How did
    that oath go?
I adore her? And how about the "she loves me"
Other part of it, why wasn't that added on? I promised
You a gift, but you've lost it; you just tossed it
Away, and I hereby declare that good deed undone.

SCAPHA: But I must say, heaven knows, I simply cannot
    imagine   220
How a clever, intelligent, worldly young woman like you
Can act like a stupid little silly.

PHILEMATIUM: Am I doing something wrong?
Do tell me, please, if I am.

SCAPHA: Heaven's name, doing wrong!
Going wrong, that's the way you're headed, as sure as my name
Means skoal, bottoms up or, in Greek, the Devoted Souse.
You are wandering, dear, by setting your cup, I mean cap
For one man alone. You wait hand and foot on him
And refuse to see all the other interested callers.
It's playing the role of a wife, not using your wiles
As a woman of the world, to yield to one man alone.   230

PHILOLACHES: (*Aside*) Super Jupiter! A snake, nourished at my
    own domestic bosom!
May all the gods, and goddesses too, while I'm at it,
Bring the whole world down on my head if I'm not the man
To kill off that hag by exposure, and hunger, and thirst.

PHILEMATIUM: Now, Scapha, no naughty advice!

SCAPHA: He'll leave you stranded,
I warn you right now, when your youth and beauty are ended
And his pleasure palls at repetition. To think of the current
    condition
Of his friendship and generous behavior as lasting forever
Is to be monumentally dumb.

PHILEMATIUM: Well, I hope not.

SCAPHA: Reality consists for the most part of things
    unhoped for.   240
  If you're quite incapable of being persuaded by words
  To believe what I say is true, just estimate the facts
  On the basis of my experience. You see, for instance, my face,
  As it is now and you remember how I used to look.
  No less than you I once was loved and adored
  By a person I exclusively chose for my master and lord.
  When a few years went by and the hair on my head changed its
    color
  I was abandoned, left stranded. That's your future with this
    fellow.

PHILOLACHES: (*Aside*) I can hardly keep my fingers from flying at
    that vixen's eyes.

PHILEMATIUM: I still think I ought to accommodate this man
    alone.   250
  It was he who set me free, after all, to have for his own.

PHILOLACHES: (*Aside*) Gods, what a woman! Intelligent and
    modest and charming.
  Hercules, no joke: for her I'm glad to go broke!

SCAPHA: But heavens, girl, you don't seem to know yourself.

PHILEMATIUM: Because . . .

SCAPHA: You're so busy
  Making sure he'll like you.

PHILEMATIUM: Why shouldn't I want him to
  like me?

SCAPHA: Because you're free. You have what you wanted and what
    can he do

But keep right on loving you? Otherwise he's bound to lose
Both you and the whole heap of silver he paid for your head.

PHILOLACHES: (*Aside*) Hercules, I'll be a bum if I don't tear
    her limb from limb.   260
She's ruining my wonderful girl plying her with advice
Of the kind a procuress would use to bid up the price.

PHILEMATIUM: I'll never be able to repay the kindness he has
    shown
In the measure he fully deserves. So don't make me think
Any less of him. Anyway, that's impossible.

SCAPHA: But the plausible
Thing to think of is this: if you're a slave to him only at present
As a pretty young thing, your old age will be unpleasantly
    lonely.

PHILOLACHES: (*Aside*) I wish I could turn into quinsy, angina of
    the voice box,
And throttle the poisonous jaws of that sinful old fox.

PHILEMATIUM: Well, I think I ought to behave the same way
    toward him   270
When I've got what I wanted as when I was wheedling it out
    of him.

PHILOLACHES: (*Aside*) Let the gods do whatever they will with
    me, for better or for worse
If I don't set her free all over again, fair Philematium
As a reward for that noble oration—as for Scapha,
I'm planning to bash in her skull once and for all.

SCAPHA: If you're perfectly sure in your mind that this lover of
    yours
Will be yours alone for the rest of your life, and provide
For you unfailingly, you should sleep with this man
And only with him, and braid your hair like a bride.

PHILEMATIUM: If a person's a good credit risk he can always
>   get a loan;   280
>   If I have a good reputation I'm wealthy enough.

PHILOLACHES: (*Aside*) By Hercules, if my father had to be sold
>   Into slavery, I'd sell him outright, long before you
>   Ever went in need or were forced to beg for a thing,
>   So long as I lived.

SCAPHA: But what about your other admirers?

PHILEMATIUM: They'll admire me even more when they see how
>   grateful I am
>   To the one who deserves my best thanks.

PHILOLACHES: (*Aside*)   I wish the news
>   Of my father's death were announced to me this very minute
>   So I could disinherit myself and confer on her
>   The claims as heiress to all my goods and possessions.   290

SCAPHA: But his money is practically gone: the lavish dinner
>   parties
>   And drinking bouts lasting all day and most of the night
>   Show how little he knows about how to put money aside.
>   The pile of provisions in the larder is flat as a pancake.

PHILOLACHES: (*Aside*) By Hercules, I'll prove how close-fisted I
>   can be,
>   Beginning right now with you: your ration of food and drink
>   For the next ten days at our house will be cut down to none.

PHILEMATIUM: If you care to say something pleasant about
>   Philolaches
>   You'll be listened to gladly. If you keep lacing into him, though,
>   By Castor, your nasty remarks will get you a beating.   300

PHILOLACHES: (*Aside*) Hooray for the house of Pollux! If I'd
>   written a check

To Jupiter on High in the amount I paid out for her
It still would have been nowhere nearly so sound an
    investment.
It's obvious how very much she loves me down deep in her
    heart.
What a masterstroke that was to set free my future patron
In the form of this lovely lawyer to plead a case for her client.

SCAPHA: I see that all other men come to nothing for you
    When compared to Philolaches. And I don't want a beating for
      my pains.
    So I'll be the cheerful chorus to your lovelorn refrains.

PHILEMATIUM: Will you hand me the mirror and my jewelry
    box, Scapha?   310
    I want to look my best when my favorite person comes home.

SCAPHA: A woman who can't trust herself or her looks has a use
    for a mirror.
    What need have you for a mirror, when any mirror would
      prize,
    Above anything else, a chance to gaze in your eyes?

PHILOLACHES: (*Aside*) Those fair words, Scapha, I assure you,
    won't go unrewarded.
    And to make sure I'll draw something out of my privates
      account
    And present it this very day to you, Philematium darling.

PHILEMATIUM: Am I all in order? Do have a look at my hair, and
    tell me
    If it's staying prettily in place.

SCAPHA: You are so well disposed
    As you are, that your hair couldn't fail to be neatly
      arranged.   320

PHILOLACHES: (*Aside*) Ugh! Can you think of anything lower than
    a woman like that?
A moment ago all scowls, and now all wreathed in smiles.

PHILEMATIUM: That jar of face powder.

SCAPHA: Face powder? Whatever for?

PHILEMATIUM: To touch up my cheeks.

SCAPHA: You might just as well expect
    To whiten the shade of ivory by applying some lampblack.

PHILOLACHES: (*Aside*) Oh, very well said, Scapha. I must applaud
    that remark
About improving on ivory by blackening it.

PHILEMATIUM: Well, then, the
    rouge, please.

SCAPHA: No, I refuse. That's not at all clever of you
    Do you want to daub over a beautiful work of art
    With streaks of new paint? No false colors should touch   330
    Your exquisite youth, no powder, paint, or cosmetics
    There, take the mirror.

PHILOLACHES: (*Aside*) Oh dear, oh me, missing this!
    She's giving the mirror a kiss! If I had a stone
    I'd bash in the silver face of that mirror.

SCAPHA: Now, use a linen cloth to wipe your hands clean.

PHILEMATIUM: But whatever for?

SCAPHA: You've held the mirror in
    your hands.
    I don't want the smell of silver clinging to your fingers.

PHILOLACHES: (*Aside*) I haven't seen a shrewder procuress
    anywhere around.
Astonishingly astute, that thought about the mirror on her
    hands.

PHILEMATIUM: I could do with the delicate gloss of this
    fragrant scent,   340
Don't you think?

SCAPHA: Not a drop, not a dab.

PHILEMATIUM: Oh? Why not?

SCAPHA: A woman smells best when she doesn't smell in the
    slightest.
Think of those old gals constantly refinishing their surfaces,
Lavishing lotions on their skins: they're shriveled and toothless,
But, concealing their bodily blemishes, they're dyeing to take
    you in.
When the sweat mixes in with the grease and lotion and cream
Well, it's like a cook making one sauce by concocting several;
What it smells like you can't say precisely but you do know it
    smells.

PHILOLACHES: (*Aside*) She certainly has it all doped out: there's
    no higher learning
Than this learned lady displays.
(*To audience*)
                        And it's perfectly true   350
As most of you husbands know who have old wives at home
Who put down a dowry for the privilege of marrying you.

PHILEMATIUM: Tell me if my robe and jewels are becoming
    to me.

SCAPHA: That's none of my business.

PHILEMATIUM: Well, whose is it then?

SCAPHA: It's his,
  Philolaches'. He shouldn't buy anything unless he's sure
  It's something you want. The lover purchases the favors
  Of his mistress by showering her with jewelry and expensive
     clothes.
  And it isn't the presents he wants, so there's no use parading
  The gifts before his eyes. Expensive clothes
  Disguise old age and gold is for the ugly duck.   360
  A beautiful girl without a stitch on her back outshines
  A woman well wrapped in the latest costliest cloth.
  For if she is pretty, she is well enough dressed as is.

PHILOLACHES: (*Aside*) I've kept out of this long enough.
  (*Comes forward*)
                                    What are you two up to?

PHILEMATIUM: I'm dressing up—I want to look nice for you.

PHILOLACHES: Whatever you wear looks wonderful just with you
     in it.
  Scapha, you may go, and take this stuff away, too.
  But Philematium, darling, I'm longing to stretch out here
  And have a drink with you.

PHILEMATIUM: Heavens knows I want
  To be with you. Whatever your heart desires   370
  I want just as much as you do, my dearest darling.

PHILOLACHES: That remark is worth $500 cash.

PHILEMATIUM: Oh, take it
  For $250. You deserve a remarkable bargain.

PHILOLACHES: The $250 is in your bank right now. And balance
     the account:
  I paid $750 for you.

PHILEMATIUM: (*Dismayed*) Oh, must you remind me?

PHILOLACHES: Me remind you? When I'm hoping others will
    insist
On reminding me of it? It's been an awfully long time
Since I made such a handsome investment.

PHILEMATIUM: I'm perfectly sure
I could not have better employed my heart than by falling
In love with you.

PHILOLACHES: Then our books do balance precisely;   380
Expenses against receipts—you really do love me
And I love you and each thinks that's how it should be.

PHILEMATIUM: Now come balance me here on the couch. Slave
    boy, some water
At once, for our hands! And bring us a table. Find the dice.
(*To* PHILOLACHES)
Some perfume?

PHILOLACHES: I've no need of that with Fragrance herself
Breathing sweetly beside me. Oh, look someone's coming
    there:
Isn't that my friend bearing down on us, with his girl?
Yes, it's Callidamates, with his girlfriend to boot:
So here come our comrades-in-arms for a share in the loot.

Scene 4

CALLIDAMATES: (*To* PINACIUM, *slave attendant*) Now boy,
    you call for me on time   390
At Philolaches' house. Get that? Oof!
(*Swings at him but misses*)
There! That'll make you do what you're told, you goof.
That fellow whose house I was at—
What a D-R-I-P drip!
No wonder I gave him the slip.

And the conversation? Even drippier.
So, I thought I'd skip over here
Where I'm sure to be so much hippier.
I mean happier, I mean Philolaches
He's a tickler, he's no stickler . . .   400
Say Delphium, old Sybil syllable
Do I sound pickled? I mean Philolaches
He's as jolly as he's . . . *hic* . . . *haec* . . . *hoc.*
That's an old Greek joke; put it in your tripod and smoke it
With laurel sauce on it. He's no drip; he's free as a faucet!

DELPHIUM: Steady, old chap. We ought to be heading *that* way.

(*Steers him around toward* PHILOLACHES' *house*)

CALLIDAMATES: Les pray on each other, whadda ya say?
    You and me, me and you?

(*Embraces her intricately*)

DELPHIUM: Sure thing, heartbeat. I'm your clinging vine.

CALLIDAMATES: You're so charmin' I want go arm in arm
    in arm in cetera   410
    Oh be my guide eight times, octopussy mine.

DELPHIUM: Whoops! You nearly gave me the slip.
    Watch it there! Atten-*shun!*

CALLIDAMATES: (*Hums*) Oh, when the iris of my eye is smiling
    I'm your bosomy boy, honey bee.

(*Weaving and buzzing*)

DELPHIUM: Look out! You'll be stretching out here on the street
    Before we make it to the rather more strategic retreat
    Prepared for us at Philolaches' headquarters. Don't shilly, Calli.

CALLIDAMATES: I can't wait to recline in comfort somewhere.
   Feel like declining and falling right here   420
   By this wall. I'm all in. A sleep.
   Lemme go. Drop right here in a heap.

DELPHIUM: All right. Look out, *below!*

CALLIDAMATES: Oh no you don't; not without what I'm holding
   Here in my hands I'm not folding.
   (*Laces his arms around her*)
   United we falls, divided we stands.

DELPHIUM: If you do fall, you won't unless I go down too.

CALLIDAMATES: Well, some pasherby will pick us both up
    later on.

DELPHIUM: This man is most mashed.

CALLIDAMATES: Whom? M-m-me?
   M-m-mashed, you shaid?

DELPHIUM: There, now. Give me your hand. I don't want you
    smashing   430
   Your head on anything hard.

CALLIDAMATES: There you are.

DELPHIUM: Ready now, all together.

CALLIDAMATES: Say, where'm I headed?

DELPHIUM: You mean you don't know?

CALLIDAMATES: Oh yes, it just came back to me:
   I'm going home to have a drink.

DELPHIUM: No, no. To this house over here.

(*Points to* PHILOLACHES')

CALLIDAMATES: Of coursh, that place. Now I've got it straight.

PHILOLACHES: (*To* PHILEMATIUM) I think I ought to step out and
    greet him, don't you?
    He's my very best friend in the world. I'll be back right away.

PHILEMATIUM: That "right away" has already lasted too long
    for me.

CALLIDAMATES: Hello, there. Anyone at home?

PHILOLACHES: (*Coming forward*) Yes, anyone is.   440

CALLIDAMATES: Hey, Philolaches, Philolaches, old best friend in
    the world!

PHILOLACHES: Gods bless you, boy. Come right in here and
    join us.
    Where have you been?

CALLIDAMATES: Where a man can get mashed first clash.

PHILEMATIUM: Come sit beside us here, Delphium dear.

PHILOLACHES: Do pour old Calli a drink.

CALLIDAMATES: (*Pushes it away*)   No thanks, I feel sort
    of sleep . . .

(*Sinks to the floor and dozes off*)

PHILOLACHES: There's nothing very new or different about his
    condition.

DELPHIUM: What shall I do with him now, Philematium dear?

PHILEMATIUM: Oh you might as well leave him alone.

PHILOLACHES: (*To slave*)   Hey there, boy!
   Come pass the wine around. Delphium first,
   Then us. So we all can satisfy our thirst.   450

ACT II

Scene 1

TRANIO: Jupiter Almighty, his eagle eye fixed on Philolaches,
   The Master's son, and on me, is putting every ounce of effort
   And money he can into annihilating us. Our hopes
   Are gone. No steady place is left for self-confidence
   To take a stand. Salvation Herself couldn't save us
   Even if she wished to. At the harbor I clamped my eyes
   On the mightiest mountain of monstrous misery imaginable.
   The Master is back home from abroad. Anyone here
   Want to make some quick cash? Where are all you tough guys?
   Heroes tattooed with chain gang insignia, or rangers   460
   Ready to assault the enemy ramparts for practically
   Nothing a month? I'll offer a thousand to the first man
   Who volunteers to carry my cross. But on this condition:
   That he climb up there twice and let both arms and legs
   Be nailed to the wood two times. When the second time shows
   That he really means business, he has only to apply
   In person for the money. It'll be ready and waiting for him.
   As it is, I'm not so well off, am I? Shouldn't I
   Be loping off to my own little home at full tilt?

PHILOLACHES: The provender for the festive board! Here's
    Tranio back   470
  From the harbor.

TRANIO: Philolaches!

PHILOLACHES: What's up?

TRANIO: You and I.

PHILOLACHES: You and I what?

TRANIO: We're up, that's what. We're done for.

PHILOLACHES: Why so?

TRANIO: Your father is coming.

PHILOLACHES: What's that I hear?

TRANIO: We've been swept away: your father's coming, I say.

PHILOLACHES: Where is he?

TRANIO: Down at the harbor right now.

PHILOLACHES: Who says so?
  Who saw him?

TRANIO: Well, I say I'm the one who saw him.

PHILOLACHES: Oh me, oh my . . . father. What am I supposed
    to do?

TRANIO: Why ask me? You're supposed to be sitting at table.

PHILOLACHES: Did you see him yourself?

TRANIO: I'll say I saw him myself.

PHILOLACHES: Are you sure?

TRANIO: Sure I'm sure.

PHILOLACHES: I'm done for if that's
  the truth.   480

TRANIO: What good would it do me to lie?

PHILOLACHES: What can I do now?

TRANIO: Have all this stuff removed. Who's that asleep?

PHILOLACHES: Callidamates. Wake him up, Delphium.

DELPHIUM: Callidamates!
  Wake up, Callidamates!

CALLIDAMATES: I'm awake. Hand me a drink.

DELPHIUM: Wake up! Philolaches' father has just come home
  From abroad.

CALLIDAMATES: Goodbye, Father.

PHILOLACHES: It's hello to him,
  And he's fine, thank you. I'm the one you can kiss goodbye
  After I show you inside.

CALLIDAMATES: Show who suicide? At my age?

DELPHIUM: Come on, for heaven's sake, get up! His father's
  coming.

CALLIDAMATES: (To PHILOLACHES) Your father? Coming.
  T-t-t-tell him t-t-t-to   490

G-g-go away ag-g-g-gain. What business does he have coming
  back here?

PHILOLACHES: What will I do? My father's going to come here
    and catch me
  Drunk, the house full of guests and girls. What's the use
  Of digging a well when you're already dying of thirst?
  That's how much chance I see for my own survival
  Now that I'm faced head on with my father's arrival.

TRANIO: Look! He's laid his head down and gone to sleep again.
  Revive him.

PHILOLACHES: Won't you wake up? My father'll be here
  Any moment, I tell you.

CALLIDAMATES: Your father, you say? Well, hand me
  My shoes, I want to get dressed for battle. By God,   500
  I'll run him through, that father.

PHILOLACHES: Yes and ruin us all.

DELPHIUM: Quiet, honey child.

TRANIO: (*To attendants*)   Get your hands on him, you two,
  and hustle
  Him inside, right away.

CALLIDAMATES: (*To attendants*) I gotta go and I'll use you
  For a pot if you don't bring me one.

(*Staggers off with them*)

PHILOLACHES: It's the end of me.

TRANIO: Now cheer up. I've got just the medicine for your fears.

PHILOLACHES: I'm finished and done for.

TRANIO: Shhhhh. I'm thinking of
    a scheme
To crack the case. Is it all right with you if I manage to make
Your father, when he comes, not only not enter the house
But run away as far as he can? Now all of you get inside
And clear away this stuff, but fast.

PHILOLACHES: And where will I be?   510

TRANIO: Where you like it best, right next to her, and to her?

(*Points to* PHILEMATIUM *and* DELPHIUM)

DELPHIUM: Don't you think we ought to get away from here?

TRANIO: No farther
    Than that, Delphium.
    (*Indicates a tiny distance with his thumb and forefinger*)
                        Keep the party going inside the house
Just as if this slight rearrangement had never occurred.

PHILOLACHES: I'm soaking wet with sweat just thinking how hot
    Those cool words of his will turn out to be for me.

TRANIO: Can't you be still and do what I tell you?

PHILOLACHES: Yes, I can.

TRANIO: Now Philematium and Delphium, you go in first please.

DELPHIUM: At your service, sir.

(*They exit*)

TRANIO: I rather wish you were.
    Now, you pay attention to what I want you to do.   520
    First of all, you're to close the house and shut it up tight:
    Don't let a soul make the slightest sound inside, not a whisper.

PHILOLACHES: Right.

TRANIO: As if there wasn't a living thing inside.

PHILOLACHES: Count on me.

TRANIO: When the old man raps on the door, don't answer.

PHILOLACHES: And what else?

TRANIO: Tell them to bring out the front
    door key
  To me here. I'll lock the house up from outside.

PHILOLACHES: To your safekeeping I entrust myself and my
    hopes.

TRANIO: (*Strolling about looking confident*)
  A feather of a difference it makes if a man
  Is in charge of, or in the charge of another,   530
  If he isn't daring at heart.
  Anyone at all, the best or the worst,
  Can easily hatch a plot in a burst
  Of inspiration and get things off to a bad start fast.
  But the mark of a man of genius is seen
  When he steers the complicated mess
  On through its mischievous confusion
  To a calm and innocent conclusion
  And suffers no punishment, not even deep embarrassment.
  And I propose to handle what's at hand,   540
  And has gotten a bit out of hand at present,
  So as to bring our rollicking ship to land:
  Clear weather after the storm is always pleasant.
  I don't want events upsetting our noble band.
  Hey, Sphaerio, how dare you drift out of there?

SPHAERIO: The key, sir.

TRANIO: Oh yes, of course, the key. You're obeying my orders
    Precisely.

SPHAERIO: Himself says please sir, please to ask
    You to frighten his father somehow, so he don't come in
    And catch him.

TRANIO: You tell him this for me, do you hear?
    The old man won't even dare to look at the house: 550
    He'll take to his heels with his head wrapped up in his cloak
    In an absolute panic—that's how I mean to manage it.
    Now give me the key, and get in there and bar the door
    While I lock it outside, here.
                    Now let the old master appear!
    I'll put on a play right now before his eyes
    That will cost him so much he won't have a cent when he dies
    To pay for the funeral games. So let him enjoy
    The festivities while he's alive. I'll dive over here,
    Away from the house and take up my station, so when
    He comes in soon and heads for his home destination   560
    I can make him the comic hero of this situation.

Scene 2

THEOPROPIDES: (*Dryly offering thanks to Neptune in a satisfied
grumble*)
    Neptune, I suppose I owe you a great debt of thanks
    For letting me out of your clutches at least long enough
    To come back home still alive. If ever again
    You hear that I've ventured so much as a foot from the shore,
    You have my permission to do to me then what you tried
    This time. Get thee behind me, thou Saline Tempter!
    And begone henceforth forevermore, starting now.
    Whatever I intended to entrust to your hands, I have.

TRANIO: (*Aside*) Good Lord, Neptune, you've made a ghastly
    mistake,   570
  Letting an opportunity like that slip through your fingers.

THEOPROPIDES: After three years I've finally come home from
    Egypt,
  Eagerly awaited, no doubt, I'll walk in on the household.

TRANIO: (*Aside*) The messenger bringing news of your death
    would enjoy
  A more enthusiastic welcome at the hands of your family.

THEOPROPIDES: What's this? Here's the front door closed in broad
    daylight.
  I'll knock. Hey there! Anyone in? Will you open the door?

TRANIO: (*Coming forward*) Who's that man walking up to the
    front door of our house?

THEOPROPIDES: Oh, here's my slave himself, Tranio.

TRANIO: Theopropides!
  My old master! Ciao! I'm delighted to see you back safe   580
  And sound. You *are* in sound health?

THEOPROPIDES: Why of course. You can see
  I'm fine.

TRANIO: Gee, sir, that's great.

THEOPROPIDES: Listen, what are you,
  Some kind of a nut?

TRANIO: Nut?

THEOPROPIDES: Yes, nut. Strolling
  Around in the street, and not a soul in the house
  Looking after things, no one to open the doors,

No one to answer my knock. I almost knocked a hole
In those darned double doors with my pounding.

TRANIO: You mean, you
    touched them?

THEOPROPIDES: Yes, I touched them and knocked good and hard.

TRANIO: Wow!

THEOPROPIDES: What's wrong?

TRANIO: You did something awful.

THEOPROPIDES: What's this
    "wow-ful" business
  You're giving me?

TRANIO: I can't tell you how horrible the thing is   590
  You've done, Master, how disastrous.

THEOPROPIDES: What horrible thing?

TRANIO: Get away from the house, I beg and beseech you,
    clear off.
  Come over here this way, toward me. You touched those doors?

THEOPROPIDES: How do you think I could knock on the door
    without touching it?

TRANIO: Oh Lord, you've murdered . . .

THEOPROPIDES: Murdered whom?

TRANIO: The members
  of this family.

THEOPROPIDES: For a crack like that may the gods slap your fresh
   face.

TRANIO: (*Musing*) I don't think you can do anything to make up
   for this.

THEOPROPIDES: Why not? Or are you trying to change the
   subject?

TRANIO: Just stay over here, keep well away from the house
   And tell those two gigantic attendants to back off.   600

THEOPROPIDES: All right. Back off, you two gigantic attendants!

TRANIO: (*To slaves*) And don't touch the house. Now touch the
   ground three times over here.

THEOPROPIDES: In the name of the gods will you kindly explain
   what's *going* . . .

TRANIO: On? It's been seven months since any soul planted a foot
   Inside that house, from the day we all moved out.

THEOPROPIDES: Would you explain just why you did that?

TRANIO: Give a look around.
   Is there anyone near who might overhear what we're saying?

THEOPROPIDES: No, the coast is clear.

TRANIO: Take another look.

THEOPROPIDES: No one, continue.

TRANIO: A capital crime was consummated . . .

THEOPROPIDES: I don't understand you.

TRANIO: I say, a hell of a murder was committed a long
    time ago.   610

THEOPROPIDES: A long time ago?

TRANIO: But we just found out about
    it recently.

THEOPROPIDES: What murder? Who did it? Tell me more.

TRANIO: The host in the house
    Killed his guest with his own bare hands. The same guy,
    I'm sure, who sold us the house.

THEOPROPIDES: Murdered him, did he?

TRANIO: And stripped the guest of his gold, and buried the body
    Of the guest himself right here underneath the house.

THEOPROPIDES: What made you begin to suspect it?

TRANIO: I'll explain: you listen.
    Your son had gone out for dinner and come home late
    From the party; we all went to bed and were soon fast asleep.
    Suddenly he let out a bloodcurdling cry of fear.   620

THEOPROPIDES: Who let out? My son?

TRANIO: Quiet, please, Shhhhh.
    Just listen. He said that the dead man had appeared in a
    dream.

THEOPROPIDES: In a dream? Are you sure?

TRANIO: Yes, I am. And listen to this:
    He said that the dead man had spoken to him as follows:

THEOPROPIDES: In a dream? Are you sure?

TRANIO: Look, you wouldn't
    want him walking around
And talking in broad daylight, when the whole live world
    was up,
Would you? A man who was murdered sixty years ago?
At times, Theopropides, you are positively obtusely stupid.

THEOPROPIDES: I'll keep quiet.

TRANIO: So the dead man said to your son
    in his sleep:
"I am a guest in this house from across the sea.   630
My name is Mudd D. Waters. I live in this house.
The dwelling has been duly given and granted to me.
Orcus, the king of the dead, has had to refuse
Me passage across Acheron to the land of the dead
Because I died prematurely. I was foully deceived
When I trusted my host, who killed me here in my bed,
And dug a deep hole underneath the house, and heaved
Me into it when no one was looking. Devoid of burial,
Down in the hole he dumped me, that hell of a host, and he
    stole
All my gold. Now young man, get out of here, and
    carry all   640
Your household possessions along. This house is unholy,
A hell of a place. It's hexed, and you will be next."
Gosh, it'd take me a year to describe the manifestations
This dead man demonstrated: we were almost delirious
At what he said and did, this guest his host
Mysteriously murdered and monstered into a ghost.
(A *muffled noise is heard from inside the house*)
Psst.

THEOPROPIDES: Oh God, what was that?

TRANIO: (*To ghost*)   He was the one
    Who rattled the doors, not me. It was he who knocked!

THEOPROPIDES: I'm drained. I haven't a drop of blood in my
    veins.
  The dead are coming to take me to Acheron alive.   650

TRANIO: (*Aside*) I'm done for. Those creeps inside the house will
    wreck the plot
  Of my play right now. And I just made it up. I'm panicked.
  For fear he'll catch me in the act with my plans down.

THEOPROPIDES: Why are you talking to yourself?

TRANIO: Back away from the door.
  Take to your heels, in Hercules' name.

THEOPROPIDES: Where to?
  Hadn't you better get going too?

TRANIO: Ohhhhh no, not me,
  I've nothing to fear. I've made my peace with the dead.

(*Muffled call from within*—Choo-choo! Tranio!)

TRANIO: Don't call me, I'll call you.
  I didn't do it! I didn't pound on the doors.

THEOPROPIDES: Say . . .

TRANIO: Shhhh . . . not so loud.

THEOPROPIDES: Why do you keep on
  Breaking off our conversation?

TRANIO: Thou senile Tempter! Get thee behind me!

THEOPROPIDES: What's got
    hold of you,   660
  Tranio, anyway? Whom are you mumbling that stuff to?

TRANIO: Oh?
    (*Much relieved*)
                Was it you that called? As the gods love me,
    I thought it was old dead and downcast bawling me out
    In a flap because you pounded the door of his flophouse.
    (*Laughs weakly*)
    But you're still standing there? Not following instructions?

THEOPROPIDES: What should I do?

TRANIO: Be careful not to look back,
    And run away, with your neck covered up in your cloak.

THEOPROPIDES: Why don't you run away?

TRANIO: I've made my peace
    With the dead.

THEOPROPIDES: I heard you the first time you said that. But what
    I don't get at the moment is why you acted so scared.   670

TRANIO: Don't bother your head about me, I can take good care
    Of myself. But go on as you started, take to your heels
    As fast as you can. And pray to Hercules for help.

THEOPROPIDES: Hercules! This is no joke! Your help I hereby
    invoke.

TRANIO: Me too, Hercules! Grant me with all your might
    (*Exit* THEOPROPIDES)
    The power to make this old man a prey to stage fright.
    And in the name of the immortal gods, I think I can say,
    I've cooked up a pot of terrible trouble today!

ACT III

Scene 1

MISARGYRIDES: (*Soliloquizing*) I've never seen a worse year than
  this one for lending out money.
  I work the forum from dawn to dark, but I can't   680
  Seem to interest a soul in borrowing a bit of cash.

TRANIO: (*Aside*) Well, this is it, pure and simple from now on
    perdition.
  Here's the moneylender who loaned us the cash at interest
  We bought the girl and staged our parties by means of.
  We're caught in the act if I can't come up with a plan
  To keep the old man from knowing. I'll intercept him.
  But here's Theopropides back home again too soon.
  I'm afraid he's heard something more than I saw fit to tell him.
  I'll go up and intercept *him*. Oh, what a rogue
  And peasant slave am I! And scared to death.   690
  There's no worse ill the flesh is heir to than conscience,
  Especially a guilty conscience. And I've got a beaut!
  But however it all turns out, I plan to proceed
  To continue to confuse things as chaotically as I can:
  That looks like what they demand.
  (*To* THEOPROPIDES)
  Where have you been?

THEOPROPIDES: Oh, I met the man I bought this house from

TRANIO: And told him—
  Of course, about what I had said to you?

THEOPROPIDES: Every word.

TRANIO: (*Aside*) I'm out of luck now, Poor Io! My beautiful schemes
    Are scheduled for the scrapheap one by one, I have the feeling.

THEOPROPIDES: What's that you're saying to yourself?

TRANIO: Who? Me?
    Oh, nothing.   700

THEOPROPIDES: Well, I told the whole story just as you unrolled
    it to me.

TRANIO: And he confessed to the ghost of the guest?

THEOPROPIDES: Denied it completely.

TRANIO: He did?

THEOPROPIDES: He most certainly did.

TRANIO: Now, just think back a bit:
    He did *not* admit it, you say?

THEOPROPIDES: I'd admit it, if he did.
    What do you think I should do?

TRANIO: I? Think? Do?
    Sue him. And insist on an honest judge, a good man
    Who will trust my testimony. That way, you'll win the case
    As easily and neatly as a fox can pilfer a pear.

MISARGYRIDES: Ah, Philolaches' man, Tranio. And they haven't paid a thing
    On their loan, either principal or interest.   710

THEOPROPIDES: (*As* TRANIO *starts off*)
    Where are you going?

TRANIO: Me? Oh, nowhere. I was just practicing.
(*Aside*)

How negative
Can you get? The gods must have frowned the day I was born.
That moneylender will soon be right here, talking to the
   master.
I'm so *measly!* They'll give me the business both ways.
I'll try and intercept him.

MISARGYRIDES: Ah, he's heading my way.
I'm in luck. There's a slight whiff of cash in the air.

TRANIO: He's in a good mood. Wait till he comes to his senses.
Ah, greetings, Silverdespiser. I *trust* you are well.

MISARGYRIDES: Greetings! Can you make a payment?

TRANIO: Get off it,
   you beast.   720
You walk up and start right in hitting me over the head.

MISARGYRIDES: You empty-handed, empty-headed fool.

TRANIO: And you're a
   mind reader?
No doubt. Or is it a pickpocket?

MISARGYRIDES: Why not relax
From the funny business somewhat?

TRANIO: Some what is it you want?

MISARGYRIDES: Where's Philolaches?

TRANIO: Say, you couldn't have come
At a better time than you did.

MISARGYRIDES: Oh, really?

TRANIO: *(Motions him aside)*   Rally over here.

MISARGYRIDES: *(In a loud voice)* How about the interest payment
    that's coming to me?

TRANIO: I know you've got a good voice; you don't have to shout.

MISARGYRIDES: I'll clamor like a commercial.

TRANIO: Oh come on, be nice!

MISARGYRIDES: How can I be nice to you?

TRANIO: Go on back home.   730

MISARGYRIDES: Leave now?

TRANIO: Come back around noon.

MISARGYRIDES: And the interest
    That's coming to me?

TRANIO: It'll be ready then. Now go.

MISARGYRIDES: Why should I wear myself out and waste time
    going home
And coming back again? I'll just hang around until noon.

TRANIO: No, go on home. Look, I mean it, kid. Scoot on home.

MISARGYRIDES: I don't want to until my interest . . .

TRANIO: Get under way,
    Slowpoke.

MISARGYRIDES: Why don't you pay me my interest? This negative
    Kick is making me sick.

TRANIO: That's nothing to the way
  You nauseate me. Listen, run along home.

MISARGYRIDES: Just for that I'll call your master,
    Philola . . .   740

TRANIO: (*Interrupting*) Good voice there. Feel better, now that
    you're shouting?

MISARGYRIDES: I'm only asking for what is mine. You've been
    putting
  Me off for days. If I'm a bother to you,
  Hand over the cash. I'll go. And you can be rid
  Of all these question and answers by redeeming one word.

TRANIO: What word's that?

MISARGYRIDES: Pay up.

TRANIO: That's two words at least.

MISARGYRIDES: Well, it's one thing, like principal and interest.
    Pay up what's due.

TRANIO: Say, how about if we pay the principal?

MISARGYRIDES: (*Loudly*)   *No no, I'm due*
    the interest first!

TRANIO: Did you come here to practice your scales,
  You bull-throated auctioneer? Stop moaning for your
    your money,   750
  You materialist. Make all the musical fuss you must,
  You still won't get a sniff of your note from my master.
  He doesn't owe you a dime.

MISARGYRIDES: Doesn't owe . . . ?

TRANIO: Not one bit
  Richer will you leave this place. You won't get a *frit*.

MISARGYRIDES: What's a *frit?*

TRANIO: The unformed granule at the top of
  an ear of wheat.

MISARGYRIDES: Thanks very much.

TRANIO: Well, I mean it's the principle
  of the thing.
  You refuse payment of the principal. And you think my master
  Will sneak out of town into exile because of the interest
  Due to a banker who's unwilling to accept the principal?

MISARGYRIDES: I don't want the whole sum paid, necessarily,
  now.   760
  What I do want is the interest that's due on the whole amount.

TRANIO: Don't be a pain. No one's going to give it to you,
  Whatever you do. You're not the only man in town
  Who loans money out at interest.

MISARGYRIDES: Give me my interest,
  Pay back that interest, hand over the interest, you two.
  Will you both be so kind as to pay back my interest at once?
  Will the interest now be paid to me?

TRANIO: Interest here,
  Interest there, interest everywhere.
  An interesting subject to our speaker, apparently; it's all
  He's interested in discussing. Personally, I find it
    disgusting.   770
  Get thee behind me, thou loud percentage of a beast.
  You're rude and unattractive.

MISARGYRIDES: Sticks and stones
  May bruise my bones, but tones can't touch my loans.

THEOPROPIDES: Things are getting warm. I can feel the heat
  Even way over here. Now what can the interest be,
  I wonder, the fellow's after with such a vengeance?

TRANIO: All right, here's Philolaches' father just back from abroad.
  He landed today. He'll pay off the interest and principal
  Both, so you don't try to take us for more. You'll see
  If he keeps you waiting.

MISARGYRIDES: I suppose I should take what I can get.   780

THEOPROPIDES: What's going on?

TRANIO: I beg your pardon?

THEOPROPIDES: Who is that,
  And what is he after? Why is he shouting the name
  Of my son and starting this brawl with you? Do you owe
  Him some money?

TRANIO: Ah, splash the cash in his face, the fish—
  Shove it down the filthy shark's throat. That's an order.

THEOPROPIDES: That's a what?

TRANIO: No, it is not a what, it's an order,
      for money.
  Plaster the fish in the face with a fist full of cash.

MISARGYRIDES: A wonderful way to go.

TRANIO: You heard that didn't you?
  A typical moneylender: no sense of shame.

THEOPROPIDES: I don't care about the man's professional
    status   790
Or what names you call him. I want to be told, and by you,
What this cash debt is that Philolaches owes.

TRANIO: Oh, a trifle.

THEOPROPIDES: How big a trifle?

TRANIO: One thousand bucks.
   You don't mean to say you think that's a big amount?

THEOPROPIDES: What's your definition of a trifle?

TRANIO: A lot less than a lot.

THEOPROPIDES: Thanks very much. Now, I seem to have heard
    that credit
Has also been advanced in the amount of the interest.

TRANIO: Well, that's forty *minae* [*pronounced miney*] plus four.
    Eeeny, meeny, miney
And one mo', well, let's see that's about 1,100 chunks,
More or less, the principal and the interest.

MISARGYRIDES: That's right.   800
   That's the sum of it. That's all I'm after.

TRANIO: I dare you
   To ask for a half-as more. We could sue and you know it.
Tell him you'll pay it, so he'll go away.

THEOPROPIDES: Tell him
   I'll *pay* it? I never carry more than two and a half asses
In cash.

TRANIO: Yes, you tell him you'll pay it.

THEOPROPIDES: *I'll* pay it?

TRANIO: Yes, your very own sweet little self. Now just tell him.
    Listen to me. Promise him you'll pay, go on now,
    That's an order.

THEOPROPIDES: Oh I get it, a money order. Answer me this.
    What have you done with the money you borrowed?

TRANIO: It's safe,
    perfectly safe. An investment.

THEOPROPIDES: If the money's intact,   810
    You people can pay back the loan.

TRANIO: Your son bought a house.

THEOPROPIDES: A house?

TRANIO: A house.

THEOPROPIDES: Well, good for Philolaches!
    Looks like he's filial; taking after his father, becoming
    A good businessman.

TRANIO: When this house turned out to be haunted,
    As I told you, he went out and bought another at a bargain.

THEOPROPIDES: Bought a house, did he?

TRANIO: A house. And you can imagine
    What a property, too!

THEOPROPIDES: I don't quite see how I can.

TRANIO: Wow, what a place!

THEOPROPIDES: What kind of a place?

TRANIO: Don't ask.

THEOPROPIDES: Why not?

TRANIO: A phenomenal buy. A marvelous place!

THEOPROPIDES: Sounds like a good deal. How much did
        it cost?   820

TRANIO: Two talents: Me plus you, three thousand bills.
        But he paid down the forty miney, or one thousand bills.
        Do I make myself clear?

THEOPROPIDES: Sounds like a very good deal.

MISARGYRIDES: Gentlemen, it's noon.

(*Flourishing his hourglass*)

TRANIO: Pay the guy, to stop his puking.

THEOPROPIDES: Just apply to me for the miney, I mean money.

MISARGYRIDES: You?

THEOPROPIDES: Come see me tomorrow.

MISARGYRIDES: I'll go, and suffer no sorrow
        If I'm going to get it tomorrow.

(*He exits*)

TRANIO: Procrastinator!
        May all the gods (and goddesses too, while I'm at it)
        Do him in promptly for his "Borrow today, pay later."
        There's no more repulsive a race of men than these
        bankers,   830

Always hankering to get back their money. They're
    unreasonable.

THEOPROPIDES: Where is the house located, the one my son
    bought?

TRANIO: (*Aside*) Here I go down for the fourth time.

THEOPROPIDES: Will you answer
    my query?

TRANIO: Yes, that's some query. I'm trying to think of the name
    Of the owner.

THEOPROPIDES: Well, think . . . or thwim.

TRANIO: (*Aside*)   Going down for the fifth.
    I can't think. Oh, buoy! I've come up with it! Next-door
        neighbor!
    Why not call that the house his son has acquired?
    They say the lie you have just cooked up and serve
    While still piping hot, is the best. What *has* to be said
    It is perfectly proper to say.

THEOPROPIDES: How about it? Remember?   840

TRANIO: Damn the man! I mean *that* one.
    (*To audience, pointing to* THEOPROPIDES)
                                        Our next-door neighbor
    It was whose house your son acquired.

THEOPROPIDES: A good buy?

TRANIO: If you make the loan good, a very good buy, if you won't
    It's goodbye to us. You'll admit the *location* [*French
        pronunciation*] is good.

THEOPROPIDES: À *merveille!* I'd love to go have a look.
   Rap on the door and call someone out, Tranio.

TRANIO: (*Aside*) I'm in for some hard knocks. I'm dashed if I know
   What to say at this point. The waves are washing me back
   All over again, and dashing me on the same rocks.

THEOPROPIDES: What's holding you up?

TRANIO: (*Aside*)   You are, you pirate.
   I'm stranded.   850
   I can't figure out what to do. I'm caught barehanded.

THEOPROPIDES: Go ask at the door for someone to show us
      around.
   Come on, get a move on.

TRANIO: Don't you know there are ladies
      present?
   We'll have to inquire if they're willing, or not so willing.

THEOPROPIDES: Well, that's a sound suggestion. Go over and
      request it.
   I'll wait outside right here while you go in.

TRANIO: (*Aside*) May all the gods (and goddesses too, while I'm
      at it)
   Do you in for once and for all, old *chap,* from now on.
   Your resistance meets my attacks at every turn.
   Hoo-oo-l-y Smoke! Just in the nic-o-tine!   860
   The owner of the house is coming out: yes, it's Simo,
   And he's going for a stroll. I wonder, will the stroll get away?
   I'll duck over here for a moment and plan what to say:
   I'll summon the senate of my mind to congress today
   And then prime Simo in the part I want him to play!

Scene 2

SIMO: (*Soliloquizing*) I haven't had so good a time all year
  At home, or a meal that pleased me more.
  My wife prepared a banquet here,
  And she's hauling me off to bed. I swore
  I'd go, but oh *no*, you don't. Enough is enough!   870
  I knew there was some ulterior motive
  In setting that marvelous meal before me:
  She wanted to lure me to bed like a votive
  Lamb to the slaughter in the sheets. I tore free.
  Anyone knows it's bad for the health
  To go to bed after eating. Myself,
  I refuse, Get thee behind me, old girl of the ruffled fluff!
  So I sneaked out the door, and the coast is clear.
  Inside the house my old woman is fully aroused,
  With fury at me, I fear. Let the fur fly, you overused stuff.   880

TRANIO: (*Aside*) But there's something unpleasant in store for the
    old rod tonight.
  Neither dinner nor bed will deliver him much delight.

SIMO: (*Continues the* canticum)
  The more I ponder the problem
  The fonder I become of my conclusion:
  You marry an older woman for her money,
  You *don't* have a lot of sleep breathing down your neck.
  Funny: Husbands with rich old wives do not adore them.
  Rather than curl up in bed they head for the forum
  Where the non-uxorious form a formidable quorum.
  Of course I don't know how the wives of you husbands out
    there   890
  Behave, but considering how mine always raises the roof
  With me, I'm in bad enough. After this I'll be even worse off!

TRANIO: Well, old fellow, if your getaway gets you in trouble
  At least there won't be one of the gods to blame.

You can only in all due fairness indict yourself.
Now it's time I went up and had a few words with my victim.
He's had it! I've thought of how to deceive the master:
A masterstroke, in brief, that will keep my grief at bay.
I'll approach the man now. May the gods shine on you, Simo.

SIMO: Good health, Tranio.

TRANIO: You're fine?

SIMO: Not bad.   900
    What's on?

TRANIO: I'm on, to you, taking the hand
    Of the finest of fellows.

SIMO: Well, aren't we the friendliest?
    Handing out compliments!

TRANIO: It's only gladhanding a man
    Who deserves it.

SIMO: But I'm not holding a worthwhile slave
    By the hand, Herc knows.

TRANIO: Who's Herc?

THEOPROPIDES: (*From across stage*)   You jerk,
    Snap back to me!

TRANIO: (*Yells*) I'll whip right over.

SIMO: I say,
    Now, how much longer . . .

TRANIO: What's that you say you say?

SIMO: Do you think you can keep on like this?

TRANIO: What's that you say
  You say?

SIMO: You know quite well what I'm talking about.
  Life is short and you're succeeding in making it sweet.   910

TRANIO: What's that? Oh, yes . . . Er . . . I really wasn't aware
  You were discussing us particularly.

SIMO: It's got some *style,*
  The way you map your menus like a gourmet
  And choose choice wines and snare your seafood fresh
  At the fanciest prices. Ah, that's the life to be living!

TRANIO: That is the life we used to be living till now.
  At this point our pleasures have positively petered out and
    pancaked.

SIMO: Ah, soooo?

(*Rising inflection*)

TRANIO: We're torn down, Simo, down to the ground.

SIMO: Nonsense, boy! Everything has gone just right
  For you both so far.

TRANIO: I won't deny those words.   920
  We've lived the way we wanted and lapped up the luxury.
  But, Simo, now the wind has dropped and left
  Our ship becalmed.

SIMO: Ah, sooooo? How so?

TRANIO: Well, no so so-so. It couldn't be worse.

SIMO: But the ship
  Was safe, high and dry on land.

TRANIO: Don't remind me of landings!

SIMO: Why not?

TRANIO: Someone landed, all right, and landed on us.

SIMO: Ah, sooooo?

TRANIO: (*Prose interruption*) Look, cut out that "ah, sooo"
    stuff will
  You? This is supposed to be a *Roman* comedy.
  Some ship, a master vessel, could be,
  Could it not? crashed into and crushed our yacht.   930

SIMO: I sympathize with you, my boy. What happened exactly?

TRANIO: I'll tell you: the master came home today from abroad.

SIMO: From abroad? He did? Well the old past master! I predict:
  One: Your hide is in for a good bit of stretching;
  Two: The chain gang will see that you're all right for ironing;
  Three: You'll be crucified, later.

TRANIO: Sway now, die later!
  Procrastinator! Look, Simo, you won't tell on us?

SIMO: He won't learn a thing from me, don't you worry your
  head.

TRANIO: Oh, newfound patron, your client salutes you!

SIMO: Client?
  I can't use a client like you.

TRANIO: About the business   940
  My master sent me to see you about . . .

SIMO: Tell me first,
How much does he know of the way you've been carrying on?

TRANIO: Not a *frit*.

SIMO: Not a what? He isn't one whit annoyed
With his son?

TRANIO: Oh no, the weather is clear, as sunny
And fine as weather can be. Halcyon days,
When the kingfisher plans for his fledglings on calm waves.
Now my master urgently asks that he be allowed
To come and look at your house.

SIMO: It isn't for sale.

TRANIO: I know that. But my old man wants to build an addition
To his own place, quarters for women, with baths,   950
A cloister, and walk.

SIMO: So? What is he dreaming of?

TRANIO: I can tell you. He wants his son to marry a wife
As soon as it can be arranged. And that's the reason
He wants a new women's wing. Some architect told him,
He says, that your house was a gem of model construction.
So he now wants to use your place as a model for his,
And particularly wants the advantages of your design
For trapping the maximum shade—yours is superb,
Or so we've heard—no matter how bright the day.

SIMO: By God, I can tell you, when there's a good shade
        everywhere else   960
The sun is hitting my house from dawn to dusk
Like a salesman at the front door. There's never any shade
Anywhere on my place, except in the shaft of the well.

TRANIO: If you haven't got some colored shade to serve as
    umbrella,
  Perhaps you've got a nice light *jade,* a kind of high yellow?

SIMO: Oh, very funny: but that's how it is.

TRANIO: All the same,
  He wants to look around.

SIMO: Let him look around,
  If he likes. If he likes what he sees, he can build
  Himself something on those lines.

TRANIO: Shall I go call him, then?

SIMO: Go call him, you're vocal enough!

TRANIO: (*Monologue as he crosses the stage*)
  Vocal? I'm a local Leonardo!   970
  And proudly lay claim to my fame! Single-handed, I frame
  These fiendish designs that will live on to future times
  And make me remembered as one who, like Alexander,
  Was Great, or like Agathocles, the noble but late
  King of Sicily. These two old men I have busily
  Saddled with bags, my bundle of tricks. Each one
  Is now carrying out his share of my plan. What fun
  To get them to work for me! And I think I've found
  A new source of income, too. Mule drivers pound
  Their mules along the road loaded down with freight,   980
  But I have men to shoulder and move the weight
  Of my bundles of tricks. And as if it were their fate,
  Men are strong and patient and capable of carrying on,
  No matter how much or how long they're imposed upon!
  (*Beat*)
  I'm not quite sure whether to . . . yes, I'll go
  And speak to him.
  (*Clears his throat*)
                  Ahem! Theopropides!

THEOPROPIDES: (*Clears his throat*) Harumph! Who's that calling
   me by name?

TRANIO: A slave who serves his master in the most amazing
   Manner.

THEOPROPIDES: Ah, so? Where in the hell have you been?

TRANIO: Where you sent me. I beg to report, sir: mission
   accomplished.   990

THEOPROPIDES: Does it take all day to tender a simple request?

TRANIO: The old man wasn't free, so I waited around.

THEOPROPIDES: Up to your same old tricks. Taking an olive break,
   I bet.

TRANIO: Now listen, sir, take this saying to heart:
   "You can't blow on your soup and slurp it simultaneously."
   That's from Euripides' fragments, Theopropides.
   I couldn't be there and here at the same time, could I?

THEOPROPIDES: And what now?

TRANIO: Come and look, just as much as
   you wish.

THEOPROPIDES: All right, escort me.

TRANIO: Shall I follow you over?

THEOPROPIDES: No, I'll follow you.

TRANIO: Ah, here's the owner himself.   1000
   Waiting in front of the door for you, downcast
   Because he's sold the house.

THEOPROPIDES: What's that to me?

TRANIO: He's asked me to ask Philolaches, please
  To sell it back to him.

THEOPROPIDES: I should *say* not.
  Every man must mow his own field. If we'd bought the house
  At an unfair price we'd have no right to return it.
  Money in hand is better than beating around the bush.
  The quality of mercy should not be strained
  To apply to money matters.

TRANIO: Stop dragging your feet,
  And dragging in those famous quotations. Keep up
    with me.   1010

THEOPROPIDES: Coming, slave, coming.

TRANIO: (*To* THEOPROPIDES)   Here he is.
  (*To* SIMO)
  Ahem! I present my master, Simo.

SIMO: Theopropides!
  Welcome home from so long a time overseas.
  How are you?

THEOPROPIDES: Fine, thanks, how are you?

SIMO: He says
  You'd like to look around my domicile.

THEOPROPIDES: If it's not too much trouble.

SIMO: No trouble at all. Enter!
  Look around!

THEOPROPIDES: But the ladies . . .

SIMO: The hell with the ladies,
   God bless 'em! No woman's worth her weight in feathers.
   Just walk around, as if you owned the place.

THEOPROPIDES: "As if"?

TRANIO: Now don't rub it in. Can't you see
      how sick   1020
   He feels about your buying the place? It's written
   All over his face.

THEOPROPIDES: I can read it.

TRANIO: So don't make a show
   Of being content with the bargain, or terribly cheerful.

THEOPROPIDES: I quite understand. I think the point's well taken
   And shows a considerate and truly human nature
   On your part, my lad.
   (*To* SIMO)
                              And now?

SIMO: Why not walk in
   And look around at your leisure? Make yourself at home.

THEOPROPIDES: Thanks so much. You're being terribly kind.

SIMO: I want you to do as you wish.

TRANIO: See the front entrance   1030
   Here, and the walk it affords along the gallery;
   Isn't that lovely?

THEOPROPIDES: Absolutely, a marvelous feature.

TRANIO: (*Pointing slyly at* THEOPROPIDES *and* SIMO)
                                    And cast your eyes

Over these two great big uprights—
Aren't they terrifically thick, and dense, and wooden?

THEOPROPIDES: I've never laid eyes on such beautiful blocks of
    timber.

SIMO: And they cost me a pretty price, by God, originally.

TRANIO: Did you hear that "originally"? He can hardly contain
    His tears.

THEOPROPIDES: How much, originally?

SIMO: Seventy-four dollars
    And fifteen cents, f.o.b., for the pair.

THEOPROPIDES: I'll be darned
    If they don't look a lot more faulty than I felt at first.   1040

TRANIO: Really, how so?

THEOPROPIDES: Termites. They've been bored into
    Darned deep.

TRANIO: Cut down out of season, no doubt,
    With worms still in them. But that's all that's wrong with them.
    They'll be perfectly good if they're coated all over with pitch.
    No oatmeal-eating Roman crucifix carpenter
    Put this house together. Look at those two blockheads
    At the door joints? You see they're fast asleep?

THEOPROPIDES: You mean, they're sleepers?

TRANIO: Yes, the way they
    stick together:
    Impenetrable, nothing could ever get through them.

THEOPROPIDES: The more I see, the better I like the place.   1050

TRANIO: And oh, look at that! It's a mural showing a crow
    Tearing two vultures apart.

THEOPROPIDES: Afraid I don't see it.

TRANIO: But I do. The crow is standing behind two old buzzards
    And nipping his beak in one, ducking back and doing
    The same to the other.

THEOPROPIDES: Sounds like a pretty fast picture.

TRANIO: Look in my direction: perhaps you can pick out the
    crow?

THEOPROPIDES: I can't see a sign of a thing that looks like a crow.

TRANIO: Train your eyes in the direction of yourself and Simo;
    If you can't spot the crow, perhaps you can see the vultures.

THEOPROPIDES: Oh never mind the art lesson now. I can't
    see a thing   1060
    That looks like a painted bird anywhere around.

TRANIO: Oh all right. Skip it. I can't blame you, at your age,
    If your eyes are not up to scratch.

THEOPROPIDES: Well, what I do see
    Certainly pleases me very much, I must say.

SIMO: But you haven't seen half of it yet, just wait for the rest.

THEOPROPIDES: Yes of course how true.

SIMO: Ho, houseboy! Here!
    Conduct this gentleman around the house: let him see
    All the rooms, I'd take you in myself, and around,
    But I'm expected down at the forum on a matter on business.

THEOPROPIDES: (*Good-humoredly*) Oh, that doesn't matter. But I
    don't want to be *taken in*.   1070
  Get this leader behind me! I don't need conductors
  To tell me where to get off. Misleading advice
  Won't help. I prefer to go astray by myself.

SIMO: I meant, take you into the house.

THEOPROPIDES: I'll just walk on in,
  And do without the conductor.

SIMO: Of course, as you wish.

THEOPROPIDES: So here I go.

TRANIO: Wait just a minute! I want to see
  If a watchdog . . .

THEOPROPIDES: Take a quick look.

TRANIO: Sssst! Woof!
  Get going, you mutt: Go find the nearest tree.
  Come on, lope! Still lying there, you son of a dogma?
  Make tracks! Follow your nose!

SIMO: She's not dangerous.   1080
  You can walk right up and she won't do a thing but lie there
  Like any other pregnant bitch. Just go on in
  And march right past her. I must be off to the forum.

THEOPROPIDES: Have a nice walk downtown. You've been very
    kind.
  (*Exit* SIMO)
  Tranio, make someone take that hound away
  Even if she isn't dangerous.

TRANIO: Can't you see
  How peacefully she's laying there? What's wrong
  With you? Are you nervous?

THEOPROPIDES: All right, all right, all right!
  Follow me in here, will you?

TRANIO: Will I? I'll dog
  Your tracks, unshakable off. That's a fact.   1090
  I wouldn't want anyone getting into my act.

ACT IV

Scene 1

PHANISCUS: Slaves who are easily cowed,
    Even when not to blame,
    Are useful to the master.
    But those who are saucy and proud
    Cause trouble, and then proclaim
    Innocence in the teeth of disaster.
    They get good exercise
    By running away, but caught,
    They pay a heavy price   1100
    For the mischief they have wrought.
  They ought not to act this way.
    When they follow their own advice
    Instead of fearing the worst,
    They get chased and then chastised.
    Had they been timid first,
  They'd burst before acting that way.
    I've long since come to prefer
  Keeping my skin intact, unbeaten, unbruised.
    And by making my body defer   1110

To my wishes I have a roof of sorts, to be used
    To protect me from the rain
When troubles descend on all the rest of the crew.
    The master, I maintain,
Reacts in the way his servants most want him to:
    If they're good, he behaves,
If they act wicked, he turns into a fiend.
    Now at our place all the slaves
Are the worst kind of rascals and wastrels born to be beaned.
    They're lazy, inclined to say "No!"   1120
When told to meet the master. "I can't be bothered,"
    They chant, "I just *Won't Go!*
New fields to conquer, eh? Something further to be fathered
    In greener pastures, eh, master mule?
I'm staying right here. You go ahead and roam!"
    So I left them there—after all, I'm no fool—
And came on the errand to escort my master home.
In that whole bunch of slaves, there's only me
With enough get-up-and-go to meet him here.
Tomorrow when the master comes to see   1130
What's happened, they'll be whipped with cowhide gear.
In short, I value my back more than theirs.
They can do wholesale business in cowhides, who cares?
I'd rather see all the leather used up on their rears
Than do any business myself in whips and tears.

(*Enter* PINACIUM)

PINACIUM: Wait, up, Phaniscus! Hey, you with the whiskers!
    Can't you hold it a minute?

PHANISCUS: Don't be a pain
    In the neck, you inner limit.

PINACIUM: Well, watch Phaniscus
    Whisk us away, with a sweep of his tail, oh joy!
    Hold it! Wait for me, parasite boy!   1140

PHANISCUS: Parasite am I?

PINACIUM: That's right, dusty: anyone
  Can lead you around as long as it ends in dinner.

PHANISCUS: It's my own business if I happen to like to eat.
  What difference does it make to you?

PINACIUM: Oh, aren't we *tough!*
  And Master simply dotes on us.

PHANISCUS: If dotes
  Is all he does on me that's not too bad.
  Ow! My eyes are watering!

PINACIUM: Oh, does the eyes
  Hurt the poor little fellow, does they smart?
  I wonder why?

PHANISCUS: The general effect of gas
  Created when you're in range.

PINACIUM: Your jokes are as current   1150
  As counterfeit money.

PHANISCUS: Well, stupid, I refuse
  To stoop to your level of insult, and besides, I enjoy
  The master's confidence.

PINACIUM: Aren't we just making our bed
  And aren't we just lying in it?

PHANISCUS: If only you weren't
  So gassed you wouldn't be so crude and rude in your thoughts.

PINACIUM: Why should I play up to you when you won't play up
  to me?

PHANISCUS: Oh, come on with me, you pessimist, go in and call
   Callidamates and tell him we're here.
   And for God's sake, lay off the disgusting talk.

PINACIUM: All right, I'll go right up and pound on the door.   1160
   Hey there! Anyone at home in there to protect these doors
   From assault and battery? Somebody, open the door!
   Well, not a soul who dares to venture outdoors;
   Understandably, since they're all out cold
   Inside: but all the more reason not to be too bold:
   Someone of these grumpy grouches might slouch out
   With a hangover and clout me right on the snout.

Scene 2

TRANIO: Look like a good buy to you?

THEOPROPIDES: I'm utterly delighted!

TRANIO: You don't think it's too expensive?

THEOPROPIDES: If I've ever seen a house
   Thrown away, it's this one.

TRANIO: And so, you do like it?

THEOPROPIDES: Like it?   1170
   I love it.

TRANIO: How about the women's quarters, and cloister,
   That colonnade, I mean?

THEOPROPIDES: T-rific, it's larger
   Than any portico you'll find anywhere in the street.

TRANIO: As a matter of fact, we compared the dimensions with those
    Of all the others in town, Philolaches and I.

THEOPROPIDES: How did they stack up?

TRANIO: Ours is longer by a long shot.

THEOPROPIDES: What a heavenly buy! If someone offered me cash
    And three times as much, I'd never part with the place.

TRANIO: And if you wanted to sell, I wouldn't let you.

THEOPROPIDES: Our money is well invested in a house like this   1180
    At a price like that.

TRANIO: And thanks to me, for *insisting*,
    And urging your son on to drive a good hard bargain—
    I forced him to borrow the cash we needed at interest
    To make the downpayment.

THEOPROPIDES: Then you certainly saved the ship.
    And we now owe eighty *minae?* Two thousand more?

TRANIO: And *no*
    change.

THEOPROPIDES: He shall have it today.

TRANIO: A good idea. That way,
    The lender won't have any cause to sue.
    Or, I tell you, count the money out now, to me:
    I'll count it out and pay it over to him.

THEOPROPIDES: I'm not completely convinced there
    wouldn't be a catch   1190
  Somewhere along the line if I paid you.

TRANIO: Have I ever, in word or deed, been false to you,
  Even as a kind of practical joke?

THEOPROPIDES: Have I ever
  Dropped my guard long enough to trust you an inch?

TRANIO: That's because after I became your slave, I never
  Gave you a bit of trouble.

THEOPROPIDES: Because I took care
  To see that you couldn't.

TRANIO: For that you have me to thank,
  And my good character.

THEOPROPIDES: Don't drag in some character:
  It's all I can do to keep a sharp eye out for you.

TRANIO: I'm with you there.

THEOPROPIDES: Now, off to the country with you.   1200
  And tell my son I've arrived.

TRANIO: Just as you say, sir.

THEOPROPIDES: Tell him to come right back into town with you.

TRANIO: Yes, sir!
  (*Aside*)
          I'll go around back and call a meeting
  Of my colleagues, reporting this situation all quiet,
  Then bring the son to this destination. Isn't this a riot?

(*Exit* TRANIO)

PHANISCUS: Strange! I don't hear the usual sounds emanating
From the party in progress, the girl on flute,
Or anyone else, doing anything at all, in fact.

THEOPROPIDES: What in the world's going on? Why are
those men
Hanging around my door? What can they want?   1210
Why are they looking in?

PINACIUM: I'll try pounding.
Hey, unlock the place! Hey, Tranio! Open up!

THEOPROPIDES: What kind of a comedy is this?

PINACIUM: Hey, you
In there! Come and open up! We're here
To pick up our master Callidamates.

THEOPROPIDES: Hey, you boys! What do you think you're doing?
Why are you battering down that building, tell me!

PHANISCUS: Hey yourself, pop! Why are you prying into
Something that has nothing to do with you?

THEOPROPIDES: Nothing to do with me?

PHANISCUS: Oh, perhaps you're
the mayor   1220
Just been elected to office, prowling around
Prying into other people's business, asking them questions,
Eavesdropping.

THEOPROPIDES: It's not other people's business
That house isn't, it's mine.

PHANISCUS: Oh really? Philolaches
Sold it, did he? Or pop's making fun of us.

THEOPROPIDES: I'm telling you the truth—but what about you?
   What's your business here?

PHANISCUS: The explanation
   Is simple: our master is in there having drinks.

THEOPROPIDES: Your master is in there having drinks?

PHANISCUS: I explained
   All that to you.

THEOPROPIDES: Aren't you the fancy one!   1230

PHANISCUS: We've come to pick him up.

THEOPROPIDES: Pick whom up?

PHANISCUS: Not whom, him, the master: how many times
   Do I have to tell you whom?

THEOPROPIDES: But listen, lad,
   No one lives there. I'm sure you mean well, but . . .

PHANISCUS: Young Philolaches doesn't dwell in that domicile?

THEOPROPIDES: He used to, but he moved out, long ago.

PINACIUM: I'm afraid the old jar's cracked.

PHANISCUS: You're quite wrong, pop.

THEOPROPIDES: Stop calling me pop . . .

PHANISCUS: Unless of course yesterday
   Or today was his moving day. I happen to know
   As a matter of actual, that this is where young Phil lives.   1240

THEOPROPIDES: For six months now, no one has lived in that
    house.

PHANISCUS and PINACIUM: *Wakeup!*

THEOPROPIDES: Whom? Me?

PINACIUM: Yes'm, youm.

THEOPROPIDES: (*To* PINACIUM)   Don't horn in, you.
    Let me talk to the boy.
    (*To* PHANISCUS)
                No one's living there.

PHANISCUS: Oh yes, someone is, and yesterday, and the day
    Before, that's three; and the fourth and fifth and sixth
    And so forth; every day since his father left.
    And they haven't let three days in a row go by
    Without a drinking session.

THEOPROPIDES: I'm not sure I'm hearing
    Things right.

PHANISCUS: I said, they haven't let three days go by
    Without a party's getting started, drinks, and eats,   1250
    And girls, and conducting themselves like Greeks, and music,
    And girls to play the music, and . . .

THEOPROPIDES: And who was in charge?

PHANISCUS: Philolaches.

THEOPROPIDES: Philolaches who?

PHANISCUS: The son of Theopropides.

THEOPROPIDES: Oof! I'm done for if what you say is true.
   But I must insist on persisting in investigating.
   Philolaches formed the habit, you say, of holding
   Wild parties with your master, right here?

PHANISCUS: Yes, right in that house.

THEOPROPIDES: I'm afraid you're a good deal dumber than I first
    realized,
   Young fellow. You must have stopped somewhere on the way
   And tossed off a few too many.

PHANISCUS: What makes you think so?   1260

THEOPROPIDES: Because you've obviously wound up at the wrong
    house.

PHANISCUS: But I know where I'm supposed to be: I recognize
    the place
   I left not so long ago. Here liveth Philolaches
   Whose father iseth Theopropides, and lefteth
   To go overseath on busineth, so Philolaches
   Setteth free a lovely young lady on the premiseth.

THEOPROPIDES: Premises? Philolaches?
   Is that who you mean?

PHANISCUS: That's the very exact same person, and the pretty
    young woman
   Who is now about his closest relation, that is "Philematium."

THEOPROPIDES: Uhh, how much did it cost to buy her freedom?

PHANISCUS: Sixteen . . .   1270

THEOPROPIDES: Sixty?!

PHANISCUS: Heavens, *nein!* I mean sixteen miney.

THEOPROPIDES: He bought her freedom, you say?

PHANISCUS: That's what he
   bought.
And it cost him sixteen *minae*.

THEOPROPIDES;   Now, let's see, you say
   Philolaches acquired a mistress, that was at a cost
   To him of sixteen *minae*?

PHANISCUS: So I say.

THEOPROPIDES: And he manumitted the girl?

PHANISCUS: So I say.

THEOPROPIDES: And after his father went overseas
   He drank a good deal in the company of your master?

PHANISCUS: So I say.

THEOPROPIDES: And what do you say about this: he bought
   The house next door?

PHANISCUS: No I *don't* say.

THEOPROPIDES: And paid forty *minae* down to the owner?

PHANISCUS: No I *don't* say.   1280

THEOPROPIDES: It's absolute ruin.

PHANISCUS: What the young man has done
   In fact is ruin his father.

THEOPROPIDES: How true a tune
   You're singing now!

PHANISCUS: I wish it were slightly off key.
   Perhaps you're some kind of friend of his father?

THEOPROPIDES: I must say, I feel sorry for the man whose ruin
   You're describing so definitively.

PHANISCUS: But *her* price was *nothing*,
   A mere sixteen miney, compared to the cost of the feed
   And wine for those fabulous parties and the entertainment.

THEOPROPIDES: Financially, then, his father's a failure.

PHANISCUS: And of course
      there's that slave,
   Tranio's his name, an absolute fiend of a spender,   1290
   A sieve with money. He could spend Hercules' whole hoard
   Overnight, if he had it. Heavens, how I sympathize
   With Philolaches' father! When he finds out what's happened
   Searing sorrow will scorch his heart and reduce it
   To a cardiac cinder.

THEOPROPIDES: Of course, if you're telling the truth.

PHANISCUS: But why should I lie? I've nothing to hide.

PINACIUM: Hey, kids!
   Won't someone please open up the door?

PHANISCUS: Don't pound
   Anymore, there's nobody home. They've probably gone
   To somebody else's place to continue the action.
   So let's be off . . .

THEOPROPIDES: Hey, lad . . .

PHANISCUS: And keep on looking,   1300
   Wherever they are. Keep up with me.

PINACIUM: I'm coming.

THEOPROPIDES: Oh, lad, are you leaving?

PHANISCUS: Freedom is a good thick cloak
    For *your* back, sir, and you have that to wear.
    But I am only a slave, with a master to fear
    And to care for, and so of course I crave his protection.
    If I'm slack nothing can save my back from detection.

Scene 3

THEOPROPIDES: This is the finish of me. Why even discuss it?
    From what I hear, I would say I did not depart
    On a trip to Egypt: I went to the ends of the earth
    And traveled to the outermost rims of the world.   1310
    Where I am now I don't really know for sure,
    But I'll find out, perhaps, for here comes the man
    My son bought the house from. Ah, hello, how goes it?

SIMO: It goes back home from the forum.

THEOPROPIDES: Oh, anything new
    Turn up at the forum today?

SIMO: Yes, one little thing.

THEOPROPIDES: Oh yes? What was that?

SIMO: They were hauling a
    dead man away.

THEOPROPIDES: Ugh! That doesn't strike me precisely as new.

SIMO: Well, I saw them lugging this recent corpse outside.
    He had been alive a moment ago, they were saying.

THEOPROPIDES: So that's what turned up! I didn't mean it
    quite that way.   1320

SIMO: Have you nothing to do but stand around listening to news?

THEOPROPIDES: I've only returned from abroad today.

SIMO: I'm sorry,
    But I can't ask you to dinner. I'm promised elsewhere.

THEOPROPIDES: Oh, I wasn't expecting you to.

SIMO: But tomorrow, let's
    see . . .
    Yes . . . I'll be free to come to your house.

THEOPROPIDES: Actually,
    I wasn't planning on that, either. Do you have a minute?
    There's something I wanted to ask you about.

SIMO: Why, of course.

THEOPROPIDES: So far as I know, you received from Philolaches
    A payment of forty *minae?*

SIMO: So far as I know,
    I never received a cent.

THEOPROPIDES: From Tranio, then?   1330

SIMO: From *him?* I received even less, a more negative nothing.

THEOPROPIDES: And this was a downpayment?

SIMO: What are you
    dreaming about?

THEOPROPIDES: Me? You're the dreamer, to think you can hoodwink me
And nullify the deal by claiming to know nothing of it.

SIMO: What deal?

THEOPROPIDES: The transaction my son completed with you
While I was away.

SIMO: To think that I would conclude
Some sort of business with him while your were away!
What in the world for? And on what date was it done?

THEOPROPIDES: Look, I owe you the sum of eighty *minae*
in silver.

SIMO: Look, you *don't.* Of course, if you do owe me that   1340
You can hand it right over. A promise to pay must be honored.
I wouldn't want you to think that you could deny it.

THEOPROPIDES: Well, I don't deny it. I owe and will pay you this
money.

SIMO: Now wait just a minute.* I've got a few things to ask you.
What is this about the money your son and the slave
Supposedly paid out to me? And this big transaction
Supposedly sealed and signed while you were away?

THEOPROPIDES: Tranio says they paid half the sum in advance
As a binder, to you when you sold your house to him.

SIMO: To whom? Philolaches? But I still live there,   1350
As you saw for yourself. And I don't intend to move out.

THEOPROPIDES: But the money . . .

Now wait just a minute: There is a gap in the manuscript here of twenty-one lines.

SIMO: Don't be funny. Not a ghost
   of a shadow of a cent
   Has passed between me and Philolaches. How could it?
   My house was never for sale.

THEOPROPIDES: He didn't buy it?

SIMO: Either that or I didn't sell it. You take your choice.

THEOPROPIDES: But the money that's owed to the banker . . .
   Oh, Lord . . .

SIMO: What the hell
   Does your son need two houses for?

THEOPROPIDES: Well, this one is haunted,
   So they moved out, six months ago.

SIMO: Oh, they've been moving
   All right; they've been moving along pretty fast ever since
   You first left for Egypt. They've been hosts to some lively
     ghosts   1360
   If you ask me. Nobody ever seems to sleep in there,
   It sounds like a wake to me. They didn't move out,
   But they sure moved around, and moved in a gaggle of girls.

THEOPROPIDES: But Tranio said . . .

SIMO: (*Imperturbably*)   He told me you wanted to see
   The inside of my place . . .

THEOPROPIDES: When he said that we were the owners,
   Naturally, I was curious . . .

SIMO: Especially the women's quarters . . .

THEOPROPIDES: I'll quarter those women after I get my hands on
   that slave.

SIMO: (*Still imperturbably*) Because, he said, you wanted your
    son to marry
And wanted to build an addition, as quarters for the women,
There in your house in time for the wedding, he said.   1370

THEOPROPIDES: I wanted to build an addition?

SIMO: That's what he said.

THEOPROPIDES: It's all up with me.
    (*Gulp!*)
                                  I haven't a thing to say,
Or voice left to say it except these three little verbs:
    I lived.   I died.   I was buried.

SIMO: Has Tranio perhaps
    Created some kind of catastrophe?

THEOPROPIDES: Just complete chaos,
    That's all, and he's made ridiculous fools today
    Of you and me.

SIMO: You mean the joke's on us?

THEOPROPIDES: More or less—less on you, more on me.
    I see it now.
He's made an absolute fool of me today,
And as far as I can see, in the visible future.   1380
Now look, would you help me plan some means of revenge?

SIMO: What would you like me to do?

THEOPROPIDES: Come along with me.

SIMO: I'm coming.

THEOPROPIDES: Lend me a couple of slaves, with whips.

SIMO: Take them from my supply; I've plenty of both.

THEOPROPIDES: And while we plan the revenge I mean to have
    I'll give you more examples of the way
    That rascal made a fool of me today.

ACT V

Scene 1

TRANIO: The man who is faint and fearful in a crisis
    Is just not worth his salt; he is "as naught."
    But what that means, "as naught," I have no notion.   1390
    Now after the master packed me off to the country
    To summon his son, I veered back through this alley
    To our garden, secretly, and opened the little gate
    That leads from behind our house into the alley.
    I led forth my legions, masculine and feminine.
    Right now I'm having a conference with myself
    About calling a congress of some clever cronies of mine.
    For I had called a meeting of the senate of my friends
    In there, but they refused to let me come to it!
    I realized I was being taken advantage of, so   1400
    I got busy immediately getting ready to do
    What any intelligent, strong-minded person would do
    In my situation so fraught with peril and confusion.
    Create even more confusion, surely that's the solution!
    Keep it all moving around and around. I'll be found
    Out, of course, the old man can hardly be kept from knowing
    Much longer, but I can still hope to get to him first,
    And head them off and make some sort of a deal.
    I haven't any time to waste. But listen, the door
    Of the neighbor's house is rattling; yes they're coming

this way   1410
I'll hide in this corner and hear what they have to say.

Scene 2

THEOPROPIDES: You men, stand back inside the doorway;
     be ready
When I call, to jump out and slap the handcuffs on him.
I'll wait in front of the house for my funny man.
His skin will feel even funnier by the end of the day.

TRANIO: The cat's out, Tranio. You'd better see what there is
You can do about it now.

THEOPROPIDES: Now I want to be subtle in getting him into
     my net
When he shows up. I won't let him see the hook,
Just the bait, while I reel in the line. I'll pretend I don't know
Anything about what's going on.

TRANIO: You clever man!   1420
No one in Athens is any wiser than you.
It's as hard to take advantage of you as it is
To get a rise from a rock. Now watch me approach
This masterful man and proceed to get his attention.

THEOPROPIDES: I wish the fish would show his head.

TRANIO: The catcher
Is looking for me awry, and I'm standing by.

THEOPROPIDES: Oh there, good old Tranio! What's the news?

TRANIO: The rustics are returning from the . . . uh . . . sticks.
Philolaches will soon be here.

THEOPROPIDES: Well, you've arrived
   In the nick of time for me. Good Lord, that neighbor   1430
   Of ours has his cheek, wise guy.

TRANIO: Because why?

THEOPROPIDES: He denies that he's had any dealings with you.

TRANIO: Denies it?

THEOPROPIDES: And says you haven't paid him a blessed cent.

TRANIO: Oh come on, you're kidding! I can't believe he says that.

THEOPROPIDES: Why not?

TRANIO: I know, you're just playing a joke on me.
   I can't quite believe he'd say anything like that.

THEOPROPIDES: Well, he does say precisely that, meaning no,
   And denies that he sold his house to Philolaches,

TRANIO: And also denies he was given the money?

THEOPROPIDES: Denies it?
   He's willing to affirm under oath, if I want him to,
   That he did not sell the house, that he never received   1440
   Any money.

TRANIO: When we bought it, and paid the cash down?

THEOPROPIDES: That's just what I told him.

TRANIO: And what did he say?

THEOPROPIDES: He offered to hand his slaves over to me
   For questioning under torture.

TRANIO: He's faking; he won't.

THEOPROPIDES: Yes he will, right away.

TRANIO: ·   Well, summon him to court.
   I'll dash over now and put the finger on him.

(*Heads for the altar in front of* SIMO'*s house*)

THEOPROPIDES: No, wait here, I've decided to check up on him.

TRANIO: Just you leave him to me. Or better, challenge him
   To contest the legal possession of that property.

THEOPROPIDES: But first I want to put his slaves on the rack.   1450

TRANIO: By all means.

THEOPROPIDES: So now I'll have them brought out here.

TRANIO: By all means. Meanwhile, I'll take a seat on this altar.

THEOPROPIDES: Oh no. Why do that?

TRANIO: You're so darned dumb.
   To keep the slaves from having this as a refuge
   When they come out to be questioned. I'll preside over things,
   To make sure the investigation proceeds properly.

THEOPROPIDES: Oh, come off it! I mean climb down from
      the altar.

TRANIO: En oh.

THEOPROPIDES: Come on now, I'm asking you not to take over
      that altar.

TRANIO: Why not?

THEOPROPIDES: Because that's what I *want* them to do,
   Take refuge there. So let them. It'll be clear evidence   1460
   Before any judge, and a means of getting him fined.

TRANIO: Look, you're going to do something; all right: do it.
   Why confuse the issue? You just don't know
   How involved these matters are when you take them to court.

THEOPROPIDES: Come down from there, over here to me. There's
       something
   I need to consult you about.

TRANIO: I dispense advice
   Very well from a sitting position. I seem to know more
   When I'm seated. From the holy seats of the gods, after all,
   The counsels are all the more binding.

THEOPROPIDES: Don't fool around.
   Come down. Just look at me: You have nothing to fear,   1470
   You see,

TRANIO: I'm looking.

THEOPROPIDES: You see?

TRANIO: Ah, I see you there!
   If a third person tried to come between us two,
   He'd die of starvation.

THEOPROPIDES: How come?

TRANIO: No source of income:
   We're both so *close!*

THEOPROPIDES: Oh good God dammit to hell.

TRANIO: Is something bothering you?

THEOPROPIDES: No; nothing but you.

TRANIO: Poor little defenseless me?

THEOPROPIDES: You've wiped me out.

TRANIO: I had to, your nose was running. It runs in the family.

THEOPROPIDES: You've wiped out my whole set of brains and taken my head
  To the cleaners. For now I've finally gotten to the bottom   1480
  Of your *clever*, frantic antics. I've dug down deep
  And gotten to the root of the trouble. I've even uprooted
  The radical region 'way down beneath the root.

TRANIO: Well, in that case I shan't arise from my heavenly seat
  This day at all, except with a promise of safety.

THEOPROPIDES: Get up! I'll have some dry kindling brought out here
  And a roaring fire started up underneath your bottom.

TRANIO: Better not: I taste much better boiled than roasted.

THEOPROPIDES: I'll make an example of you.

TRANIO: To be held up to others?
  That shows how highly regarded I am.

THEOPROPIDES: Tell me this: 1490
  In what condition was my son when I left him?

TRANIO: Let's see, he has feet and hands, two each, with fingers
  And toes, two ears, two eyes, and two Dutch flowers.

THEOPROPIDES: I was asking about something other than his
  physical status.

TRANIO: I was answering in another vein from your quizzical
    status.
    But look, here comes your son's best friend and companion,
    That charming Callidamates. See what you can do
    With me in his presence, a man who's loyal and true.

Scene 3

CALLIDAMATES: I buried myself in sleep—
(*Stretches and yawns*)
                                that was a good deep one—
    And slept off the effects of the wine. I'm feeling fine.
    Now Philolaches has told me how his father has come   1500
    Back home from abroad and how the slave had his fun
    Misleading the new arrival, or leading him on,
    Or leading him away anyway, from the true situation.
    He has asked me to make a diplomatic approach
    And plead his case and make his peace with his father.
    Ah, there he is, just the man I was looking for.
    Greetings, Theopropides! I'm glad you are back
    And looking so well. Have dinner with me this evening.
    Please do accept.

THEOPROPIDES: Good day, Callidamates.
    And thanks all the same for inviting me to dinner.   1510
    I'm sorry I must decline.

CALLIDAMATES: Oh please, do come.

TRANIO: Say you will. Or shall I go in our place?

THEOPROPIDES: You knothead, actually laughing?

TRANIO: You mean because
    I swear I'll go to dinner instead of you?

THEOPROPIDES: You *won't*. I'll have you carried to the cross:
That's where you ought to be hanging out.

CALLIDAMATES: Never mind
The slave, Theopropides. Promise you'll come
To my house for dinner? Why not simply say yes?
And tell me,
(*To* TRANIO)
                        blockhead, what's gotten into you,
To make you take refuge on the top of the altar?   1520

TRANIO: The new arrival scared the wits out of me.
Advise me what to do. For you are here
And, like a judge, can listen to both sides,
So let us try the case.

THEOPROPIDES: I say that you
Have led my son astray.

TRANIO: But now hear me:
I admit he misbehaved while you were away
And bought his mistress's freedom with money borrowed
From a moneylender, and the money is all used up,
I'll say that loud and clear. But is it *mis*-
Behavior, I ask you? Or is it standard conduct,   1530
When the sons of all great families act that way?

THEOPROPIDES: I'll have to watch my words debating you:
You're pretty shrewd when it comes to the orations.

CALLIDAMATES: Now let me rule on that point. Dislodge yourself,
Tranio. I'll sit up there and preside over things.

TRANIO: It's a trap! No, Callidamates, you must first
Assure me I won't be grabbed the moment I leave
My perch of immunity. Then you can have my place.

THEOPROPIDES: Back to the argument: I don't hold it against you,
My son's misbehavior, half as much as the means   1540
(Or is it extremes?) you've gone to in making a fool
Out of me and making me look like a dope.

TRANIO: Serves you right, sir—a jolly good show.
These are things a man of your age should know.

THEOPROPIDES: Now that I know how a white-haired man can be
    fooled
By people he takes for granted, what do I do
With the newfound knowledge?

TRANIO: Offer it to the comic poets.
If you're a friend of the writers Diphilus and Philemon
Tell them how your slave made a comic character
Out of you. That's good frustration material for them   1550
To use in their comedies.

CALLIDAMATES: Quiet, there on the altar!
It's my turn to say a few words. Listen, for a change.

THEOPROPIDES: Hear, Hear!

CALLIDAMATES: First of all, you know I'm a very good
    friend
Of your son. He's come to me—he's ashamed, you see,
To show his face or let himself in your sight
Because he knows that you know what he's done.
So I appeal to you—please pardon the boy
For his childish foolishness. He's your son, after all.
You know how lads of his age love to lark around
And live it up. And I was as bad as he was: 1560
I joined in it all. We're both completely at fault.
As for the money, the principal, the interest, the cash
He used up, the girl he bought, every bit he spent,
I will have it paid back and the expenses all made good
From my own funds and my friends', not yours.

THEOPROPIDES: No more effective
A speaker than you could present this case before me.
I'm no longer angry at him, nor do I bear
Any kind of a grudge. Let him follow his heart; make love,
Enjoy his wine, and count on my friendly indulgence.
If he's genuinely sorry he's wasted all this money,   1570
That's punishment enough for me.

CALLIDAMATES: He's abjectly sorry.

TRANIO: In the spirit of that indulgence, what fate is in store
For me?

THEOPROPIDES: The lash, you slab of mud, and then
Stringing up, for further flaying and jabbing.

TRANIO: Even if I'm genuinely sorry?

THEOPROPIDES: As I live and breathe,
You'll choke and die.

CALLIDAMATES: Why not make a clean slate
Of all your pardons, and forgive Tranio his sins,
For my sake?

THEOPROPIDES: I would gladly grant your request
For anything else, *except that* I refrain
From cracking down on this nut, to prove to him   1580
He's not so tough as he's cracked up to be.

CALLIDAMATES: Come now, do let him off.

THEOPROPIDES: *Let him off!!!*
Look at him, grinning! Nonchalant: couldn't care less.

CALLIDAMATES: If you had any sense, Tranio, you'd leave off
acting
So fresh and let things subside.

THEOPROPIDES: You can leave off asking
  Any sort of favor for him. I'll make him subside
  With a tattoo of bright body blows bounced off his outside.

CALLIDAMATES: Oh come now, let yourself be persuaded by me.

THEOPROPIDES: I don't want you to persuade me.

CALLIDAMATES: Oh please give in.

THEOPROPIDES: I tell you I don't want you to talk me
    into it.   1590

CALLIDAMATES: It's no good your not wanting me to when I
    want to!
  Forgive Tranio his sins, just this once, for my sake.

TRANIO: Why be so reluctant? As if tomorrow
  I won't cause you just as much trouble as I'm doing today!
  Then you can take revenge on me for both times.

CALLIDAMATES: Do let me convince you . . .

THEOPROPIDES: Oh *all right, then:*
  You fiend, go free! But thanks to *him,* not *me!*

ALL: Spectators, our play is over, and in this cause
  We ask you now for handfuls of applause!

Acknowledgments

Janet Burroway's translation of *Poenulus* and Palmer Bovie's translation of *Mostellaria* appeared in *Five Roman Comedies*, edited by Palmer Bovie, published in 1970 by E. P. Dutton.